English Clocks

800 YEARS OF INNOVATION

English Clocks

800 YEARS OF INNOVATION

John Cronin

THE CROWOOD PRESS

Contents

Introduction

The earliest mechanical clocks were probably built for medieval monasteries. The great Christian monastic orders, such as the Cistercians and Benedictines, did not recognise national borders; their allegiance was to Rome. Having Latin as their common language, members of these orders were free to travel throughout Christendom, so learning and new ideas spread freely across what we now call Europe. Water clocks and sundials were familiar objects, but we are unsure where the first mechanical timepieces were invented, or who built them. They were possibly developed in the twelfth century, but none of these early devices survive and what written evidence we have is not very helpful. The earliest surviving clock is in Salisbury Cathedral and dates from the late fourteenth century; it is well documented as being built by a group of Flemish craftsmen who worked in several monasteries.

From these early beginnings, English horological artisans became increasingly numerous from the sixteenth century onwards, thanks to an enlightened attitude to immigration. Protestant England welcomed skilled artisans in many trades escaping from troubled parts of Europe, particularly Huguenots and other Protestants fleeing persecution in Catholic France. By the seventeenth century, England was emerging as the main centre of clock- and watchmaking at the expense of Catholic France and the German-speaking states impoverished by a series of religious wars.

It is now generally accepted that the so-called 'Industrial Revolution' began long before the eighteenth century. Relative peace and prosperity encouraged trade and all kinds of manufacturing enterprises developed and flourished, spurred on by a new interest in experimental science and technology. English horology was always at the cutting edge of new developments, as timekeeping became ever more vital to an increasingly technological nation.

Chapter 1

The Beginnings of Mechanical Timekeeping

It has been a matter of some speculation as to why the Chinese did not invent the mechanical clock, considering that technology in China was far in advance of that in medieval Europe. Marco Polo and other early explorers regarded with wonder the achievements they witnessed on their travels to the Far East. It was, after all, the Chinese who gave the world gunpowder, paper, movable type and many other ingenious products.

WATER CLOCKS

By the eleventh century, Chinese astronomers had developed complex water clocks to reproduce the movements of the sun, moon and selected stars. The name of Su Song, a brilliant scientist, diplomat and administrator, has come down to us as organising the construction of such a clock, which was completed in 1094. The document that Su Song presented to the Emperor Daozong, together with the completed clock, has survived, although the clock itself was carried away by the invading Chin Tartars in 1126, who attempted to reconstruct it without success.

Shown overleaf is the original drawing from Su Song's manuscript, together with a modern reconstruction. The clock was built in the form of a tower. It was driven by a wheel turned by buckets filled with a controlled stream of water, a method developed by the Chinese based on ancient Greek and Roman *clepsydras*. These were simple containers filled with water that dripped through a hole in the base, the passage of time being indicated by the falling level of the water against a scale on the inside of the container.

Although Su Song's water clock was considered a wonder of its age, it represented a dead end in terms of the development of the clock, as it depended on an inherently unreliable timekeeping source. Keeping a reasonably constant flow of water to the device was a weakness with this type of clock and the Chinese made no further progress in this area of technology. By the time the Jesuits brought European clocks to China in the late sixteenth century, the great clock constructed by Su Song had been long forgotten.

Su Song.

A modern reconstruction of Su Song's clock.

THE FIRST PURELY MECHANICAL CLOCKS

The earliest completely mechanical clocks are believed to have been developed as a practical solution to a problem in medieval European monasteries. In Islamic countries, sundials during daylight and simple water clocks sufficed to fix the times for religious obligations; however, Christian monasteries were looking for a better source of timekeeping, particularly in the hours of darkness.

It was believed that the 'second coming' would occur during the hours of darkness and a night vigil, later known as Matins, became an essential element of life in a monastery. However, as the centuries passed, the timing of services tended to be left to individual houses. By the eleventh century, the strict observance of monastic rules had often become less important than the pursuit of power and wealth.

The coming of the Cistercians, with their passion for order and strict discipline, changed all this. In their new isolated monasteries, they demanded a regular and punctual prayer cycle:

- **Matins** (during the night, at about 2am), also called Vigil
- **Lauds** or Dawn Prayer (at dawn, about 5am, according to the season)
- **Prime** or Early Morning Prayer (First Hour = approximately 6am)
- **Terce** or Mid-Morning Prayer (Third Hour = about 9am)
- **Sext** or Midday Prayer (Sixth Hour = about noon)
- **None** or Mid-Afternoon Prayer (Ninth Hour = about 3pm)
- **Vespers** or Evening Prayer ('at the lighting of the lamps', about 6pm)
- **Compline** or Night Prayer (before retiring, about 7pm).

Salisbury Cathedral clock, the earliest surviving mechanical clock.

Being late for worship was unthinkable and bells controlled every aspect of the monk's life, including being awakened in the small hours of the night. Sounding the bell reliably for Matins must have been a matter of some anxiety for the Sacristan who was responsible. However, necessity is the mother of invention and the industrious and ingenious Cistercians solved the problem sometime in the thirteenth century with the invention of a mechanical timekeeper; this would sound an alarm to awaken the bell ringer to get the monks out of their beds at the appointed time. Unfortunately, none of these early clocks have survived and dating them is difficult because of the use of the term 'horologium' in monastic records, which could equally apply to other timekeepers, including sundials and water clocks. The word comes from the Greek *horologion* (time-teller), which gives us the modern term 'horology' – the art and science of timekeeping.

The first detailed descriptions of clocks to come down to us are from the early fourteenth century. These clocks were highly developed machines, with bell-striking and complex astronomical dials. By this time, mechanical timepieces were well established in Northern Europe's great monasteries and churches. The earliest surviving mechanical clock is in Salisbury Cathedral; it is believed to have been constructed in the 1380s.

Pride of place in many European cities was given to a public clock, often with astronomical features and mechanical figures – Jacks – which appeared and processed round to mark the hours. A splendid example that has survived to this day is in Prague and dates from 1410.

Astronomical clock, Prague.

Chapter 2

The Mechanisms of the First Clocks

This chapter will cover the elements that make up the construction of the first mechanical clocks. It will then look in detail at the construction of two examples, the Salisbury Cathedral clock and Giovanni de Dondi's clock.

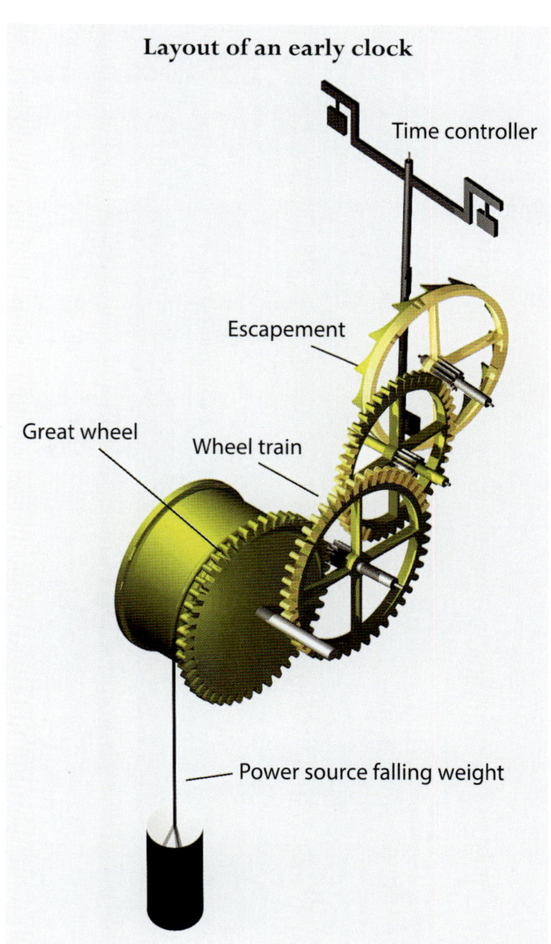

THE BASIC ELEMENTS

There are four main elements in the construction of all mechanical clocks:

- **The power source** A falling weight suspended on a rope wound around a barrel, or a coiled spring, provides the power to drive the clock.
- **The gear train** The power is transferred from the great wheel attached to the barrel to a group of gears known as the train, which drives the escapement.
- **The escapement** This device, in conjunction with the time controller, allows the mechanism to unwind at a fixed rate so that it can release a striking work that sounds a bell at pre-determined intervals.
- **The time controller** The earliest device to provide a way of slowing the unwinding of the train was an oscillating bar known as a foliot. This is a weighted bar caused to swing to and fro at a more or less constant rate by the escapement.

The detail of the Salisbury clock shows the various components in place. Note that the great wheel gears directly to the escapement and the length of running depends on the drop of the weight. Later clocks had more gear wheels in the train to extend the time between winding. The rest of the mechanism is the striking work, which will be described later.

THE POWER SOURCE

The Weight Drive

As we have seen, the first clocks used a falling weight to drive the gear train. The rope, or other form of cord, was wound around a drum attached to the great wheel. In order to raise the weight, the drum had to be provided with a ratchet system connecting the drum to the great wheel.

Salisbury Cathedral clock mechanism detail.

The winding drum and ratchet wheel are a single unit. The great wheel is connected to the drum by the ratchet. When the winding square is turned, the drum rotates and the rope winds on to the drum, raising the weight. The click, operated by the click spring, locks into the ratchet wheel and connects the great wheel to the drum, driving the gear train.

Despite the simplicity of this power source, it had one disadvantage – the clock had to be fixed to a framework or on to a wall. A new power source was needed to make the clock portable.

Coiled Spring

The spring was one of the earliest inventions of humanity; prehistoric hunters well understood the capacity of the bow to store the energy of the arm and release it to propel an arrow. By 1400, metal springs were used in all kinds of devices and weapons. The invention of a spring that could be coiled so that it could be 'wound up' to store energy probably came from locksmiths. When released, the spring's stored energy would provide several turns of rotary motion. By the mid-fifteenth century, spring-powered domestic clocks began to appear, but none of the earliest springs has survived; they were probably made from a strip of hammered brass. Brass can be 'work hardened' by hammering to make it more elastic than in its cast state. These early springs could only have powered the clock for short periods and probably needed winding twice daily. Iron was too brittle to make springs. However, if iron is alloyed with a small percentage of carbon, it produces steel, which can be worked in its soft state, then hardened and tempered by heating and quenching the metal to make it resilient and flexible.

Before the seventeenth century, steel was mostly used for the production of weapons and other cutting tools. Wootz steel – iron with a carbon content of around 1.5 per cent – originated in India and was widely exported to Europe and the Middle East in pre-Christian times, where it was often known as Damascus steel. Swords made from Damascus steel became highly prized for their strength and elastic properties; it was possible to bend one of these swords through 90 degrees without breaking. Early spring makers would have used the techniques of the swordsmith to hammer out a thin ribbon of steel, which would be hardened and tempered before coiling and enclosing it in a barrel.

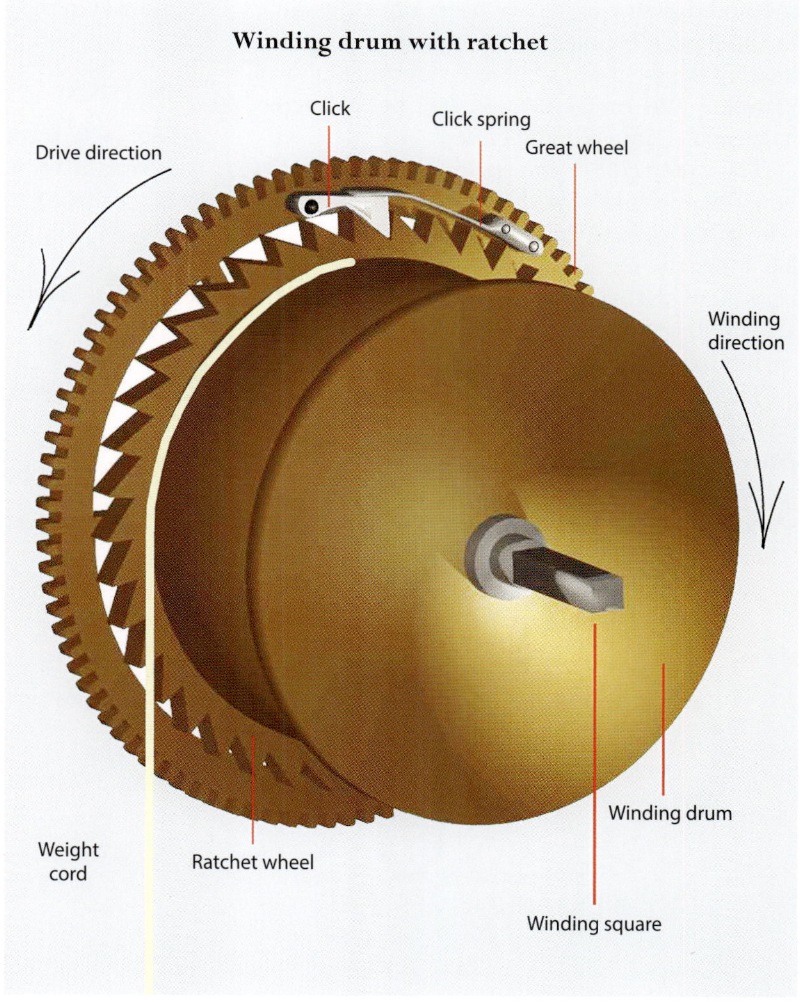

Making clock mainsprings, from the Encyclopédie de Diderot et d'Alembert, *1751–80.*

The above illustration of mainspring making is from the mid-eighteenth century, but the method shown would have been much the same in the fifteenth century. We can see a forge for heating the steel and craftsmen hammering and grinding the metal into strips, before being hardened, tempered and coiled.

The outer coil of the spring is attached to a hook on the inside of the barrel and the inner coil is hooked to the barrel arbor. The arbor has a square section that allows the spring to be wound with a key. The square on the arbor also holds the ratchet wheel, which prevents the spring from running down.

The problem with using a coiled spring as a power source is that it provides progressively less power (torque) as it runs down. This variation in power would result in poor timekeeping, so some form of compensation was needed to lessen this effect. Very soon after spring-driven clocks and watches were developed, an ingenious device appeared in the mid-sixteenth century.

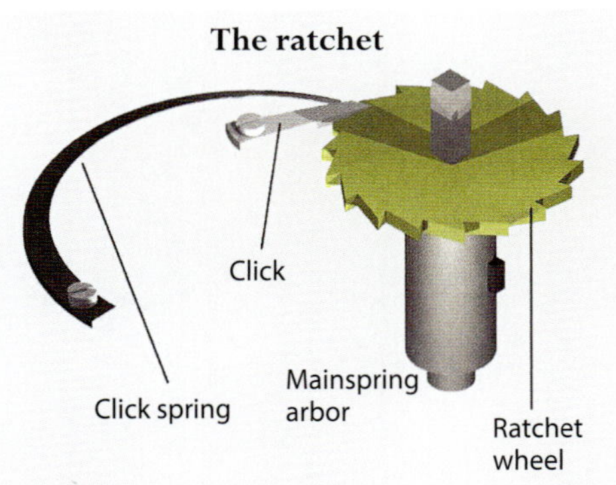

The Fusee

There is a theory that the fusee was a device that may have originated in a type of tapered windlass used to tension powerful crossbows.

A normal windlass was a cylinder turned with levers around which a rope was wound. If the cylinder was replaced with a cone, then the pulling power would be increased as the rope wound around the narrower part of the cone, providing extra torque as the tension of the bow increased.

The spring is tensioned by a gut line wound around the mainspring barrel. As the fusee is turned, the line is wound round the fusee spiral, tensioning the mainspring. When the mainspring is fully wound, the fusee line pulls on the narrow section of the cone. As the spring runs down, it pulls on progressively larger sections of the fusee cone, gradually increasing the torque to the gear train and compensating for the decreasing power of the spring. Not all of the turns of the spring are used; when the fusee is run down, the mainspring is still under power so that the last turn or so is not used. Likewise, when the fusee is fully wound, the spring in the barrel still has a turn or so of winding left. This avoids the coils of the spring in the barrel becoming tightly pressed together, thus giving a smoother release of power. The system can also be 'set up' by varying the number of turns the spring is given when the fusee becomes run down, providing a little more or less power.

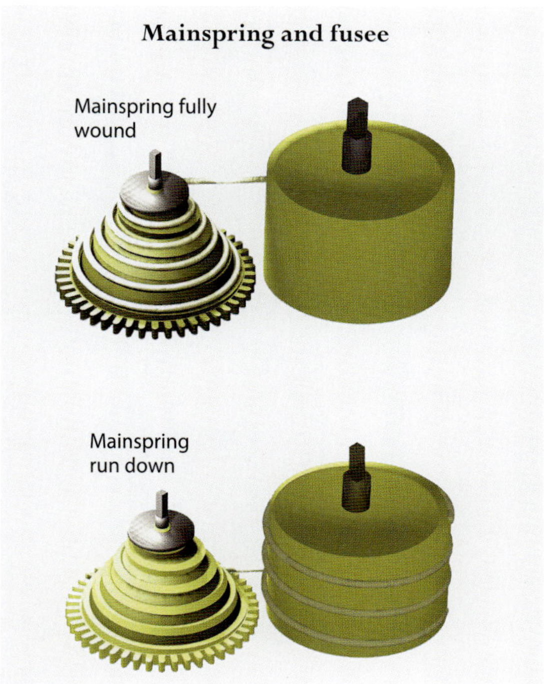

The fusee was one of the most ingenious devices of the period and it became an essential component of all precision spring-driven timepieces. Horologists soon learnt that by closely matching the shape of the fusee to the properties of the mainspring, it was possible to eliminate almost all variations in torque. During the eighteenth century, chains replaced the gut fusee lines for high-grade clocks and watches.

The early iron table clock illustrated here was made in Germany, *c.* 1580. It has a verge escapement and is powered by a mainspring and fusee.

THE GEAR TRAIN

Two or more gears working in sequence are known as a 'gear train'. In mechanical timepieces, a gear train has the dual purpose of:

- Transmitting the energy from the weight or spring to the escapement
- Transferring the beats of the time controller (for example, a pendulum) to the hands indicating the time.

Sixteenth-century table clock.

Cage gearing.

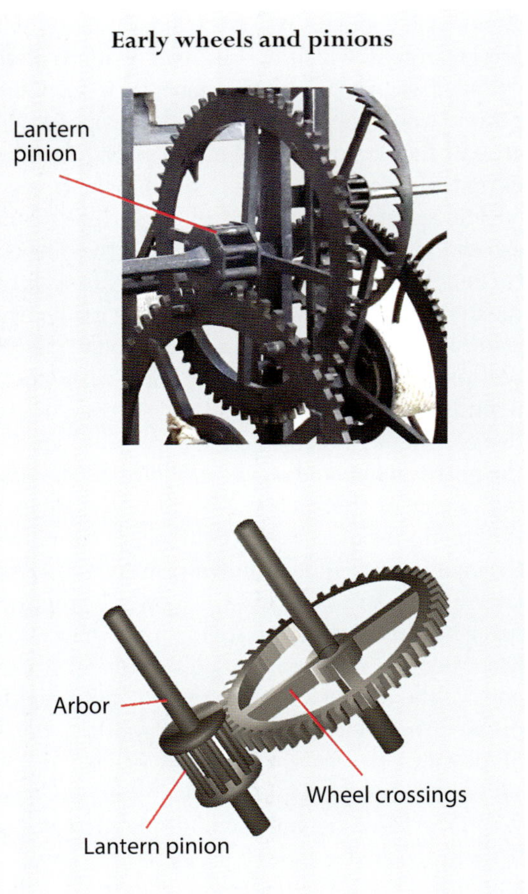

In medieval times, simple gearing, generally made of wood, was commonly found in various kinds of mills, transferring water or wind power to drive pumps and grindstones.

The earliest reference to 'segmental gears' – circular gears with peripheral teeth – comes from the Islamic scholar and engineer Ismail al-Jazari (1136–1206) in his *Book of the Knowledge of Ingenious Mechanical Devices* of 1206, which describes 50 mechanical devices with instructions for building them. The manuscript shows a drawing of a water pump and a modern reconstruction.

Early clocks generally used a combination of spur gears, that is, wheels with peripheral teeth

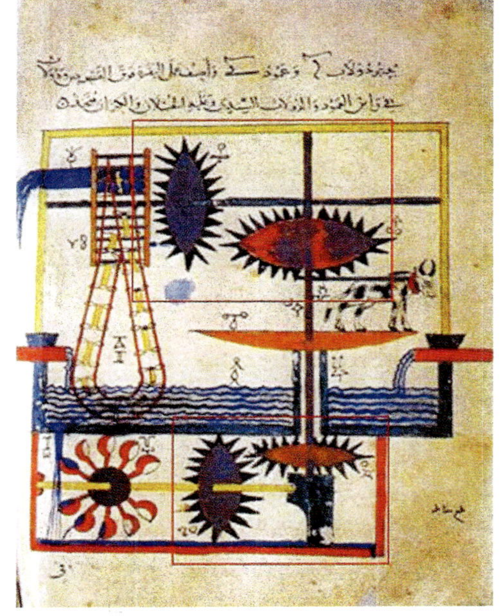

Al-Jazari manuscript and reconstruction.

and lantern pinions. The wheel teeth would be marked out with dividers and filed out by hand; the smaller pinions were made by inserting forged iron rods into a cage. This can be clearly seen in the fourteenth-century Salisbury Cathedral clock mentioned earlier.

The complex gearing used in these early astronomical clocks showed, among other things, the location of the sun and moon, dates of eclipses, star maps, the current zodiac sign and much else. The origins of this method of displaying astronomical information using gears is lost in the mists of antiquity, but certainly long predates the first clocks.

We know of complex gear systems from ancient Greece and in 1901 an object was discovered in a shipwreck off the coast of the Greek island of Antikythera, which transformed our knowledge of ancient mechanics. It consists of 82 crust-encased fragments of a bronze mechanism and the remains of a wooden box. At that time, the purpose of this machine was a mystery. However, with the aid of modern X-ray techniques, it has been possible to reconstruct the instrument, with its complex gearing consisting of over 37 bronze gear wheels; the largest of these is 13cm in diameter with 223 teeth. The gears are turned with a handwheel and various dials with pointers can be used to predict astronomical positions and eclipses in future decades, based on the calculations of the second-century BC astronomer Hipparchus of Rhodes. The chance discovery of such advanced use of gearing for mathematical calculations gives us a tantalising glimpse into ancient Greek engineering.

The Antikythera mechanism, first-century BC

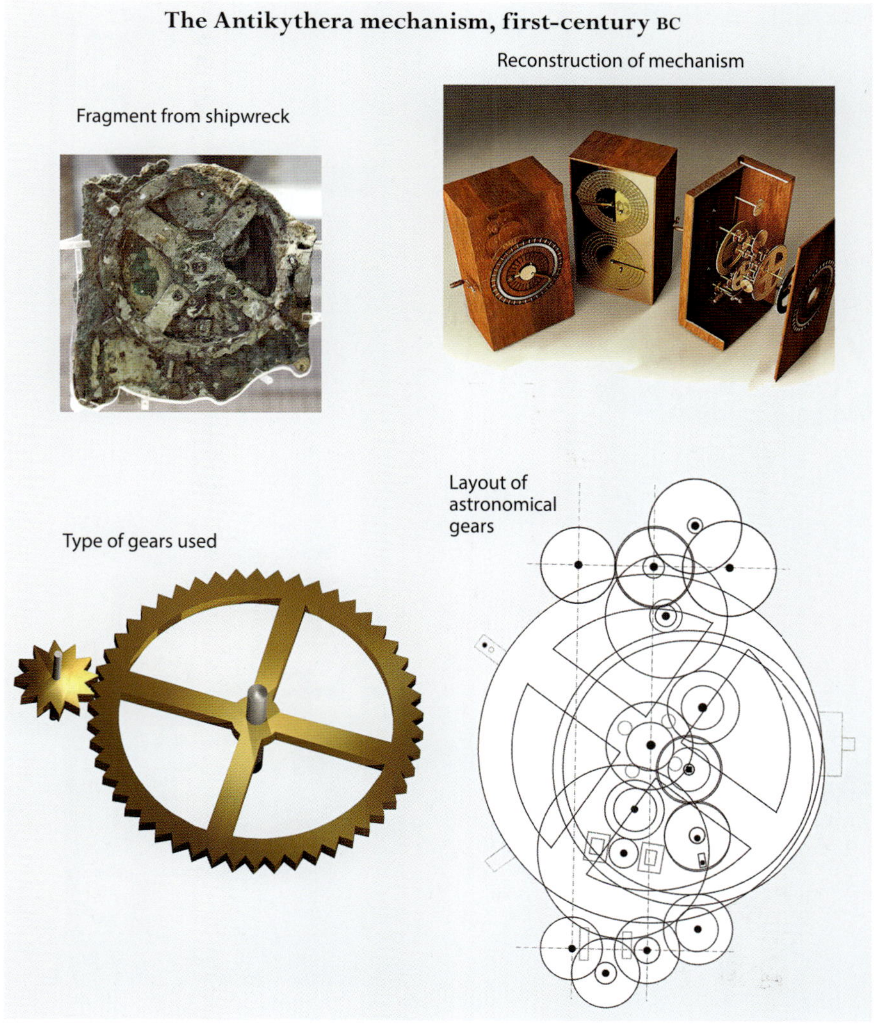

THE VERGE ESCAPEMENT

The name of the earliest form of escapement probably came from the medieval use of the Latin word *virga*, describing a rod or staff carried as a symbol of office by one in authority, such as a verger. It seems to have first appeared in the thirteenth century and was the key invention in the development of clocks and watches. It has been suggested that it may have been developed from a mechanism for sounding bells.

In the verge escapement, the two pallets are fixed to a rotating bar and are pushed alternately by the teeth of the crown wheel. In the illustration, figure A shows one pallet coming into contact with the wheel tooth; the pallet is pushed anticlockwise as the wheel rotates and the tooth escapes. Figure B shows the opposing tooth locked on to the other pallet and beginning

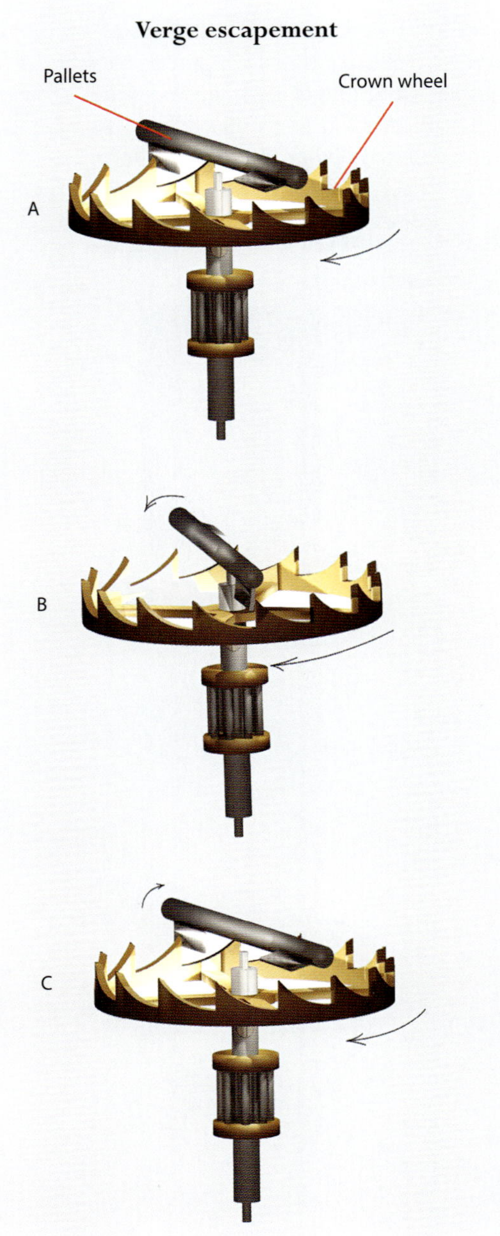

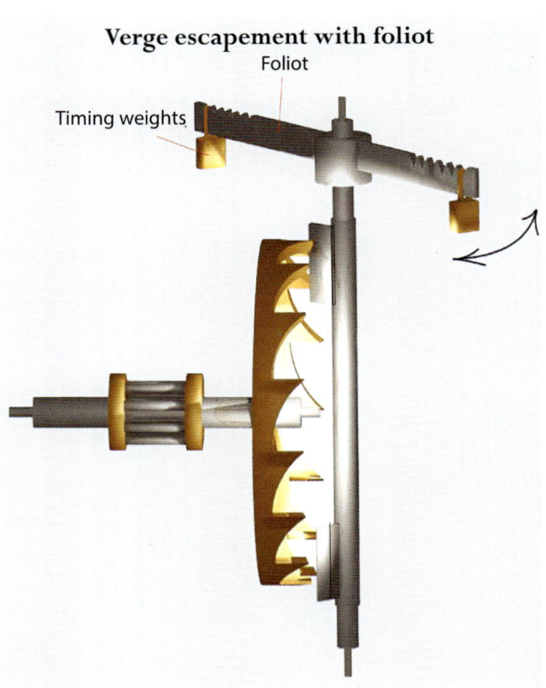

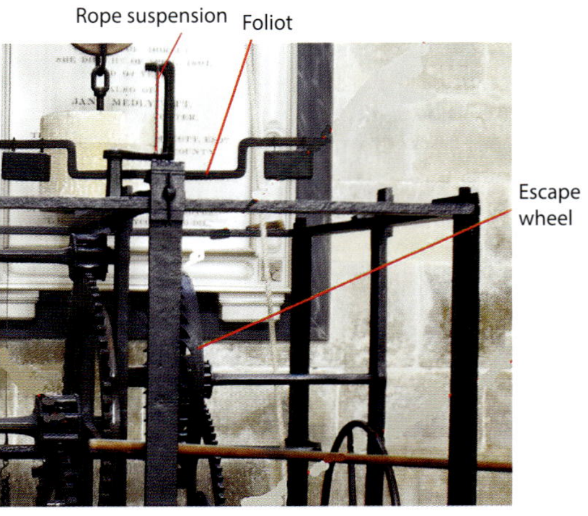

Salisbury Cathedral clock foliot detail.

to push the bar in the opposite direction until this tooth escapes and brings the opposing pallet into contact with the opposite tooth in Figure C. Thus, a rocking motion is set up, with the bar oscillating through about 60 degrees.

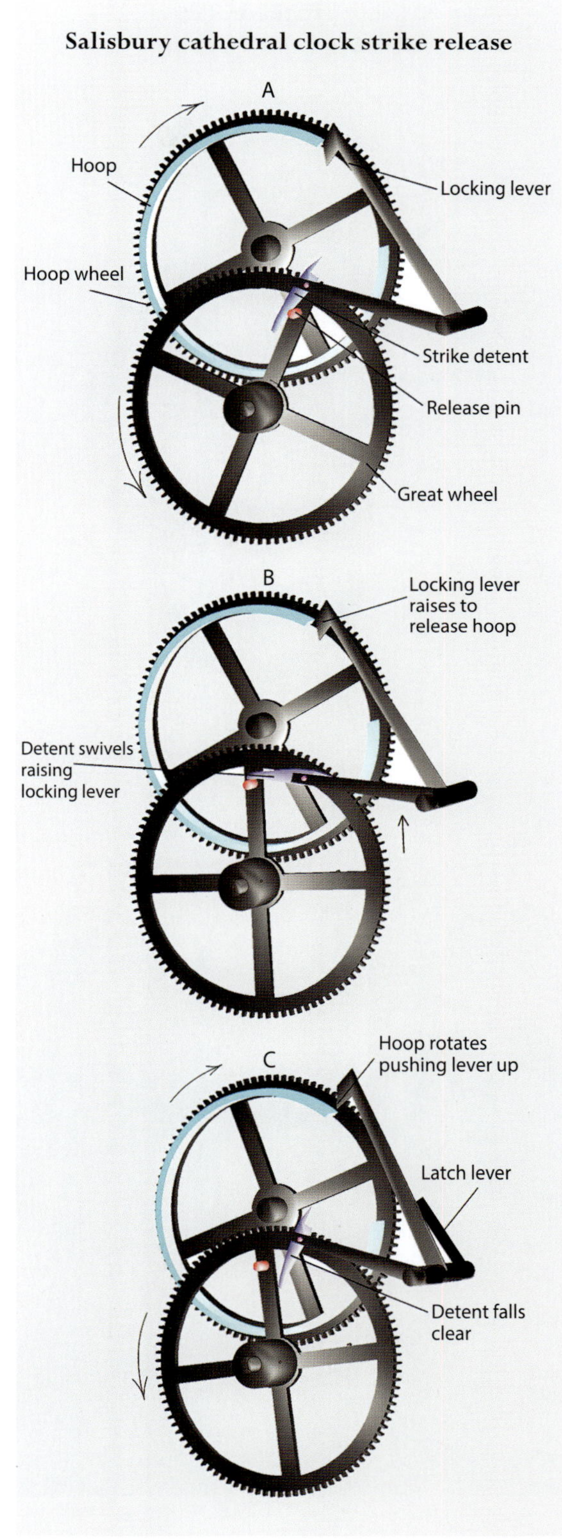

THE TIME CONTROLLER

The Foliot

The first description of this oscillating bar probably comes from a poem written in 1369 by Jean Froissart, in which he uses the word *foliot* (from the French *follet* – to dance about madly). The poem *'L'Horloge amoureux'* describes the various parts of a clock compared to aspects of love. The illustration shows a foliot suspended on a rope, allowing the assembly to twist. The rate of oscillation was adjusted by moving timing weights along the foliot bars: moving the weights outwards would result in a slower rate; inwards would make the clock gain.

STRIKING MECHANISMS

The earliest surviving clocks all have striking mechanisms; indeed, the word 'clock' comes from the German *glocke* – bell. As the invention of the mechanical timepiece was probably for the purpose of sounding a bell, it would seem that some kind of device to strike a bell was part of the earliest mechanisms. If we look again at the Salisbury Cathedral clock, we see that it is divided into two sections, one for timekeeping and the other for sounding the hours. All of the earliest surviving clocks use some variation of this arrangement. These early clocks did not have a dial – their function was simply to sound each hour by striking a bell for the appropriate number of blows. During daylight hours the clock could be set using a sundial, leaving the mechanism to run on, striking the hours to ensure that the various divine offices happened at the appointed times, particularly Matins in the early morning hours.

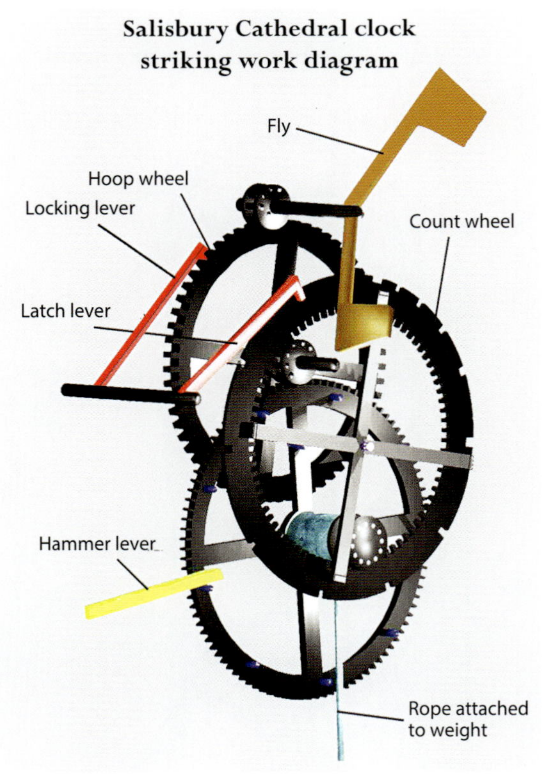

The Salisbury Cathedral Clock Striking Mechanism

As it is the earliest surviving example of a medieval clock, it is worth looking in detail at the Salisbury Cathedral clock's mechanism, bearing in mind that by the late fourteenth century, clock mechanisms must have been under development for over a century.

The timekeeping of all of these early clocks was controlled by a verge escapement with a foliot, as described earlier. This basic design continued until pendulum clocks and new escapements were developed in the seventeenth century. Designs of the striking work, however, became more sophisticated during the fifteenth and sixteenth centuries.

Most striking clocks have an arrangement of levers and wheels that set up the mechanism ready to be released at a certain hour; this is called the warning. If you turn the minute hand of most striking clocks forward, you will hear a click slightly before the hour, then as the hour is reached, the striking train is released – this is the warning. The Salisbury Cathedral clock has a much simpler method of

Salisbury Cathedral clock striking mechanism.

releasing the strike train and gets the job done with fewer parts. Although the actual release would not be as accurate as the later systems, it was entirely suitable for early clocks without hands.

The great wheel turns once per hour; the hoop wheel is part of the strike train and is locked by the locking lever against the hoop.

A. Shows the strike in locked position; the locking lever holds the loop. The strike detent (usually a lever that locks a wheel by catching its teeth) is being raised by the release pin.
B. Shows the detent, pushed by the release pin, swivelling to start raising the locking lever, which unlocks the hoop. The hoop turns, lifting the lever further and allowing the detent to fall away from the pin.
C. Shows the hoop wheel rotating, causing the bell to sound once per rotation. The latch lever is controlled by the count wheel (*see* the striking work diagram), which keeps the locking lever raised until the latch lever falls into the next slot on the count wheel, allowing the locking lever to fall into the gap in the hoop, stopping the strike train.

The diagram of the clock's striking work shows the complete striking train. As described earlier, the strike train is held by the

English lantern clock, c. *1640.*

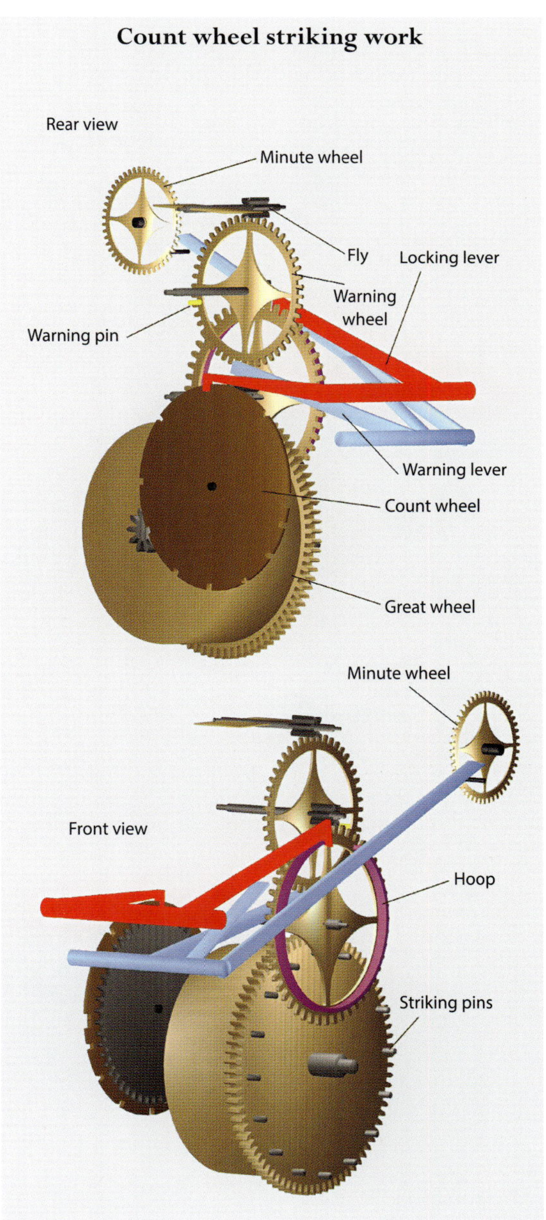

locking lever. The latch lever is locked into a slot in the count wheel. When the hoop wheel is released by the locking lever, the latch lever is also raised. The striking train runs, controlled by the fly until the next slot in the count wheel is reached, when the latch lever drops into the slot, causing the locking leaver to lower into the hoop, stopping the train. The hammer lever is connected to the bell to strike the hours, measured by the distance between each slot on the count wheel.

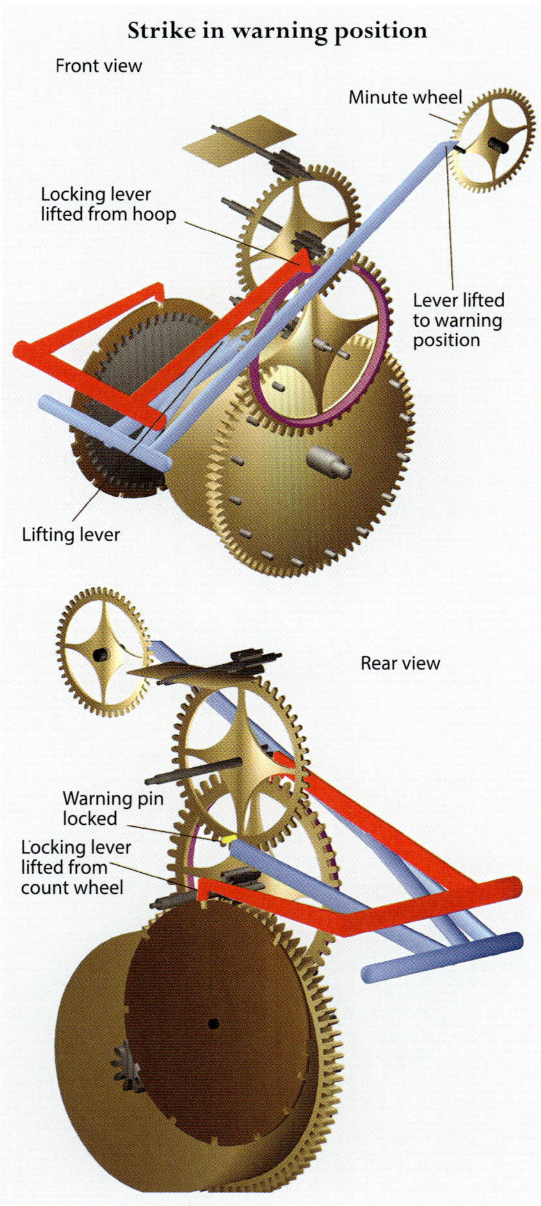

Count-Wheel Striking

As we have seen, the earliest striking systems used a count wheel to determine the number of blows struck each hour. At some time during the sixteenth century, a more advanced system was developed than that used in the early tower clocks; the main improvement was the introduction of the warning wheel. As explained earlier, at a few minutes before the hour the clock 'warns', and you will hear a click; this is the striking work being set up, ready to sound on the hour.

The illustration is of a typical early seventeenth-century lantern clock. The mechanism is divided into two parts; the going train is directly behind the dial, with the striking work at the rear. The main components are shown in the diagram.

The illustration shows the components of a typical count-wheel striking system. The great wheel is driven by a weight or mainspring and has a series of pins that lift a hammer to strike the hours. The rear view shows the count wheel, which is geared to the great wheel and controls the number of strikes. The front view shows the locking lever (red) locked into a gap in the hoop (violet), which turns clockwise once per single strike. The minute wheel is part of the going train and turns clockwise once per hour; it lifts the warning lever, which starts the striking sequence that begins with the warning.

Also illustrated here is the striking work in the warning position, ready to be released to commence striking. Note that the minute wheel is lifting the group of levers (blue) and the centre lever has lifted the (red) locking lever, which has two functions: one, to release the hoop wheel; and two, to lift the locking lever from the count wheel. The rear view shows that the warning pin (yellow) has moved anticlockwise to lock against the blue lever. The striking train is now being held ready to commence working when the minute wheel has turned to exactly the hour. At this point, the blue lever drops and releases the warning pin. This sets the strike train running until the next slot in the count wheel is reached, when the locking lever (red) falls into the hoop and locks the train until the next hour.

GIOVANNI DE DONDI'S CLOCK

All of the previously described elements can be found in the earliest surviving detailed description of a mechanical timepiece, which was written by Giovanni de Dondi (1318–89), who was professor of astronomy, logic and medicine at Padua University. In his *Tractatus astarii* of 1364, he describes an astronomical clock that he had constructed between 1348 and 1364. Most of the manuscript concerns details of the various astronomical and calendrical indications, and although it gives a brief description of the clock's workings, it is simply described as 'a common clock ... with the usual beat'. This implies that a detailed description was unnecessary because basic clock mechanisms were so well known at that time.

The detail from the manuscript clearly shows the verge escapement with a wheel-shaped time controller, rather than the usual foliot. It has been possible to build a working reconstruction of this clock from the description in the manuscript.

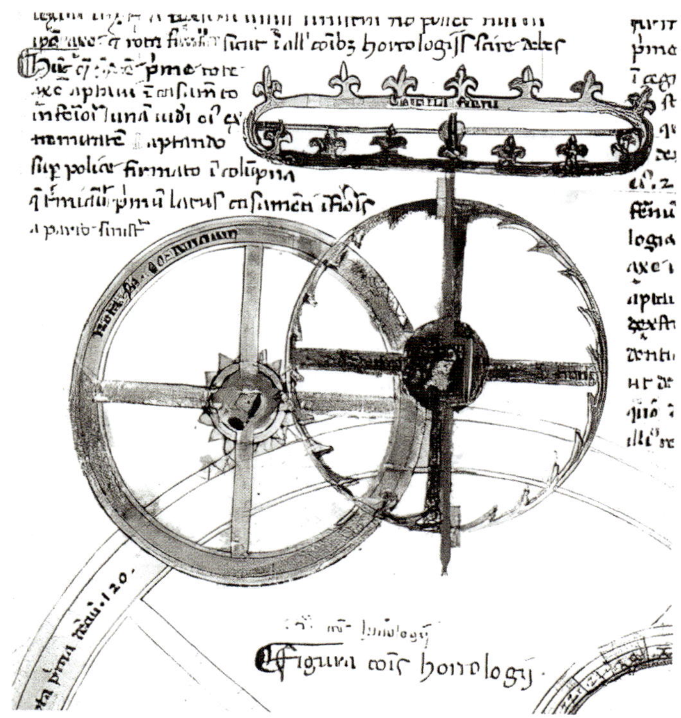

Giovanni de Dondi manuscript, Tractatus astarii.

Reconstruction of de Dondi's clock.

Chapter 3

The Early Clockmakers

Craftsmen have constantly developed specialist tools and equipment. A master was paid to introduce his apprentices to the 'secrets' of the trade; innovations were generally closely guarded and few details of how early clocks and watches were made have survived. Horologists of the sixteenth and seventeenth centuries produced intricate and beautiful devices, seemingly with the aid of simple hand tools. Descriptions of the tools and equipment they developed are rare, so we need to treasure what few sources survive to shed even a little light on the work of these early artisans.

CLOCKMAKING TOOLS

Files and Saws

The steel file was one of the most important tools in clockmaking, as it was in other crafts, such as making locks and weapons. Archaeologists have discovered bronze rasps from ancient Egypt dating from 1400BC, and from the seventh-century BC iron rasps are known to have been used by the Assyrians. Advances in steel making by the Middle Ages resulted in the development of hardened steel files, which were very similar to modern files. File blanks were originally forged, then the teeth were cut into the surface with a chisel. The file was then hardened by heating and quenching the steel.

By the sixteenth century, file-making had reached a high degree of perfection and skilled craftsmen could produce small precision files with teeth numbered in the thousands. The illustration shows a complete workshop with a forge in the background. The file cutter uses an angled hammer to strike a chisel made from high-carbon steel – another hammer can be seen beside the anvil. The file blank, in its soft state, was held on a lead block with a strap, which was tensioned with a lever operated by the artisan's foot. When it was finished, the file was heated to a high temperature in the forge (this is shown in the drawing), then quenched in oil or water to harden the steel.

File-making became concentrated in several areas, including Nuremberg in Germany, Florence in Italy and Sheffield in England. By the sixteenth century, the Lancashire town of Prescott had also become renowned for the quality of its files. The file cutter's hammer in the illustration is from the nineteenth century, but is identical to those in the sixteenth

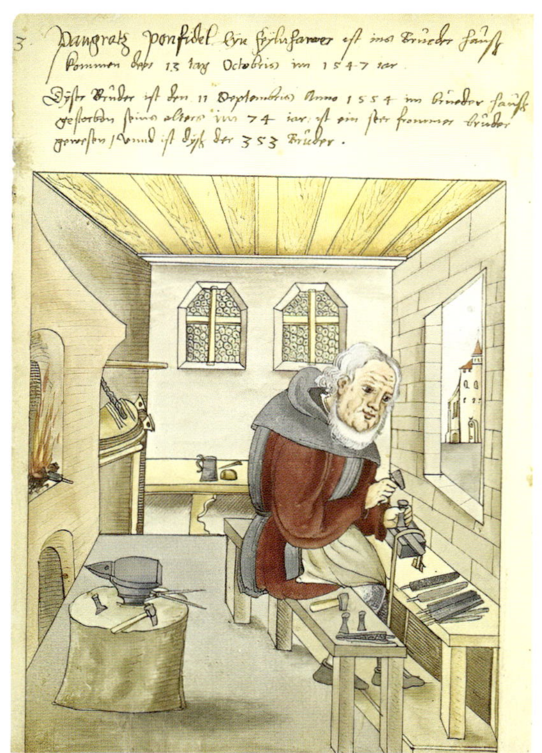

File maker from the Housebook *of Mendel, Nuremberg, 1554.*

century; Sheffield makers used it to cut files in exactly the same way as the Nuremberg file maker.

The *Encyclopédie de Diderot et d'Alembert* of 1751 is one of the earliest sources of detailed drawings of many tools, including files and a piercing saw (Fig. 1). Tools such as these would still be familiar to artisans today.

Saws have an even longer history. Copper saws from as early as 3000BC are known to have been used in ancient Egypt to cut stone using quartz sand as an abrasive. Later, steel saws were made in a similar way to knives, with teeth filed into the edge before hardening. Fine saw blades were developed, probably by clockmakers in the sixteenth century for use in piercing saws to

File cutter's hammer, English, nineteenth century.

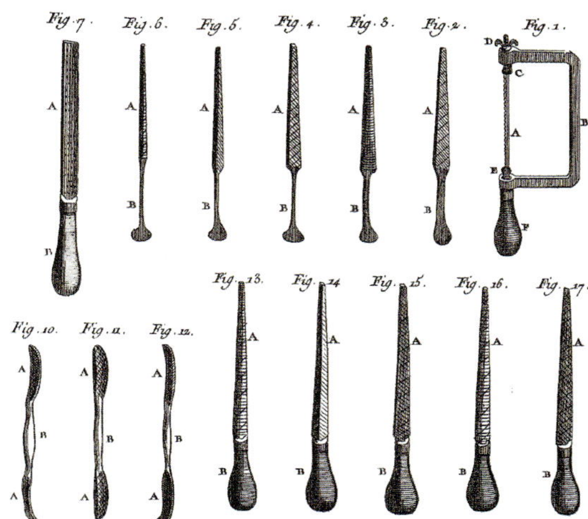

Files from Encyclopédie de Diderot et d'Alembert, *1751.*

Saw maker, sixteenth century.

cut out complex shapes from sheet metal, such as crossing-out wheels – cutting out the metal between wheel spokes.

Drills

The earliest type of drill, the bow drill, was well known to the ancient Egyptians and in one form or another, has been used until the present day. The ancient Egyptian bow drill shows the operator spinning the drill bit with a bow, whilst his assistant supports the upper end of the drill with a wooden block.

Various types of hand-operated drills were in use by the sixteenth century. The illustration from the *Encyclopédie de Diderot et d'Alembert* (Figs 40–42) shows simple bow drills with pulleys attached. The drill bit was held in place with a block placed at A, the bit B was placed on the work and the bow string wound around the pulley. Fig. 43 shows a pump drill still popular with jewellers today; the flywheel B helps with stability.

Ancient Egyptian bow drill.

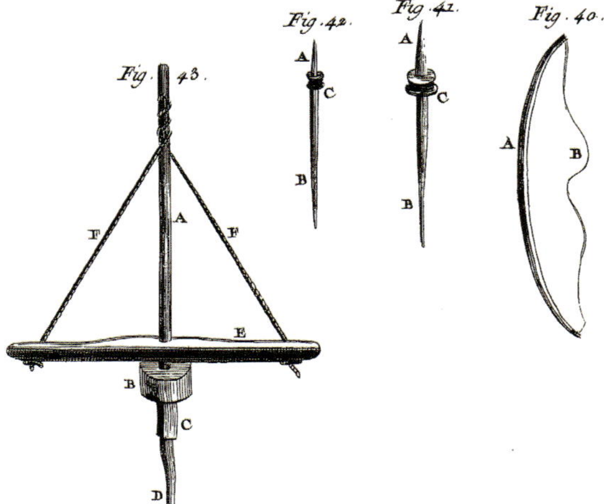

Drill types from the Encyclopédie de Diderot et d'Alembert.

Turning

Many parts of a clock or watch, such as wheels and pinions, were turned in the same way as furniture makers produced items such as chair legs. Turning was an essential skill to be mastered by an apprentice watch- or clockmaker. The illustration of an eighteenth-century watchmaker shows him using a bow in his left hand to spin a small part between centres. He uses a cutting tool called a graver in his right hand to remove metal.

This way of turning is simply a precision form of the earliest method of producing cylindrical objects developed over 3,000 years ago. Images have been discovered from ancient Egypt, such as the two-man lathe shown here from the tomb of a priest, *c.* 300BC. This shows one man spinning the object to be turned between centres with a rope, whilst the other holds the cutting tool.

Eighteenth-century watchmaker.

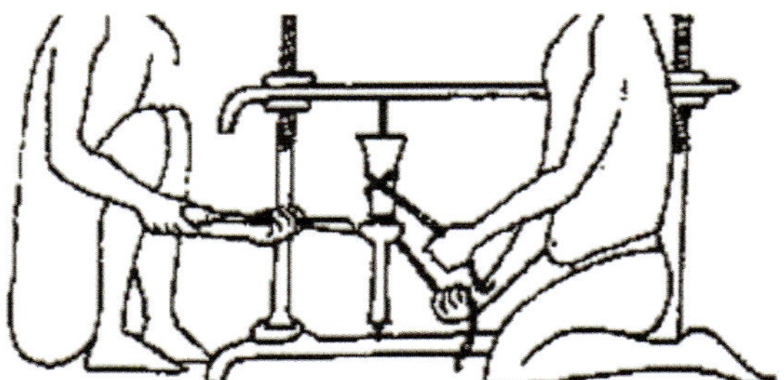

Egyptian two-man lathe.

Various types of lathes were familiar to the ancient Greeks and Romans, and by the Middle Ages pole lathes for turning wood and other

Pole lathe, 1554.

Set of turns.

materials would have been in regular use. A single operator using a foot treadle attached to a sprung pole could turn out items like chair legs with great rapidity.

The use of turns to make and finish parts such as wheel arbors and pillars was practised well into the twentieth century – a skilled craftsman could produce work of an incredibly high standard with this simple tool.

CLOCKMAKERS IN MEDIEVAL ENGLAND

The makers of the early tower clocks for religious houses were probably itinerant craftsmen who set up on site, bringing with them specialist tools and materials. Most monasteries would have had a forge and blacksmiths on hand to provide facilities for fashioning the ironwork of the clock as it was constructed. The accounts of Salisbury Cathedral show that the Bishop of Salisbury, Ralph Erghum, in the mid-1380s invited three clockmakers from Delft, Johannes and William Vrieman and Johannes Lietuijt, to construct the Salisbury clock. In 1386, a house was provided for the clock keeper. The same team was sent to Wells by Bishop Erghum in 1388 to build another clock there; this clock is now in the London Science Museum. It is also believed that designs, or possibly complete clocks, were imported from the Low Countries in the late fifteenth century and a number of these clocks, known as the Dover Castle Group, have survived in the south of England. Many of these early clocks had elaborate astronomical dials.

The Late Fifteenth-Century Cotehele Clock

A peculiarly English style of tower clock appeared in the fifteenth century. Instead of the usual bird-cage construction, like the Salisbury Cathedral clock, the wheels were mounted in a vertical frame, with the escapement and foliot at the bottom. These appear to have been made mostly in the West Country and the Midlands.

The chapel of this well-preserved medieval house was remodelled after 1485 when Sir Richard Edgcumbe, a supporter of the new King Henry VII, returned victorious from the Battle of Bosworth Field. At this time, a clock, which rang a bell on the hours, was installed in a cupboard-like alcove in the corner of the chapel.

This remarkable clock is, apart from the Salisbury and Wells Cathedral clocks, the earliest surviving in England and, unlike the other clocks, is in almost entirely original condition. Jonathan Betts (National Trust, *Cotehele Journal*, Vol. 8) notes that the well-preserved state of the mechanism indicates that it was not run for

Wells Cathedral astronomical clock dial.

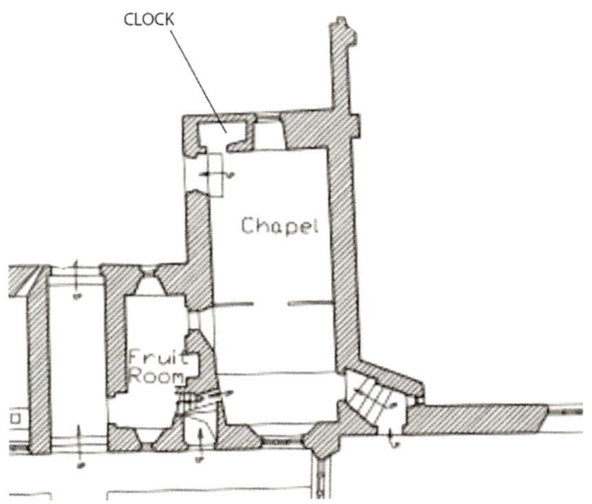

Plan of Cotehele Chapel.

Cotehele House, Cornwall.

much more than a century. He ascribes this to the fact that the clock needed daily winding and regular oiling and maintenance to keep it working, so it was probably replaced by more reliable eight-day clocks from the seventeenth century onwards. The clock's location, out of sight behind a heavy door, explains why it appears to have been forgotten until it was rediscovered in 1952. Various restoration projects, notably by Thwaites & Reed in 1962, have restored the timepiece to working order.

The clock is shown here in its alcove, together with a diagram of the main working parts. All of the components are made from iron and a wooden framework supports the assembly. The two stone driving weights hang to the right of the movement and a rod goes upwards through the ceiling to ring the bell on the chapel roof.

Cotehele House clock, late fifteenth century.

The going train with just a great wheel and escape wheel is below the striking work, with the foliot hanging suspended below the mechanism rather than the usual arrangement.

The construction of the mechanism is similar to that of the Salisbury Cathedral clock in many ways. The hoops of the wheels are mounted on two crossbars riveted in place. Before the teeth were marked out and filed, the arbor must have been fitted so that the wheel could have been spun in some kind of framework. This would have enabled the rim to be trued up by filing. Note that the wheel teeth are in the ancient triangular form.

The striking work is of an unusual form, known as flail locking; this is one of the earliest known forms of striking work. It uses a rotating bar called a flail as the warning mechanism, essential to all striking clocks. The Salisbury Cathedral clock, although earlier, uses a different system to perform the same function and is more closely related to the striking work used in most clocks until the late eighteenth century. No doubt the makers of the Cotehele clock were familiar with the more usual locking system, but chose this form due to its simplicity.

The going train consists of a great wheel attached to the winding drum; this turns once per hour and a lever on the arbor releases the strike. The verge escapement is normal, apart from being situated below the striking work with the foliot hanging downwards from a rotating bolt suspension. However, it may have once had a more usual rope suspension. The verge rod is held in place by a bracket.

Detailed views of the mechanism.

Cotehele clock striking mechanism

The illustrations show the components of the striking work and when they are running. The drive comes from the weight attached to the strike great wheel and the striking pins operate the bell. The striking sequence is as follows:

- The great wheel has a lifting lever that rotates once per hour, lifting the locking lever (green). At the same time, the locking pallet is lifted out of the slot in the count wheel, allowing the flail (blue)

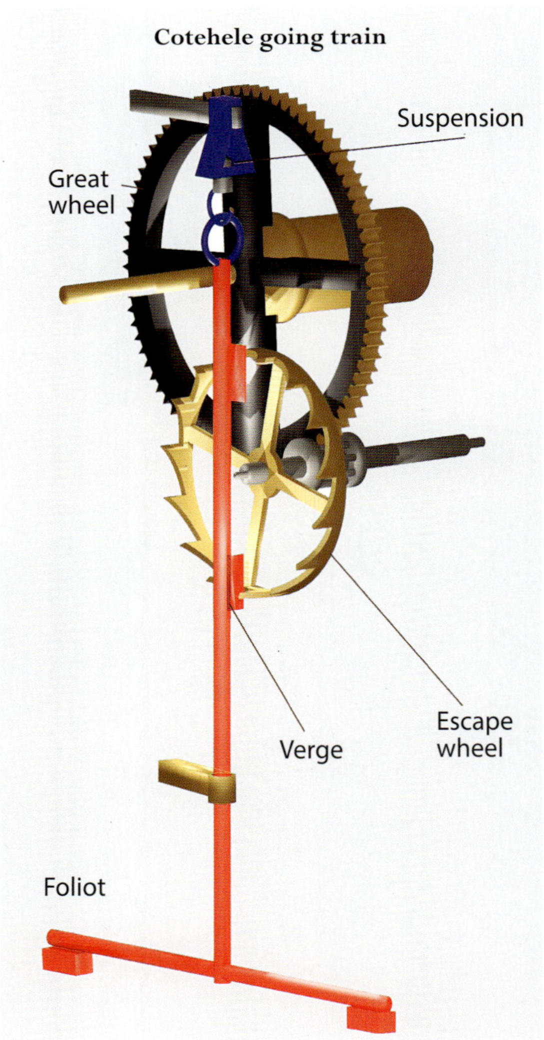

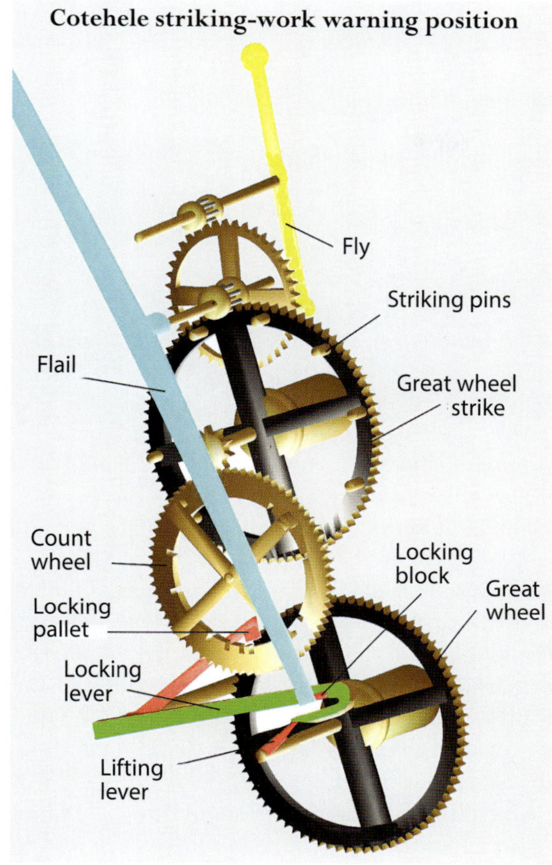

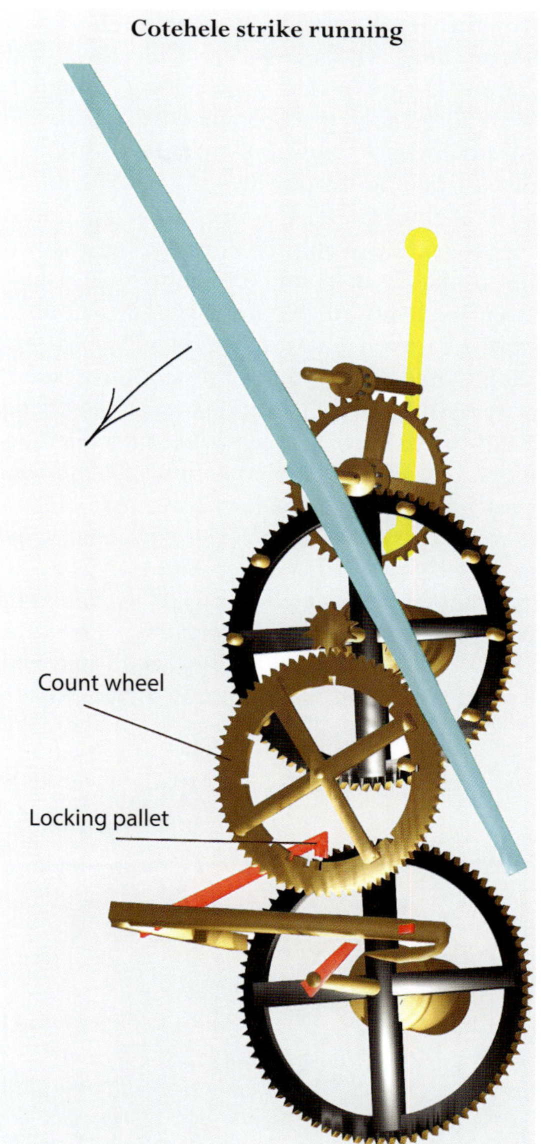

to rotate and lock on the locking block (red). This is the warning; the strike is held ready to be released at the hour, when the lifting pin rotates to release the locking lever and allow the flail to rotate.

- As the great wheel turns, it releases the locking lever and the flail (blue) rotates. The count wheel controls the number of strikes, the locking pallet (red) drops into the next slot in the count wheel and stops the striking train, ready for the next hour when the flail is released and locks in the warning position. The speed of striking is controlled by the fly (yellow).

DOMESTIC CLOCKS

As techniques of metal-working improved during the fifteenth and sixteenth centuries, and with the increasing use of brass and steel as well as iron in clock construction, smaller clocks were appearing for domestic use from the fifteenth century. The earliest surviving domestic clocks were made in German-speaking Europe in centres such as Nuremberg and Augsburg, and it is likely that the first spring-driven clocks came from this area.

The illustration of a clock workshop is a woodcut from *The Book of Trades*, published in Frankfurt am Main in 1568 by Hans Sachs (a cobbler turned poet, who was the inspiration for Wagner's *Die Meistersinger von Nürnberg*). The Swiss artist Jost Amman (1539–91) produced a set of woodcuts for the book depicting various trades in Nuremberg, including *Der Uhrmacher.* This shows a clockmaker's workshop complete with forge and workbench with a vice and an anvil where the clockmaker's apprentice or assistant is hammering out what appears to be a clock plate. The open construction of the workshop would have made the most of the available light and the shop would have been well heated by the forge. No doubt a heavy wooden shutter would close off the shop at night. The master is in conversation with a well-to-do customer who is examining a typical German sixteenth-century chamber clock of similar construction to the one shown here. This clock is mainly made of iron, is weight-driven with a verge escapement and is brightly painted.

German sixteenth-century chamber clock.

A more detailed engraving of a sixteenth-century workshop by Johannes Stradanus (1523–1605) from *c.* 1590 has survived, from a collection of prints called *Nova Reperta* (new discoveries). The images in the collection and the accompanying text demonstrated the impact of the inventions of the time. The remarkable frontispiece shows the range of the topics covered, including printing, gunpowder, the discovery of the Americas, distilling and the development of timepieces.

Johannes Stradanus, or Giovanni Stradano, was a Flemish artist active in Florence, working for the Medici court. The clock workshop depicted in the illustration, judging from the street scene visible through the open doorway, was probably in that city. In this busy workshop, we see many of the processes involved in early clockmaking. In the background is a forge with what appears to be a stone trough for quenching components; in the foreground, two artisans are seated at a bench. Clocks and watches of all kinds are displayed in various stages of completion, with a finely dressed customer examining a large clock being worked on by the master.

The younger man, depicted seated at the workbench, is filing out the teeth of a wheel held in a vice and a collection of files is to hand. However, we need to allow for artistic licence, as the wheel would have been clamped lower down in the jaws of the vice and he would have needed to support his elbows on the bench. The older man also seems to be making wheels; he has an identical vice and four files and two completed wheels can be seen on the bench. The establishment clearly produces a huge range

Der Vhrmacher.

Clock workshop, 1568.

Frontispiece of Nova Reperta.

Clockmaker's workshop, engraving by Johannes Stradanus, c. 1590.

Detail of engraving by Johannes Stradanus.

of timepieces. We see six watches hanging in a frame for testing and there are several small clocks on the bench and two completed wall-mounted clocks on the right.

The inscription gives us the clue that the engraving was not designed to represent the clockmaking of the time accurately, but as an artistic and philosophical representation of this aspect of the modern world. The Latin inscription refers to iron clocks with iron wheels that turn, to reveal both this and previous times. Nevertheless, the artist clearly modelled his image on a workshop he must have been familiar with and thus provides us with a valuable insight into sixteenth-century horology. It is interesting to compare this with the woodcut by Jost Amman, showing a much more modest establishment consisting of a master and his apprentice, which surely would have been a more typical business.

EARLY ENGLISH CLOCKMAKERS

Both Henry VIII and Elizabeth I owned many clocks and watches, mostly made in France and Germany. Clockmakers working in England include Nicholas Oursian, a Huguenot immigrant to England who served as a royal clockmaker under four monarchs. He is first recorded in 1532 and was naturalised in 1541, remaining in service until his death in 1590. The astronomical clock executed for Henry VIII at Hampton Court is signed 'N.O. 1540' and is thought to be Oursian's work.

Another Protestant immigrant, Nicholas Kratzer, a native of Munich, arrived in England around 1518 and by 1520 was described as 'deviser of the King's horloges'. He entered the service of Thomas More, who introduced him to the King. Kratzer had his portrait painted by Hans Holbein. The portrait shows him at a workbench with an unfinished polyhedral sundial and various tools. He lived in England for around 30 years, teaching astronomy and mathematics. Whether he was actually practically involved in clockmaking is not clear; however, he is believed to have contributed to the design of the great clock at Hampton Court Palace, among others.

A Clock for a Sultan

Details of an extravagant organ clock presented by Queen Elizabeth I to Sultan Mehmet III of Turkey have survived in the remarkable diary of Thomas Dallam, a Lancashire organ builder, who later built the organs for Eton College and King's College Chapel, Cambridge. The organ was 16ft high, played tunes automatically four times daily and had a 24-hour clock with various astronomical features. It was decorated on top with 'a holly bush full of blacke birds and thrushis', which 'sing and shake theire winges'. It is probable that the clock mechanism was made by Robert Harvey, who was in Oxford at the time Dallam was working on organs for several Oxford colleges. Such automata were very popular at the time, particularly in Turkey, and thus would have made a suitable gift. It was paid for by the new Levant Company that the queen had established to promote trade with the East.

Hampton Court clock.

Nicholas Kratzer *by Hans Holbein, 1528.*

Sultan Mehmet III with his court.

Dallam set sail with his great organ clock in February 1599 aboard the armed merchantman, the *Hector*. Harvey, who Dallam describes as the 'engineer', and 'Mr Rowland Buckett the paynter and Myghell Watson the joyner' were included in the party. Despite having to fight off pirates before they were clear of the English Channel, they safely entered the Mediterranean and docked at Algiers, where the King, having heard of the fabulous gift for the Sultan, demanded to see it, taking the ship's captain as hostage. It says much in favour of Dallam's diplomatic skills that he was able to negotiate his way out of this tricky situation and resume his voyage, visiting several islands and the ruins of Troy.

On docking at Constantinople, they found to their dismay that on unpacking the organ, it had suffered badly during the voyage and was in such a state that the English ambassador believed it was damaged beyond repair. However, Dallam and his team managed to restore the instrument to working order, then set it up in the Sultan's palace. Dallam was concerned to learn that the Sultan wanted to hear the organ played manually as well as automatically. He knew that as a Christian, he would not be allowed into the Sultan's presence and that it was also punishable by death to turn his back on the ruler or to touch his person. Dallam explained that the cramped space would oblige him to sit very close to the Sultan and he must also play with his back to him.

Despite his protests, the order was repeated and the terrified Dallam was thrust forward by the Chief White Eunuch. He recounts that his 'britches' brushed the Sultan's knee as he took his seat at the organ and turned his back on the royal personage and began to play some popular English tunes, and 'suche things as I coulde until the clock strouke and then bowed my head as low as I coulde, and went from him with my backe towardes him'. In the event, the Sultan was apparently delighted with the performance. He rewarded Dallam with a purse of gold coins, leaving Dallam to search for the ambassador who had been waiting elsewhere in a fever of anxiety for the last two hours, having failed to present his credentials. Eventually, the Englishmen were allowed to leave the great city and make their way home with an astonishing tale to tell.

Portrait of Sultan Mehmet III.

HUGUENOT IMMIGRATION

Protestant emigration to escape persecution in France was very important to both English and Swiss clock- and watchmaking. Huguenots, who held to the Reformed or Calvinist tradition, were a sober and industrious community and it has been estimated that over half of French horological craftsmen were Calvinist Protestants. The French Wars of Religion during the sixteenth century were a result of tensions between the Catholic population and Protestants, claiming the lives of an estimated 70,000 Huguenots. Many survivors fled to Protestant countries, with cities such as London and Geneva welcoming these highly skilled workers in many useful trades such as silk weaving, enamelling and glassmaking, as well as clock- and watchmaking. The emigration of these craftsmen resulted in a rapid expansion of the watch and clock trade in both London and Geneva at the expense of French industry. In the same period, the frequent wars that devastated central Europe caused a collapse of trade

Blackfriars, London, 1540s.

and great poverty in important centres such as Nuremberg and Augsburg. The English 'Golden Age' of horology in the eighteenth century, as well as advances in other industries, owed much to the decline of European competition and the enlightened attitude of Protestant England in welcoming foreign immigration.

In London, just outside the control of the City authorities in Blackfriars, an area known as the 'liberties' was a place favoured by many Huguenot craftsmen, including engravers and enamellers, where they could trade freely. This competition did not please a group of established London clock- and watchmakers, who objected to the Huguenot presence in a petition to King James I in 1622 to prevent them from trading – the petition failed.

Lantern Clocks

This type of domestic clock became by far the most popular in England. The name 'lantern clock' probably comes from the fact that they were predominantly constructed using brass, which was then called 'latten'. The French *Latten horloge*, or *Latten uhr* in German, was used to refer to brass clocks rather than iron; this may well have later been corrupted in England to 'lantern clock' because of its obvious resemblance to a lantern. These clocks first appeared around 1600 – the British Museum has a fine chamber clock dated 1598 by Nicholas Vallin, a Huguenot refugee who became the leading London clockmaker. This is an elaborate three-train musical clock, although simpler

Work by Nicholas Harvey.

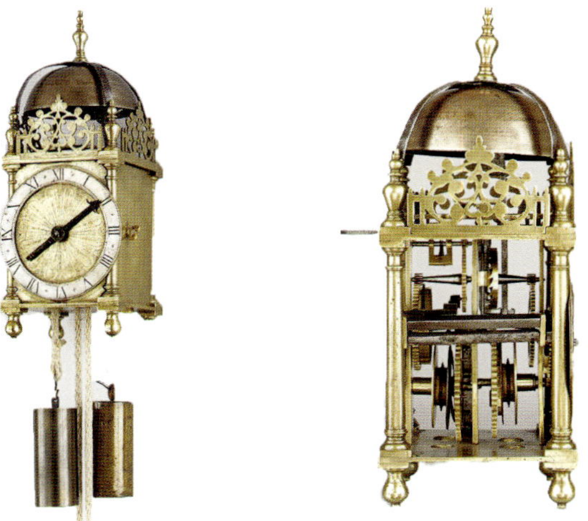

Lantern clock made by Nicholas Harvey.

Lantern clock balance.

designs based on European chamber clocks evolved from around 1600 in London and soon became the dominant form of domestic clock.

The earliest surviving lantern clock is by Nicholas Harvey, who died in 1614; the pillared construction and layout proved very successful and set the pattern for the next century. Although many examples from London and the provinces survive, very few have their original verge escapement, with simple wheel balance. Most have been later converted to anchor escapement with pendulum.

THE WORSHIPFUL COMPANY OF CLOCKMAKERS

As with most trades, guilds grew up in the centres of clock- and watchmaking, both to protect trade and control the quality of work and the training of apprentices. English clock- and watchmakers originally belonged to the Worshipful Company of Blacksmiths, founded in 1571; like other companies, they regulated membership and apprenticeships in the City of London.

Many of the growing number of clockmakers in the early seventeenth century wanted to establish their own Company. Despite opposition from the blacksmiths, they succeeded in obtaining a Royal Charter in 1631 and founded the Worshipful Company of Clockmakers. The Charter gave regulatory authority to the Company to control the horological trade in the City of London and for a radius of ten miles around. It incorporated a controlling body, which should have 'continuance for ever under the style and name of The Master, Wardens and Fellowship of the Art and Mystery of Clockmaking'.

Arms of the Worshipful Company of Clockmakers.

The first Master of the Worshipful Company of Clockmakers was David Ramsay, who was born in Dundee (date unknown) and became clockmaker to James VI of Scotland. He seems to have spent time in France as, according to his son William, he was summoned from France by the King when he succeeded to the English crown in 1603. Ramsay served both James I and Charles I; in 1613 he was given a pension of £50 a year and payments from the royal accounts are recorded during Charles' reign. When in 1631 he became the first Master of the new Worshipful Company of Clockmakers, he was described as 'of the City of London'. Ramsay died *c.* 1653 after a long career, not only making watches and clocks, but as an inventor – he obtained eight patents for inventions relating to subjects as diverse as agriculture, dyeing and metal refining. The spring-driven striking clock shown here, signed 'David Ramsay Scotland', was made around 1610 and has a French gilt and enamel case. The detail of the base shows King James with his two sons holding the Pope's nose to the grindstone, which is turned by two English bishops.

The Worshipful Company of Clockmakers limited each member to just one or two apprentices. However, C. Stuart Kelley (*Antiquarian Horology*, June 2005) points out that in the late seventeenth century many clockmakers violated this rule. It was possible to keep on apprentices when they were qualified as journeymen, who in turn could take on their own apprentices.

One of the founding members of the Worshipful Company of Clockmakers was Edward East, born in 1602 and baptised at Southill in Bedfordshire. He was apprenticed to Richard Rogers and was made a freeman of the Worshipful Company of Goldsmiths in 1627; examples of his early watches confirm that he was a fine craftsman. Despite his young age, he was appointed 'Assistant' for life in the new Company and became watchmaker to Charles I. East is first recorded as living in Pall Mall, near the Tennis Court, a convenient place to attend the King, who was said to give one of East's watches frequently as a prize. He had certainly moved to Fleet Street by 1635, when the King had a gold alarum watch fetched from East's premises there. His career was long and successful, continuing as both clock- and watchmaker until his death at the age of 94 in 1696. The illustration shows a table clock by East, *c.* 1665. It is one of the earliest clocks fitted with a pendulum and is spring-driven with a duration of 30 hours.

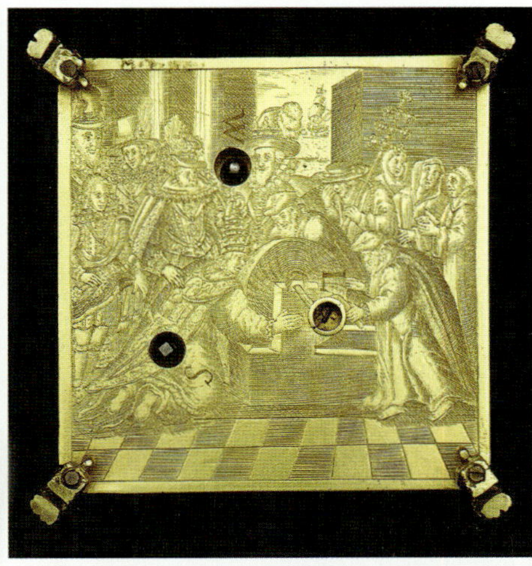

Striking clock by David Ramsay, c. 1610 (V&A Dundee).

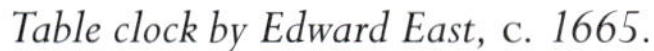

Table clock by Edward East, c. 1665.

Chapter 4

Seventeenth-Century Developments

One of the most important advances in horology was the adoption of the pendulum as the time controller, in place of the medieval foliot. It transformed the time-keeping properties of the clock, paving the way to the true precision clocks developed in the early eighteenth century.

THE INTRODUCTION OF THE PENDULUM

Galileo

Unlike the foliot, we have a good deal of evidence of the discovery of the properties of the pendulum and its application to the clock. Although some use had been made of the pendulum since ancient times and Leonardo da Vinci made drawings of the motion of pendulums, it was not until Galileo Galilei (1564–1642) began to study it seriously that the value of the pendulum for timekeeping was realised. The earliest firm date for his experiments is found in a letter to Guido Ubaldo del Monte, dated 29 November 1602, although it was later claimed by his student Vincento Vivani that the young Galileo had been inspired by the swinging of a chandelier in the cathedral at Pisa.

The crucial property that Galileo discovered is known as isochronism, which is that the time of a pendulum's swing, its period, is approximately independent of the amplitude or width of the swing. He also found that period is proportional to the square root of the length of the pendulum and is not affected by the mass of the bob. He realised that the pendulum could be useful as a timing device, simply by counting the number of swings, or vibrations (from the Latin *vibrare* – to move rapidly to and fro). Shortly before his death, Galileo gave instructions to his son Vincenzo for the construction of a pendulum clock. However, although in 1846 a drawing was discovered of the design for the clock, there is no evidence that Vincenzo was able to complete it before his death in 1649. Galileo's biographer, Vincenzo Viviani, describes the invention:

Galileo Galilei, *early portrait by Ottavio Leoni of Rome (1587–1630).*

> One day in 1641, while I was living with him at his villa in Arcetri, I remember that the idea occurred to him that the pendulum could be adapted to clocks with weights or springs,

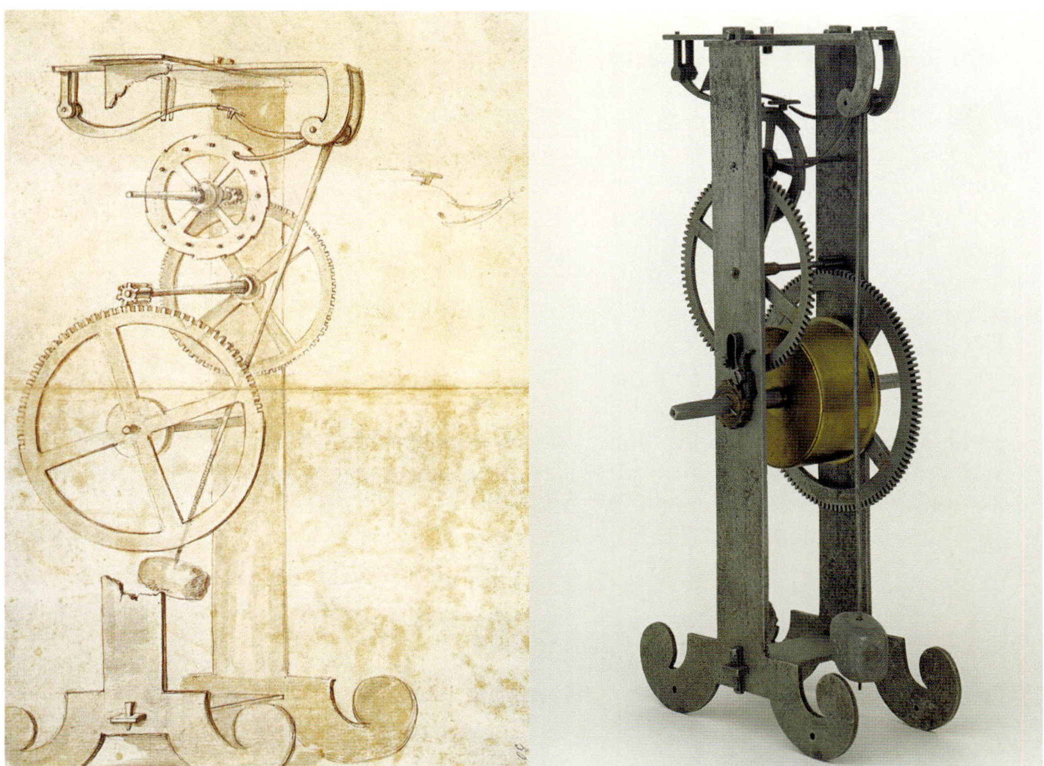

Drawing of Galileo's design for a pendulum clock, with a photograph of a nineteenth-century reconstruction.

> serving in place of the usual tempo, he hoping that the very even and natural motions of the pendulum would correct all the defects in the art of clocks. But because his being deprived of sight prevented his making drawings and models to the desired effect, and his son Vincenzio coming one day from Florence to Arcetri, Galileo told him his idea and several discussions followed. Finally, they decided on the scheme shown in the accompanying drawing, to be put in practice to learn the fact of those difficulties in machines which are usually not foreseen in simple theorising. (Vincenzo Viviani, *Historical account of the Life of Galileo Galilei*)

After the discovery of the drawing in the nineteenth century, several reconstructions were made, showing that the design was practical. However, although Galileo has the credit for discovering the timekeeping properties of the pendulum, the application to a clock mechanism came some years after his death.

Christiaan Huygens by C. Netscher, 1671.

Christiaan Huygens

The great Dutch scientist Christiaan Huygens (1629–95) was the first to apply the pendulum to a clock. The earliest experiments were probably made during 1656, although there is some doubt as to who actually constructed the first pendulum clock to Huygens' design. The Paris clockmaker Isaac Thuret has been linked with Huygens, with two surviving Thuret pendulum clocks being dated to 1656. The other contender is the Dutch clockmaker, Saloman Coster. Huygens was working with Coster in the same year, using a normal verge escapement to impulse the pendulum. The patent application was submitted in June 1657 on Huygens' behalf by Coster and seven simple domestic pendulum clocks made by him under Huygens' licence have survived.

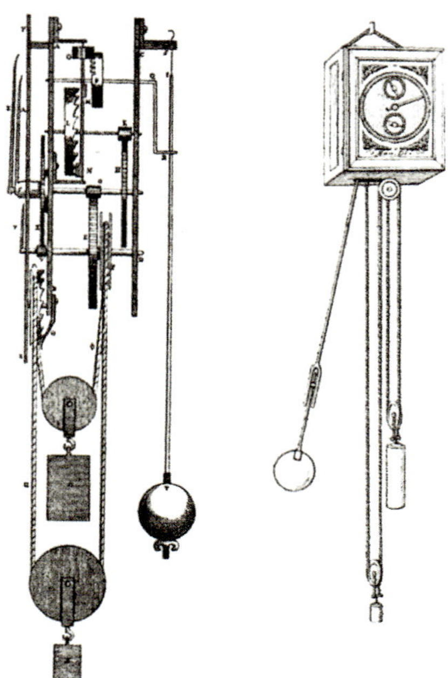

Huygens' pendulum clock from Horologium Oscillatorium, *1673.*

In 1673, Huygens published his ground-breaking book, the *Horologium Oscillatorium: Sive de Motu Pendulorum ad Horologia Aptato Demonstrationes Geometricae* ('The Pendulum Clock: or Geometrical Demonstrations Concerning the Motion of Pendula as Applied to Clocks'). This was not simply a description of the pendulum clock, but a seminal work of applied mathematics that analyses the accelerated motion of a falling body.

Huygens had become aware that the pendulum was not truly isochronous. He discovered that longer swings of a pendulum took slightly more time than shorter swings. This later became known as circular error. Providing that a clock could be relied on to keep its pendulum vibrating in a constant arc, this would not be

I

CHRISTIANI HVGENII

ZVLICHEMII, CONST. F.

HOROLOGIVM OSCILLATORIVM,

SIVE

DE MOTV PENDVLORVM AD HOROLOGIA APTATO

Demonſtrationes Geometricæ.

ANNVS agitur ſextus decimus ex quo fabricam horologiorum, tunc recens à nobis inventorum, edito libello publicam fecimus. Ab illo verò tempore cùm multa invenerimus ad perfectionem operis ſpectantia, viſum eſt ea ſingula hoc libro exponere. Quæ quidem adeo ad perfectionem ejus inventi pertinent, ut potiſſima ejus pars cenſeri poſſint, ac velut fundamentum totius mechanicæ hujus, quo prius deſtituta erat. Menſura enim temporis certa atque æqualis pendulo ſimplici naturâ non inerat, cum latiores excurſus anguſtioribus tardiores obſerventur; ſed geometria duce diverſam ab ea, ignotamque antea penduli ſuſpenſionem reperimus, animadversâ lineæ cujuſdam curvaturâ, quæ ad optatam æqualitatem illi conciliandam mirabili planè ratione comparata eſt. Quam poſtquam

A

Horologium Oscillatorium *by Christiaan Huygens, 1673.*

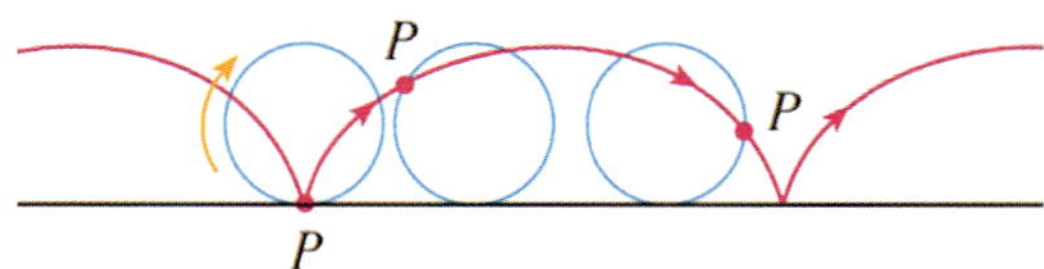

A cycloid.

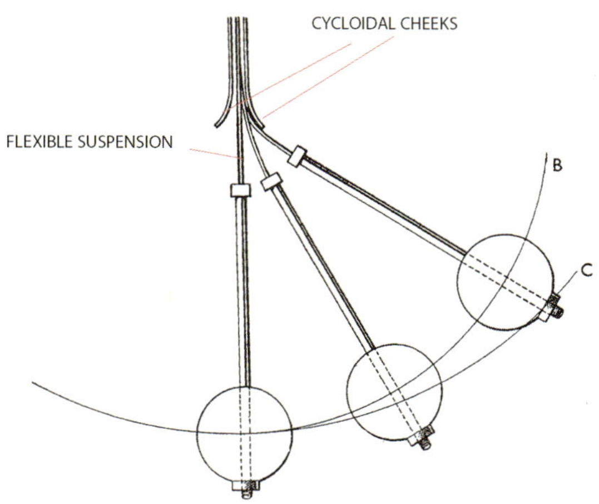

Cycloidal cheeks.

a problem. However, early clocks fitted with verge escapements allowed considerable variation in the arc of the pendulum. In an attempt to cancel out circular error, Huygens came up with an ingenious solution. He invented a way of forcing the pendulum arc to change from a segment of a circle to a cycloid.

A cycloid is a curve generated by a point on a circle rolling along a flat surface. In the diagram, point P generates the cycloidal curve as the blue circle rolls along the surface. Huygens used a pair of cycloidal cheeks on either side of a flexible pendulum suspension (usually a pair of cords), which causes the normal circular arc C to change to a cycloid B as the pendulum swings. This makes the larger arcs slightly shorter than the smaller arcs, compensating for circular error.

The illustration shows Huygens' drawing of a clock demonstrating the arrangement of the cycloidal cheeks applied to a seventeenth-century clock with a verge escapement.

The earliest surviving pendulum clock is in the Rijksmuseum Boerhaave, Leiden. It is a spring-driven timepiece constructed by Saloman Coster in 1657, displayed next to a copy of Huygens' *Horologium Oscillatorium*. Huygens claimed an accuracy of 10 seconds per day for these clocks.

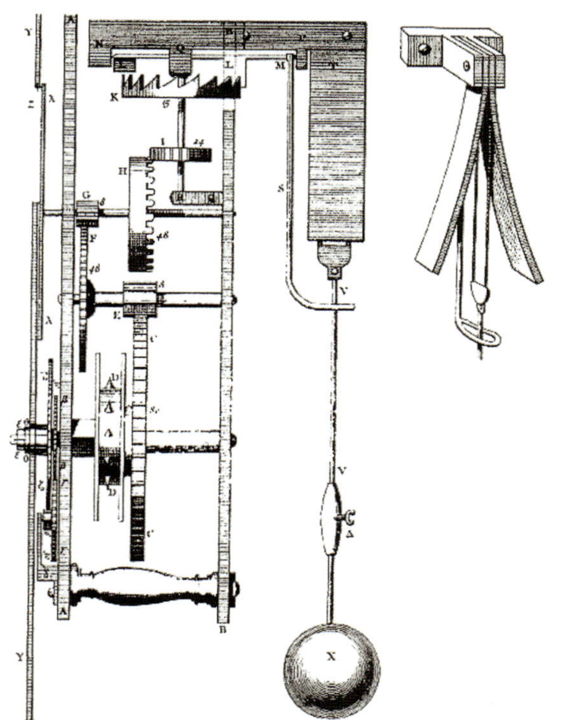

Huygens' pendulum clock from Horologium Oscillatorium.

Clock by Saloman Coster, 1657.

FROMANTEEL AND THE FIRST ENGLISH PENDULUM CLOCKS

Ahasuerus Fromanteel was the first English maker to produce pendulum clocks. He was born in Norwich in 1607 to a family who had emigrated from Flanders due to the Spanish conquest. It is not clear how he received his training as a clockmaker; author Brian Loomes suggests it was from Jacques van Berthen, later anglicised to Jacob Barton. However, it is clear that Fromanteel was an accomplished craftsman by the time he settled in London in 1629, where he joined the clockmaking community, working on tower clocks in East Smithfield. Like other clockmakers, he joined the Company of Blacksmiths in 1630, then in 1632 was accepted as a 'brother' in the new Company of Clockmakers.

From 1632, Fromanteel disappears from the records for over twenty years, until November 1658, when an advertisement appeared in *Mercurius Politicus* – a weekly publication printed from 1650 to 1660 – offering for sale all manner of timepieces, including clocks with his new 'regulator', that is, the pendulum. This was remarkable, as it was just the year after the first Coster pendulum clocks.

The Fromanteel family maintained its Dutch connection, therefore it is no coincidence that John Fromanteel, the son of Ahasuerus, had travelled to The Hague in September 1657 to work for Saloman Coster. A contract survives setting out the payments to the eighteen-year-old for making clocks on Coster's premises. It was probably in this workshop that the first pendulum clocks were constructed according to Huygens' design. We cannot be sure which clocks Fromanteel worked

Early pendulum wall clock by Ahasuerus Fromanteel, c. 1660.

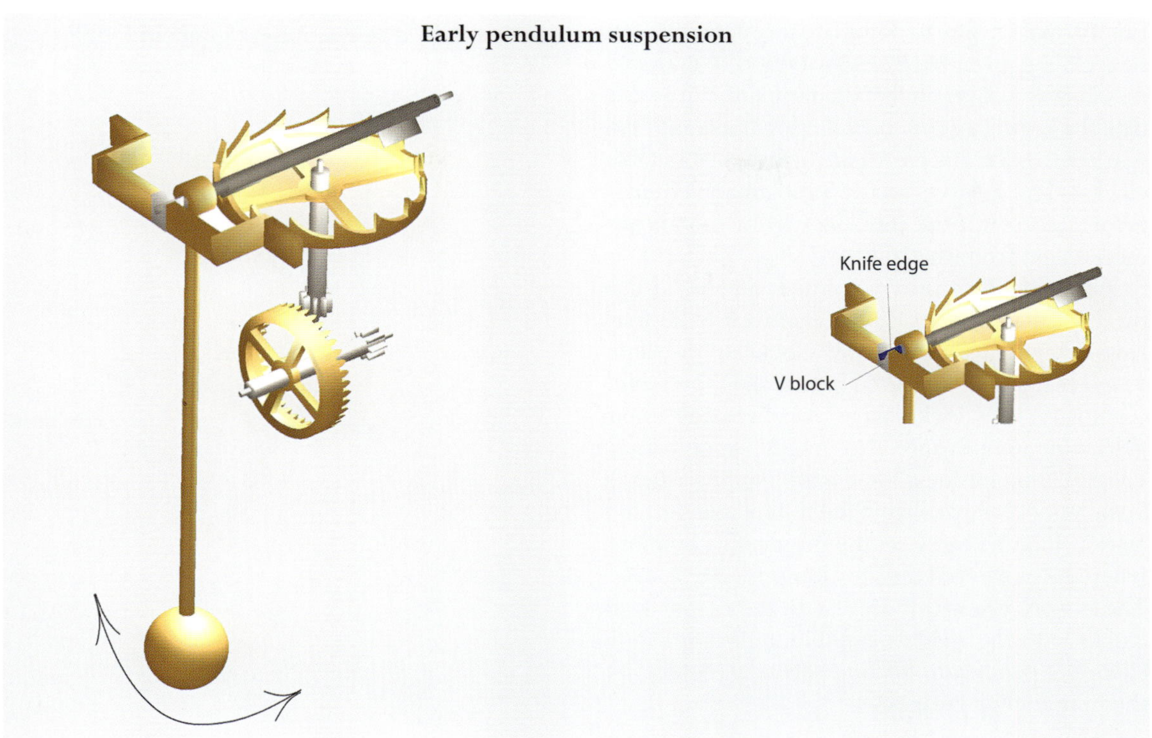

on; however, he must have been familiar with the new designs. John Fromanteel left Coster's employment in May 1658, bringing Huygens' discovery to England, where he rejoined the family firm and began producing the new pendulum clocks, soon to be copied by the rest of the trade. Illustrated here is an early Fromanteel pendulum wall clock in the Museum of Modern Art, New York. The construction is a great advance on the earlier lantern clocks. The wheels are now arranged between two brass plates and the new pendulum is attached directly to the verge pallets.

Rather than suspend the pendulum by a flexible spring or cords as shown in the Huygens drawing, Fromanteel attached a knife edge to the rear of the pendulum that rested in a steel 'V' block. This reduced friction and was very robust, allowing the clock to be moved without removing the pendulum. This method was very successful and was used in verge table clocks for over a century.

Although generally accepted as being the first to adapt the pendulum successfully to a clock, Huygens largely failed to profit from his work; he only managed to obtain a patent in Holland, leaving

John Wilkins *by John Greenhill,* c. *1670.*

English makers free to dominate the market for the new clocks. Even Huygens' invention of cycloidal cheeks was not generally taken up, due to the fact that the clock needed to be firmly fixed and was not suitable for the increasingly fashionable table clocks. The answer to the problem of circular error came with the introduction of the anchor escapement from the 1670s.

Ahasuerus Fromanteel claimed patronage from the Lord Protector, Oliver Cromwell, who may have owned one of these new clocks. In the same year, Fromanteel appeared before the Worshipful Company of Clockmakers for breaking their rules by employing too many apprentices. Clearly, his business was thriving. Ahasuerus Fromanteel eventually moved to Holland, leaving his son John to carry on the business in London, where he pioneered the new longcase clock style. These were essentially similar to the earlier wall clocks with the weights cased in, but with a long ('Royal') pendulum beating seconds enabled by the new anchor escapement.

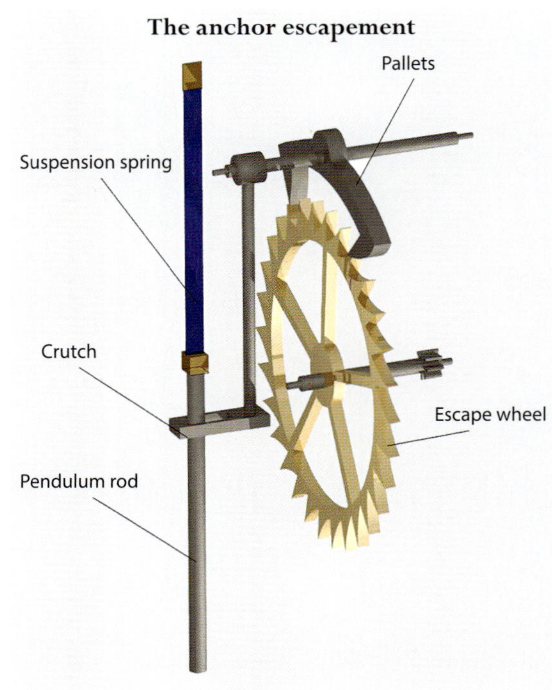

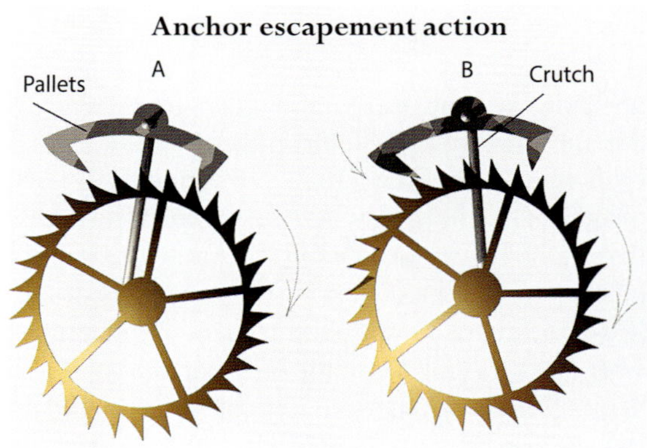

The Royal Society

In the mid-seventeenth century, a generation of 'natural philosophers', inspired by the work of Francis Bacon, were transforming experimental science. In England, John Wilkins gathered together a group known as the Philosophical Society of Oxford, including Christopher Wren and Robert Boyle, who held regular meetings from 1645 in Oxford and Gresham College, London.

By 1660, twice weekly meetings were being held in rooms at Gresham College and after a meeting in November it was proposed that a 'college' should be constituted, known as the 'College for the Promoting of Physico-Mathematical Experimental Learning', which would meet weekly to run and discuss experiments. Two years later, the King signed a royal charter, naming it the 'Royal Society of London' and Robert Hooke was appointed Curator of Experiments.

THE ANCHOR ESCAPEMENT

As discussed earlier, Huygens, who first explored in detail the properties of the pendulum, discovered that it was not truly isochronous, so added his cycloidal cheeks to provide a form of compensation, although this method never came into general use. Huygens showed that circular error could be more or less eliminated if the pendulum's amplitude was restricted to below 2 degrees; however, this was not possible with the verge escapement. A new escapement appeared in the early 1670s, replacing the earlier verge type and allowing a pendulum to work with a much smaller amplitude. It became known as the anchor escapement, due to the shape of the pallets. The escapement used a vertical escape wheel engaged by pallets connected to a crutch

Early longcase clock by John Fromanteel.

(invented by Huygens), which transferred the impulse to the pendulum.

In the diagram, A shows the impulse given to the right-hand pallet face, which pushes the pallet assembly anticlockwise, locking the left-hand pallet against the escape wheel tooth in B. The escape wheel then pushes the pallets back to the A position, locking the right-hand pallet. Thus, the reciprocating action of the pallets gives the pendulum its impulse through the crutch. After the impulse is given, the continued swing of the pendulum pushes the wheel backwards; this is known as the recoil and can be seen by observing the seconds hand of a typical longcase clock, which will move back a little after each impulse.

The anchor escapement could be constructed to keep the amplitude of the pendulum below 2 degrees, more or less eliminating circular error and enabling the earlier short 'bob pendulum' to be replaced with a much longer pendulum of approximately 1m in length, beating seconds. This was christened the Royal Pendulum and was enclosed in a tall case behind the weights. The longcase clock was thus born, capable of an accuracy of a few seconds per day. However, due to its robust design and portability, the earlier design with the verge escapement continued to be used in spring-driven table and bracket clocks for the next century.

The illustration shows one of the first of the new longcase clocks from the early 1670s; the long pendulum can be seen hanging from a flexible 'suspension spring' threaded through the crutch. The clock strikes the hours on the bell. This design was so successful that it set the pattern of domestic longcase clocks for over two centuries.

Who Invented the Anchor Escapement?

The identity of the inventor of the anchor escapement has been a subject of considerable dispute. The London clockmaker William Clement made a tower clock for King's College Cambridge in 1671, which was claimed to be the earliest example of the escapement. In 1694, John Smith, writing about the introduction of the new long pendulum in his *Horological Disquisitions*, claimed: '... that eminent and well known Artist Mr William Clement, had at last the good Fortune to give it the finishing Stroke, he being indeed the real contriver of that curious kind of long pendulum, which is at this Day so universally in use among us'. However, the anchor escapement in this clock is now known to have been fitted as part of a rebuilding in 1819.

A strong claim to the invention has been made for Robert Hooke. In 1696, William Derham (*The Artificial Clockmaker*, p.96) reported that: '... Dr Hooke denies Mr Clement to have invented this; and says that it was his Invention, and that he caused a piece of this nature to be made, which he showed the R Society, soon after the Fire of London *1666*'. As well as being a brilliant mathematician and scientist, Robert Hooke took a great interest in horology and was active in developing new ideas for the improvement of timekeeping, working with the up-and-coming Thomas Tompion (*see* Chapter 5), one of the finest craftsmen of his generation. Hooke had a habit of keeping his inventions secret, hoping to exploit them later for financial gain, whilst moving on to another problem – until someone came up with a similar idea, when he furiously claimed priority. However, no evidence has been forthcoming to confirm that he had in fact demonstrated the escapement to the Royal Society.

A third claim has been made for the great clockmaker Joseph Knibb, who was known to have been working along similar lines. Dr C.F.C. Beeson (*Clockmaking in Oxfordshire 1400–1850*) has proposed that Knibb built a new tower clock for Wadham College, University of Oxford in 1669 with an anchor escapement.

ROBERT HOOKE

One of the greatest contributors to the science of horology, Robert Hooke, was born on the Isle of Wight in 1635. From an early age, he was fascinated by mechanics and drawing. On the

Portrait of a Mathematician, *believed to be Robert Hooke, by Mary Beale (1633–99).*

Robert Boyle *by Johann Kerseboom,* c. *1689.*

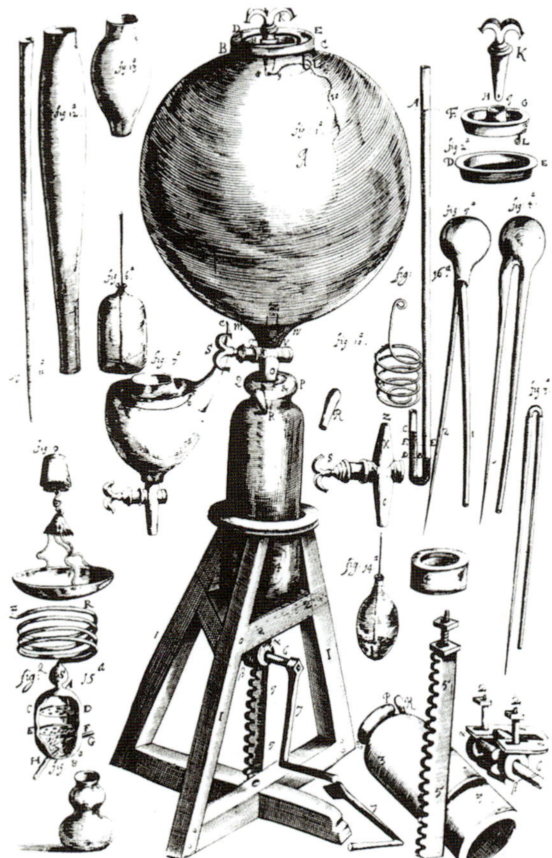

Boyles' air pump.

death of his father, an Anglican priest, in 1648, he moved to London and entered Westminster School, where he flourished, mastering Latin and Greek and beginning his study of mechanics. He also studied the organ and used this skill to secure a chorister's place at Christ Church, University of Oxford in 1653 and it was there that he met the scientist Robert Boyle, who employed Hooke as his assistant from 1655 to 1662. One of his tasks was constructing and operating Boyle's improved air pump and he probably had a hand in the development of the mathematics of Boyle's Law, concerning the behaviour of gases.

During his time in Oxford, Hooke formed close relationships with other natural philosophers apart from Boyle, including Christopher Wren, John Wilkins and John Evelyn, who became

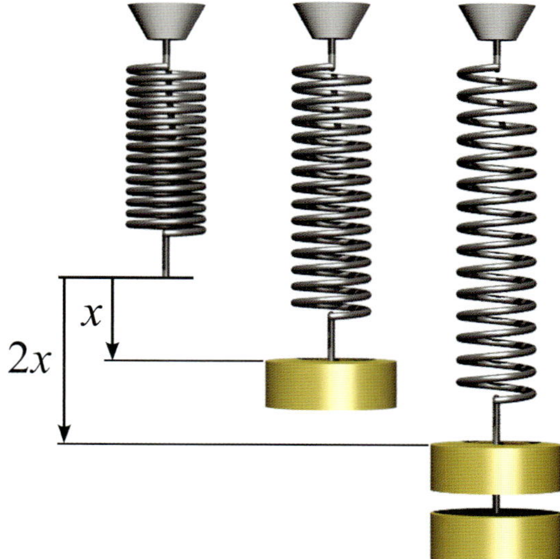

Hooke's Law.

founding members of the Royal Society. Boyle released Hooke from his employment to take up his post as Curator of Experiments at the new Royal Society. Among his duties was to arrange demonstrations and commission the manufacture of scientific instruments. An important instrument he had caused to be constructed was an astronomical quadrant. Through this commission, Hooke became associated with the rising young watchmaker Thomas Tompion, beginning a lifetime friendship; in fact, most of what we know about Tompion comes from Hooke's diaries.

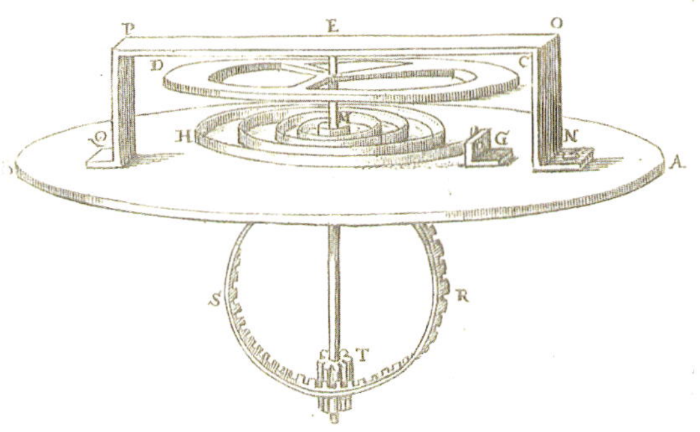

Huygens' drawing of 1675 showing a balance wheel with spring attached.

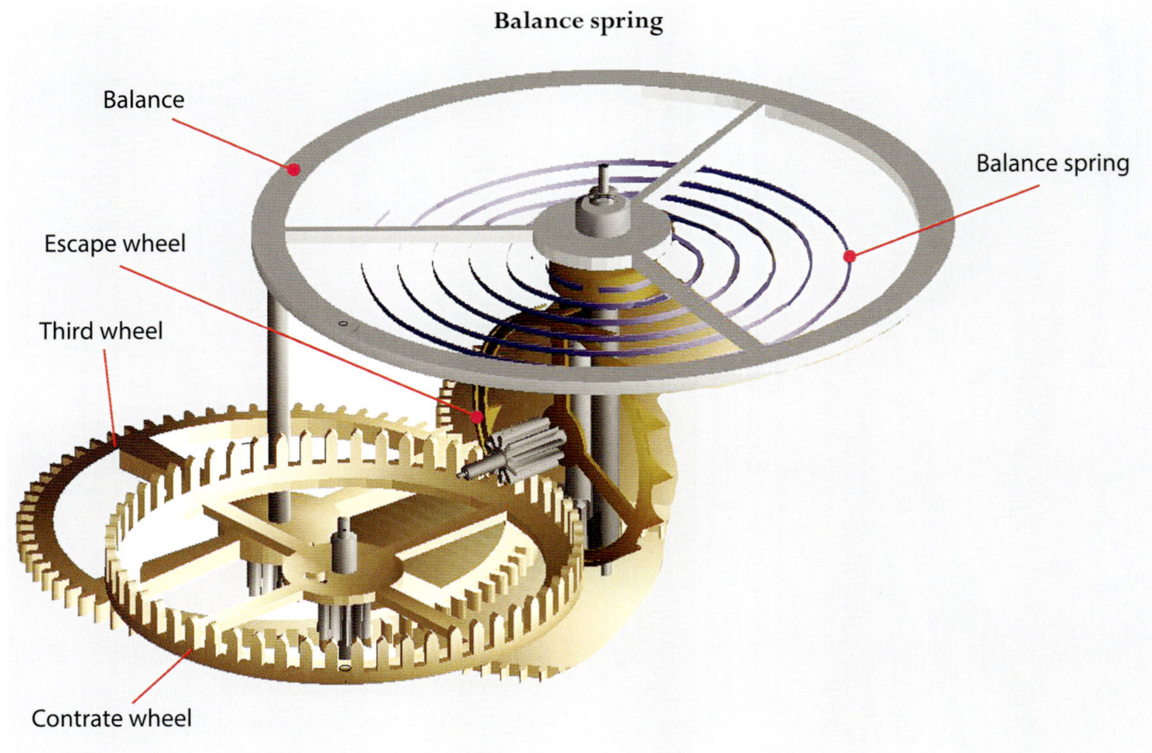

The Invention of the Balance Spring

Amongst his many discoveries in mechanics, Hooke was the first to formulate the properties of the spring. In 1660, he produced Hooke's Law, which states that the extension of a spring is in direct proportion with the load applied to it.

This discovery led to a revolutionary improvement in horology, that of the balance spring (often called the hairspring), first to the balance wheels of watches and later in marine chronometers and other portable clocks. The innovation was hotly disputed at the time. Hooke's rival, Christiaan Huygens, claimed to have invented the balance spring and he published a drawing in 1675 showing a spring attached to a watch balance, although the drawing of the escapement is inaccurate.

When a spiral spring was applied to the watch balance, the action of the spring had a profound effect on timekeeping. As the balance oscillated, the spring had a strong influence over the time taken for each turn of the wheel. The rate could now be controlled by the strength of the spring. rather than just the inertia of the wheel.

Watch by Thomas Tompion.

Tompion watch with balance spring and regulator

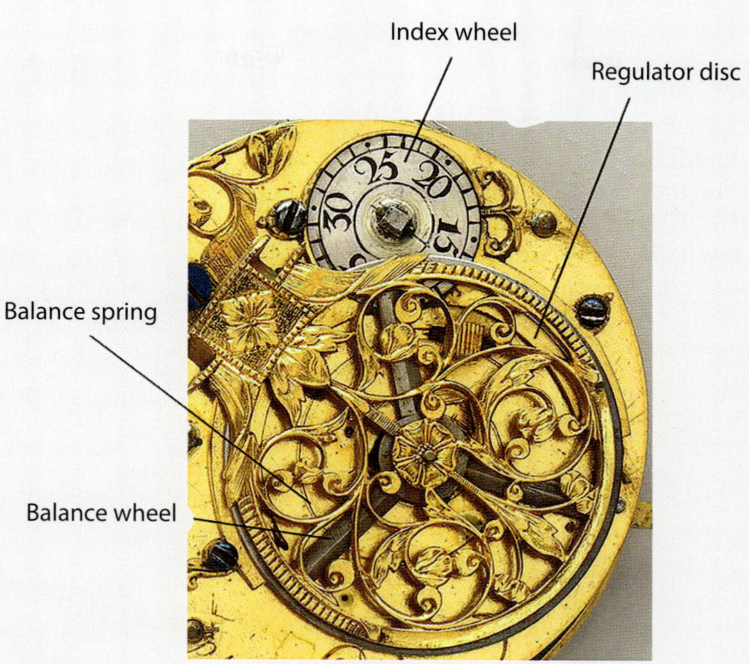

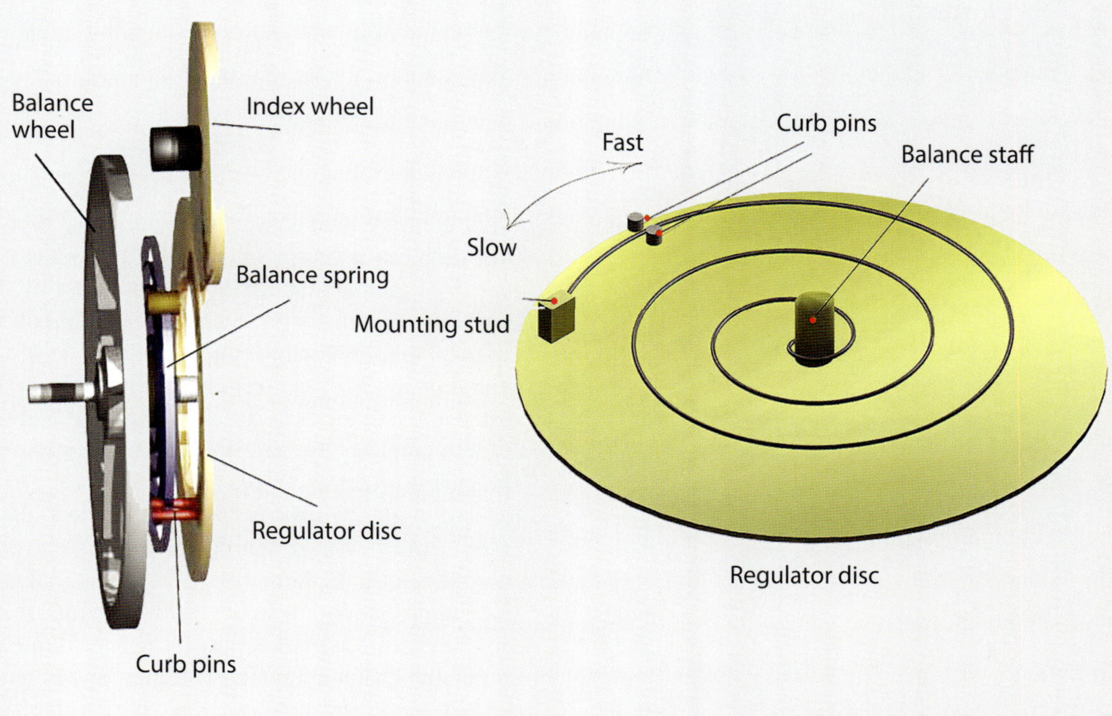

Huygens tried to obtain a Royal patent on the device; he also sent a claim as to his priority for the invention to the Royal Society in early 1675. When Hooke heard about this, he immediately made a counterclaim and produced a watch with a balance spring, probably made for him by Thomas Tompion some years earlier. Unfortunately, this watch has not survived, although we do have a witness to a demonstration of a new balance-spring watch by Hooke to the Royal Society in 1668. Lornzo Magalotti of the Florentine Academy describes the watch as: '... regulated by a little spring of tempered wire which at one end is attached to the balance wheel'.

The Metropolitan Museum of Art in New York has an extraordinary watch by Tompion from 1682, which has a balance spring of three turns and a regulator. It also has a seconds hand, a most unusual feature at that time. Tompion's design with a regulator under the balance became the standard pattern for the next century. The illustration shows a typical Tompion balance-spring watch. The effective length of the balance spring is controlled by the curb pins, which are mounted on each side of the balance spring on the regulator disc. The index wheel gears with the regulator disc. When the disc rotates to shorten the effective length of the balance spring, the rate increases; lengthening the spring slows the rate.

Rack striking work, longcase clock.

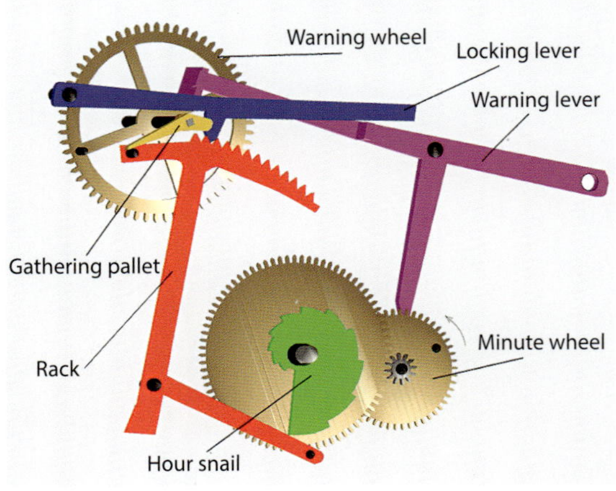

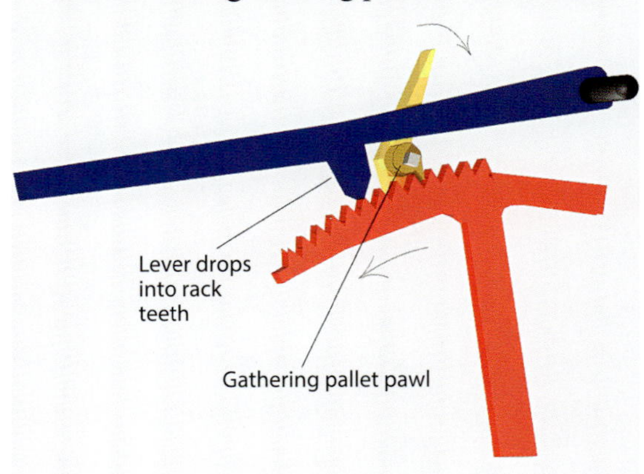

The evidence clearly favours Hooke's claim to the invention and Tompion certainly played a central role in the new design's success. All earlier single-handed watches now became obsolete; instead of timekeeping of half an hour or so per day, balance-spring watches would go to within a few minutes per day, which justified the inclusion of a minute hand.

RACK STRIKING

A considerable improvement to the earlier count-wheel striking mechanism was made in the last quarter of the seventeenth century. The inventor is unknown, although it was formerly credited to the Rev. Edward Barlow (1639–1719). The great advantage of this new system was that it separated the counting device from the striking train, unlike the count-wheel system, which always struck the next hour, meaning that if the hands were set too quickly, they would get out of sequence. The photograph shows the striking work for a typical longcase clock and this basic design has continued for all striking clocks up to the present day.

The diagram shows the main components. The gathering pallet (yellow) turns to advance the rack (red) one tooth for each turn of the warning wheel; this rotates once for each blow of the bell hammer. The arm of the gathering pallet is locked on to a pin on the rack.

The diagram of the rear view of the gathering pallet shows how, as it rotates, the pawl moves the rack one tooth per turn and the lever rises and falls to lock into each tooth as the rack advances. Before the striking work starts, the warning must take place.

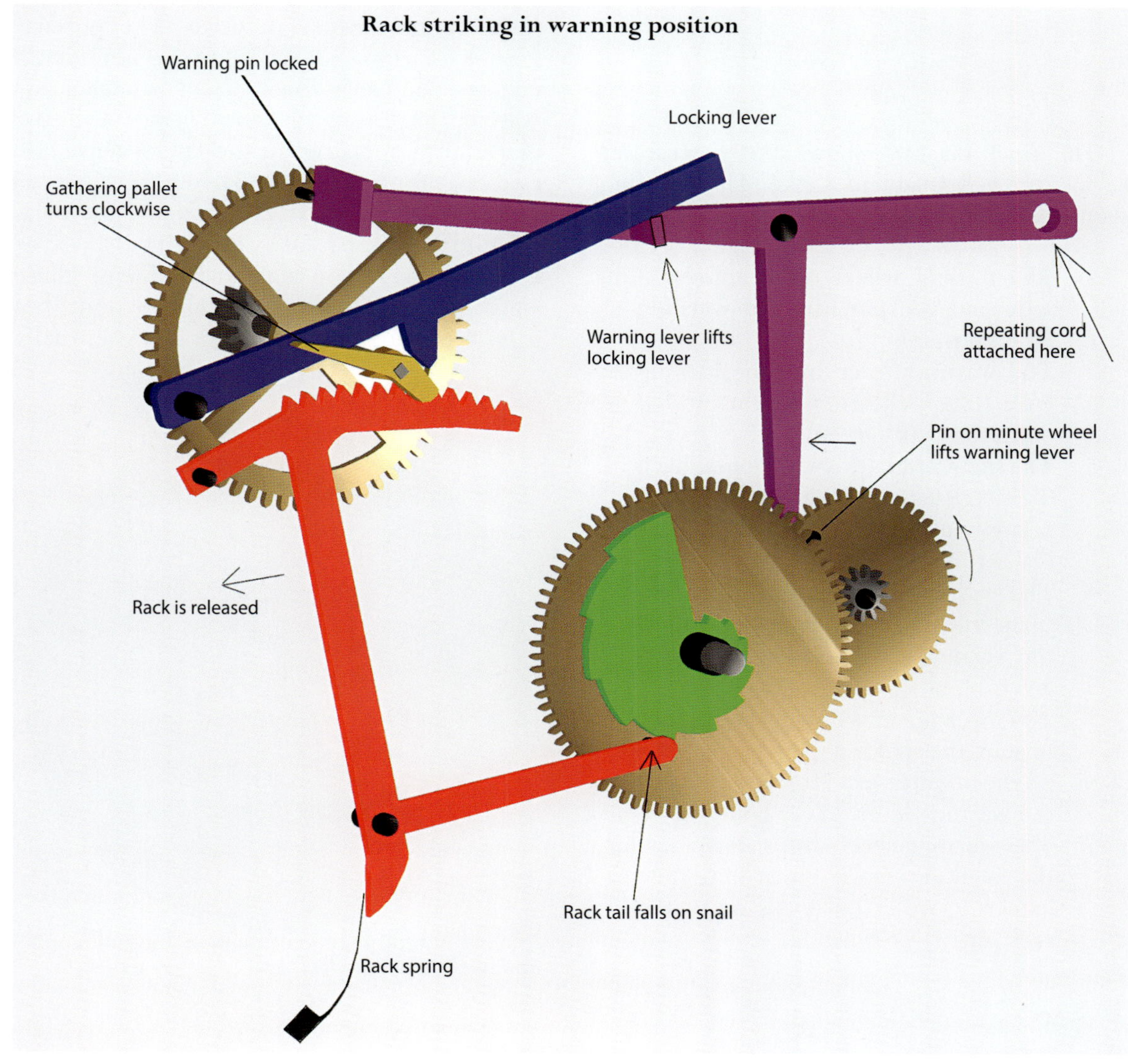

Repeating table clock by Thomas Tompion, c. *1690.*

The final diagram shows the mechanism having warned ready to strike. The warning sequence is as follows:

1. The minute wheel turns anticlockwise and the pin lifts the warning lever (purple).
2. The warning lever lifts the locking lever (blue), allowing the rack to fall on to the snail (green).
3. The snail rotates every 12 hours. Each division lets the rack fall to the appropriate hour position; it is shown here ready to strike five o'clock.
4. The gathering pallet is now free to turn with the warning wheel, until the warning pin is held by the locking lever.
5. The mechanism is now locked, ready to start the striking sequence.
6. As the minute wheel turns, it releases the warning lever on the hour.
7. The warning lever drops down and the striking train runs until the gathering pallet tail locks on to the rack pin.

Repeating Mechanisms

It was not long before clockmakers realised that this new system could be easily adapted to 'repeat' the strike, that is, strike the previous hour again. This was a very useful feature, which allowed the owner a means of getting an approximate time at night, without the trouble of using a tinder box to light a candle. A cord was attached to the extended warning lever (*see* previous diagram), the cord was threaded through an opening and hung down the side of the case. When pulled and released, the clock struck the previous hour.

The Tompion table clock shown here was spring-driven and could easily be placed near the owner's bedside. Such clocks became increasingly common from the late seventeenth century onwards. The popular French carriage clocks from the nineteenth century onwards used such a repeating system. Repeating watches using a similar mechanism appeared in the late seventeenth century. Both Edward Barlow and Daniel Quare claimed priority, although Quare was granted the first patent by James II in 1687. The major makers soon started producing these watches, at first just repeating the hour, but soon repeating quarter hours and eventually

Nineteenth-century dividing plate.

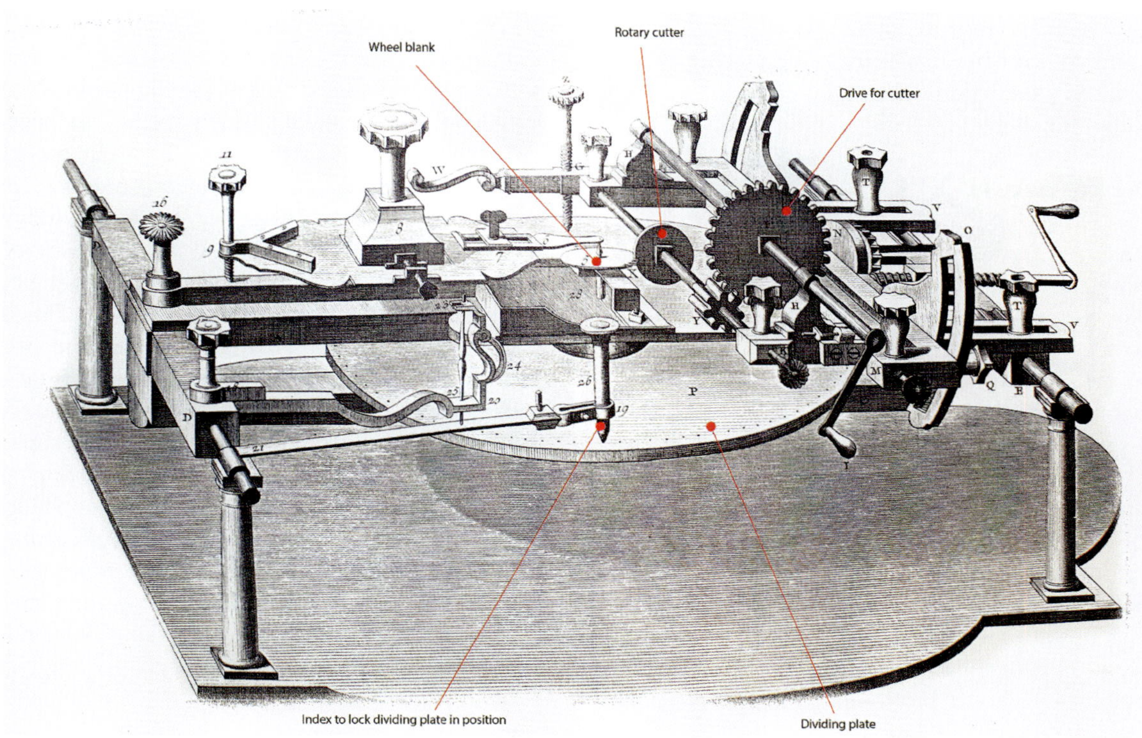

Eighteenth-century wheel-cutting machine.

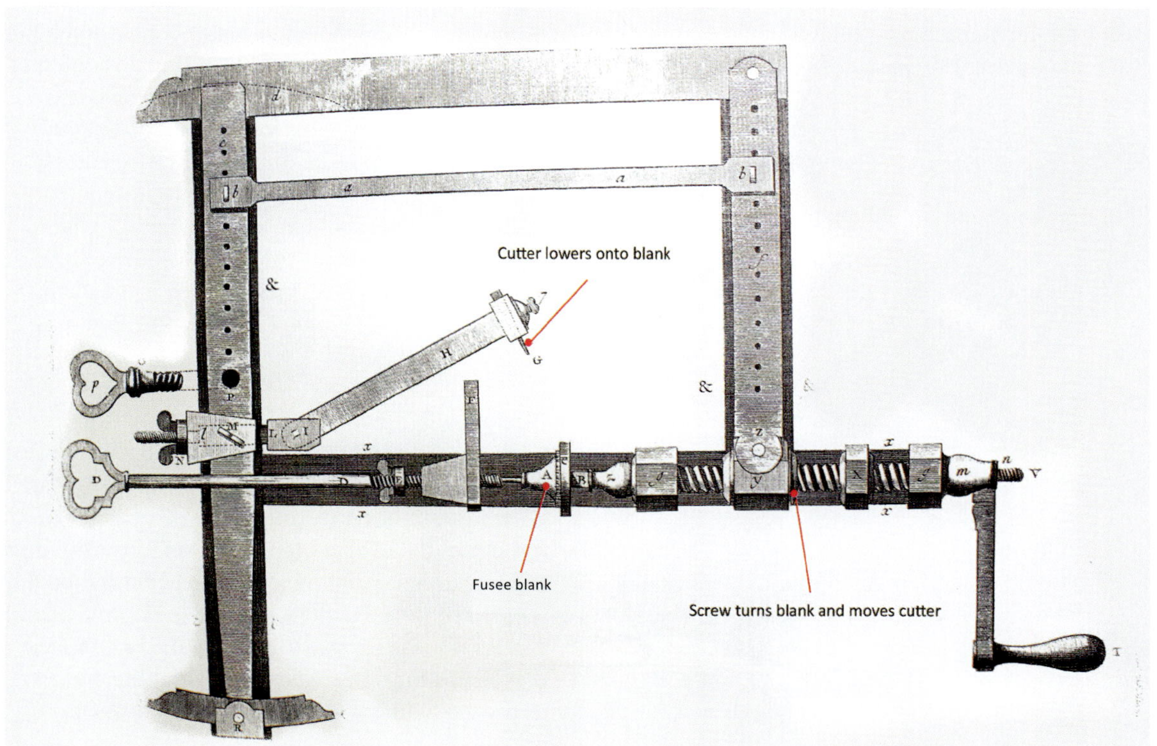

Eighteenth-century fusee-cutting tool.

the nearest minute. The great watchmaker John Arnold made a minute-repeating watch for King George III around 1768.

NEW MACHINERY

As in any trade, specialists in certain horological processes tended to keep their methods and special tools and machinery that they had devised to themselves. Passing these 'trade secrets' on to their apprentices was part of the deal with parents, who paid well for the training, ensuring a son's future in a well-paid occupation.

Wheel cutting was one of the most important processes in horological work. From the earliest times, mechanical aids were used to mark out the positions of teeth on a wheel blank before hand filing. A device called a dividing plate was used. This consisted of a metal disc with a series of holes or indentations for various wheel counts and would be linked to the wheel blank for marking out.

It would have been an obvious next step to build a machine incorporating a dividing plate that held a wheel blank and positioned it for a rotating cutter to form each tooth. Recent research by Anthony Turner (*Antiquarian Horology* Dec. 2019, p.514) has uncovered evidence for wheel-cutting machines in the seventeenth century. Letters between Nicholas Toinard and John Locke in 1680 concern the purchase of a wheel-cutting machine. Two main types are described, both for clocks and watches. The first uses files, the second uses wheels for cutting; the latter was said to be the more accurate. Tompion is mentioned as having one of his own design, which was a very large machine, fixed in his house and not transportable. From this, it would seem that by the late seventeenth century, wheel-cutting machines using rotary cutters were in regular use. The earliest detailed illustrations of watchmaking machinery come from the *Encyclopédie de Diderot et d'Alembert* of 1775. Although somewhat later, these tools would probably have been similar to the wheel-cutting machines that Tompion and his contemporaries would have used. Similarly, the fusee-cutting tool illustrated would probably be something like those used in the late seventeenth century.

Pinion wire.

John Carte, a watchmaker from Coventry who worked in London from the mid-1690s, wrote that:

> The English have invented that Curious Engine for the Cutting the Teeth of a Wheel, whereby that part of the work is done with an exactness which farr exceeds what can be performed by hand: Then there is an engine for equalling the balance wheel: Likewise the Engine for cutting the turns of the fusie: and lastly the instrument for drawing of the steel pinion wier: All which ingenious inventions were first conceived and made at Liverpool in Lancashire in England. (Manuscript by John Carte in the Bodleian Library, Oxford)

Pinion wire was made like other forms of wire, by drawing metal rods through a series of hardened steel dies. Special dies were produced with indentations in the shape of gear teeth to form lengths of steel pinion of various sizes and teeth numbers; pinion wire could be cut to the lengths required for watch and clock pinions and arbors. This is further evidence of the vital part played by the Lancashire tool-making industry in the early history of English watchmaking.

Chapter 5
The English Golden Age

In the late seventeenth century, much of Europe was impoverished due to religious wars, particularly the Thirty Years' War. It is probable that the German-speaking population halved during this period, due mainly to plague and starvation. England, from 1660, largely at peace and with a new monarch, was laying the foundations of the great power it was to become in the next century as wealth flowed in from the new colonies. At the same time, London became the home of many superb horological craftsmen, some native-born, some immigrants attracted by a stable government and religious tolerance.

Thomas Tompion *by Sir Godfrey Kneller.*

THOMAS TOMPION

Thomas Tompion was born to a Quaker family in Northill, Bedfordshire, in 1639. His early life is a mystery and nothing is known about where he learnt his trade. However, we do know that in 1671 he became a member of the Worshipful Company of Clockmakers, with a business in Water Lane, off Fleet Street. In 1674, he is recorded as becoming a Freeman of the Company and became acquainted with Robert Hooke in the same year. Fortunately, Hooke's diary has survived and from this we have most of our information about Tompion.

Hooke's Quadrant

At the age of 39, Hooke was already established as an important figure in the Royal Society, and one of his responsibilities was to commission new scientific instruments. In 1674, he designed a quadrant, which he described as 'a new kind of instrument of his own invention for the taking of heights, angles and distances of celestial bodies'. The Society asked Hooke to have the quadrant made – at a cost of not more than £10.

Hooke was an eminently practical man and knew exactly how the quadrant should be constructed. The problem was that the instrument maker employed by the Society, Tom Shortgrave, was, in Hooke's opinion, not capable of working to the standards he required. He had, however, met an up-and-coming young watchmaker with a shop in Water Lane. In his diary, he jotted on 20 April: 'Cald on Tomkins for quadrant' (it took him a while to spell Tompion's name correctly). It seems that Hooke, a man by all descriptions of an irascible nature, was impressed by the younger man (Tompion was then 35 years of age), and this visit to Water Lane eventually led to a lifetime's

Robert Hooke's quadrant.

friendship. Hooke was naturally suspicious and secretive, and his willingness to discuss his ideas and inventions with Tompion is completely out of character. His diary later records:

> Much discourse with him about watches. Told him the way of making an engine for finishing wheels, and how to make a dividing plate; about the form of an arch [*probably the shape of wheel teeth*]; about another way of Teeth work; about pocket watches and many other things.

This entry is particularly interesting as it confirms the evidence of Nicholas Toinard regarding Tompion's wheel-cutting engine (*see* Chapter 4) from just a few years later, in 1680.

Work on the quadrant proceeded slowly and when Hooke brought the astronomer John Flamsteed (soon to become the first Astronomer Royal) to inspect the partly finished instrument at Water Lane, Hooke was annoyed by Flamsteed's criticisms. He later summed up the astronomer as 'a conceited cocks combe'. By 5 July 1674, the quadrant was finished and Tompion delivered it to Hooke at his rooms in Gresham College, finding him with the fellow scientist Sir Jonas Moore;

Seventeenth-century London coffee house.

the three of them retired to Blacklocks Coffee House. Hooke later gave a lecture on the quadrant to the Royal Society and gave Tompion a fulsome recommendation for his work.

Hooke's diary gives us a vivid picture of fashionable London at that time, where the new coffee houses became the favoured meeting places, not only for the literati of the city but also for the scientific community. The Grecian Coffee House was the preferred meeting place of the Royal Society; indeed, on one famous occasion, Isaac Newton and Edmond Halley dissected a dolphin on the premises. Hooke's favourite coffee house was Garraways and his diary records many convivial evenings where Tompion would join him after a long day at his workshop, such as on 12 December 1675: 'To Garraways, I was very brisk smoked 4 pipes, Drank 2 chocolate. Discoursed with Tompion. Barrow clock. About bellows new invented and about oval watch ...'.

Tompion often visited Hooke in his Gresham College rooms: 'Mr Tompion here from 10 to 10. He brought clockwork to shew.' On another occasion: 'Tompion here all day. Bought home one watch and took another.' By now, Tompion had emerged from obscurity and was accepted in Hooke's circle, which included not only the leading scientists and thinkers of the day, but also the King and many of the nobility.

A Watch for the King

In February 1675, when Hooke heard of Huygens' claim to have invented the balance spring (*see* Chapter 4), he furiously claimed priority for the invention. He was dismayed to find that there was no reference in the Royal Society's minutes to confirm his demonstration of such a watch in 1658. He blamed the Society's secretary, Oldenburg, for the omission, claiming that he was employed as a spy for Huygens and accused him of being 'a trafficker in intelligence' for his rival.

Hooke immediately went to see Tompion with an order for a new watch to his design with a balance spring, which he intended to present to the King in the hope of being granted a Royal Patent. It was engraved 'R Hooke *invent. 1658.* T Tompion *fecit 1675*'. The construction of the watch did not go smoothly, however, and Hooke's diary records almost daily visits to Water Lane. He writes: 'Severall Disputes with Tompion urgd him forward with the watch' and later 'At Tompions I fell out with him for slownesse', indicating the pressure the watchmaker was under. On 28 July, he writes: 'Tompion shewed the watch finished', but a week later the balance spring came loose. The watch was not finally completed until 11 August. The watch was then delivered to the King and on a visit to Whitehall the following month, Hooke reported that the King 'Cald me to him and told me that my watch did very well that he had tryd it the day before and found it true with his pendulum clock to a minute.' However, later the King 'spoke to me in the park that the weather had alterd watch'. This is not surprising as the watch had no temperature compensation; it took almost a century for this problem to be solved. We have no further information on the watch, apart from an account by John Ward (*Lives of the Professors of Gresham College, 1740*) that the engraved top plate from the watch was in the possession of George Graham.

THE ROYAL OBSERVATORY

In 1674, the King's mistress, the Duchess of Portsmouth, alerted Charles that 'a bold and indigent Frenchman who called himself le Sieur de St. Pierre ... pretended no less than the absolute Discovery of the Longitude from easy celestial observation'. The King, to his credit, took the information seriously and appointed a commission to investigate the claim, and they in turn appointed John Flamsteed, a 29-year-old astronomer from Derby, to look into it.

Flamsteed reported that St Pierre's method was impracticable due to inaccurate data, writing that: 'he had only betrayed his own ignorance and we knew better methods'. He convinced the Commission that they should persuade the King to set up an Observatory, 'for making such observations as were necessary for correcting the places of the Fixed Stars, the Luminaries,

John Flamsteed *by Thomas Gibson.*

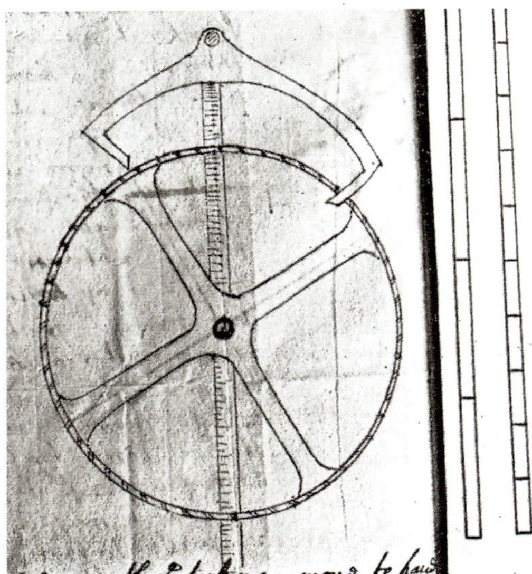

Drawing of Tompion's escapement from Flamsteed's letter, 1675.

and Planets, in order to the Discovery of the Longitude'. He modestly offered that: 'myself to be employed in it with a salary for my support'. The King took the young man seriously and in 1675 appointed Flamsteed his 'astronomical observator' at a salary of £100 to make new star charts, instructing that: 'he must have them anew observed, examined, and corrected for the use of his seamen'. The site chosen for the new Observatory was Greenwich Park and Christopher Wren was commissioned to start work on the new building. In the meantime, Flamsteed took up residence in the Tower of London and set up a temporary observatory in the White Tower.

Flamsteed's First Observatory Clock

In order to begin his observations, one of the essential instruments Flamsteed needed was a suitable clock. In March 1675, he wrote: 'I have a good pendulum making by Mr Tompion, an ingenious artificer'. Until this was completed, he no doubt used one provided by Sir Jonas Moore, the Surveyor General and Flamsteed's patron, who supplied many of the instruments for the Observatory at his own expense. In August 1675, Flamsteed moved to Queen's House in Greenwich to oversee the new Observatory building on the hill above the house and began to take observations from a balcony there. He recorded his first observation on 24 September, when he timed the passing of a star behind the Moon's disc (an occultation), presumably using his new Tompion clock. From a later description of this clock, it appears to have had a Royal Pendulum beating seconds.

A New Escapement

A recently discovered collection of letters from 1675 to 1678 (Derek Howse, *Antiquarian Horology*, Dec. 1970), from Flamsteed to the scientist Richard Towneley (1629–1707), sheds much light on the Observatory clocks. Towneley was a Roman Catholic, which isolated him from many of the scientific groups of his time, including the Royal Society. However, he did collaborate with important figures such as Boyle, Flamsteed and Hooke. He was a resident at Towneley Hall in Lancashire for most of his life.

It is clear that Tompion was experimenting with new escapement designs and it seems that for Flamsteed's clock, he dispensed with the usual anchor type and built the clock with a new form based on a design by Towneley. In his description of the escapement, Flamsteed writes to Towneley in December 1675 that: '... I hear not of any pallets for pendulums that have been made your way, but Mr Tompion likes it very well since as the other it puts not the second finger back by the girds'. His words 'made your way' make it clear that Tompion was influenced by Towneley's design. At that time, the word 'girds' meant a sudden movement or jerk; thus, he is saying that the seconds hand does not show any of the recoil, which was a characteristic of the anchor escapement (*see* Chapter 4).

The drawing in Flamsteed's letter was made when his Tompion clock was dismantled for cleaning and he carefully traced the pallets on to the paper. It is clear from the drawing that this is an early form of the dead-beat escapement that George Graham has been credited with inventing in 1715 by various authors. We should now give precedence to Richard Towneley for the design sometime before 1675. As George Graham worked for Tompion from 1696 and later became a partner in his business, he must have been familiar with the principles of this new design as used by Tompion and developed it later for his own precision clocks. If we compare the Tompion and Graham escapements, we can see that they are remarkably similar. Perhaps Tompion did not continue with this escapement because without a temperature-compensated pendulum (later invented by Graham), precision timekeeping was not yet possible and the anchor escapement was adequate for his needs. His experiments with the new Observatory clocks built for Flamsteed were his only attempt to build truly accurate clocks.

A Pair of Great Clocks for the Observatory

Flamsteed took up residence at Queen's House in Greenwich, Inigo Jones' revolutionary building commissioned in 1616 by James I in the new Classical style. From here, Flamsteed was able to supervise the construction of Wren's new Observatory, which was progressing remarkably quickly on the hill behind his quarters. He continued to make his observations from a convenient balcony, where his Tompion clock appears to have been set up. Meanwhile, Tompion was busy working on a pair of Great Clocks, which were to be installed in the new Octagon Room of the Observatory.

Unfortunately, the two Great Clocks no longer survive. They were removed after

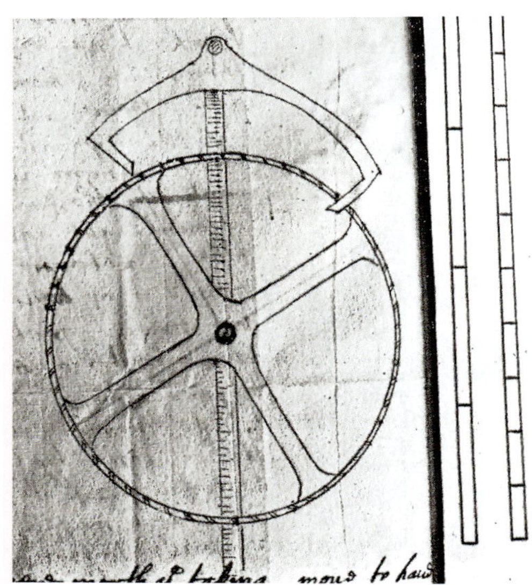

Tompion's modified dead-beat escapement taken from Flamsteed's 1675 letter.

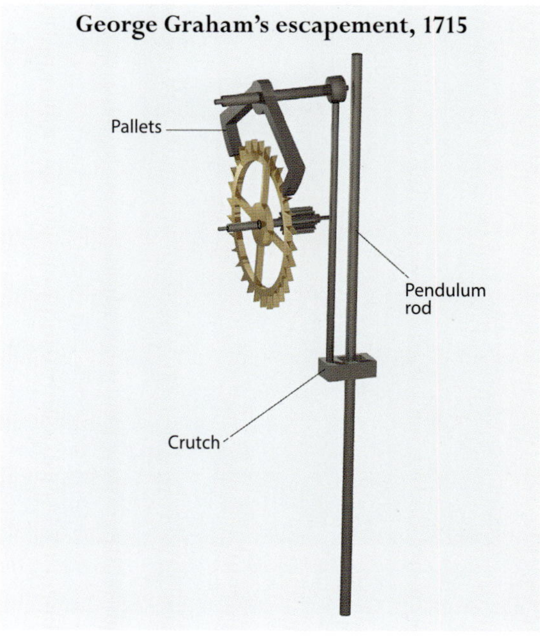

SOLAR AND SIDEREAL TIME

One of the first tasks set for the new Astronomer Royal was to confirm that the speed of rotation of the Earth was constant. To do this, he would need to set up a telescope with crosshairs to the position of a convenient star and use an accurate clock to time its reappearance each night. This is known as a 'sidereal day', which is about 4 minutes per day shorter than the normal 'solar day'. (A sidereal day is in fact 23h 56m 4.091 s.) The diagram shows the Earth's progression around the sun at the vernal equinox, when the day and night are of equal length. When the day is measured by observing a distant star, the 1-degree difference accounts for the sidereal day being about 4 minutes shorter than the solar day.

Another consideration is that because of the Earth's elliptical orbit, the solar day is longer or shorter than 24 hours at different times of the year by as much as 16 minutes – this is the time shown on a sundial. When clocks became more accurate, it was necessary to adopt Mean Solar Time, which uses an imaginary sun always equidistant from the Earth. The difference between apparent Solar Time and Mean Solar Time is called the 'equation of time'. Sundials were made with a table included to add or subtract minutes at different times of the year to allow for the difference. Clocks were also made to show the difference.

Sundial equation calculator.

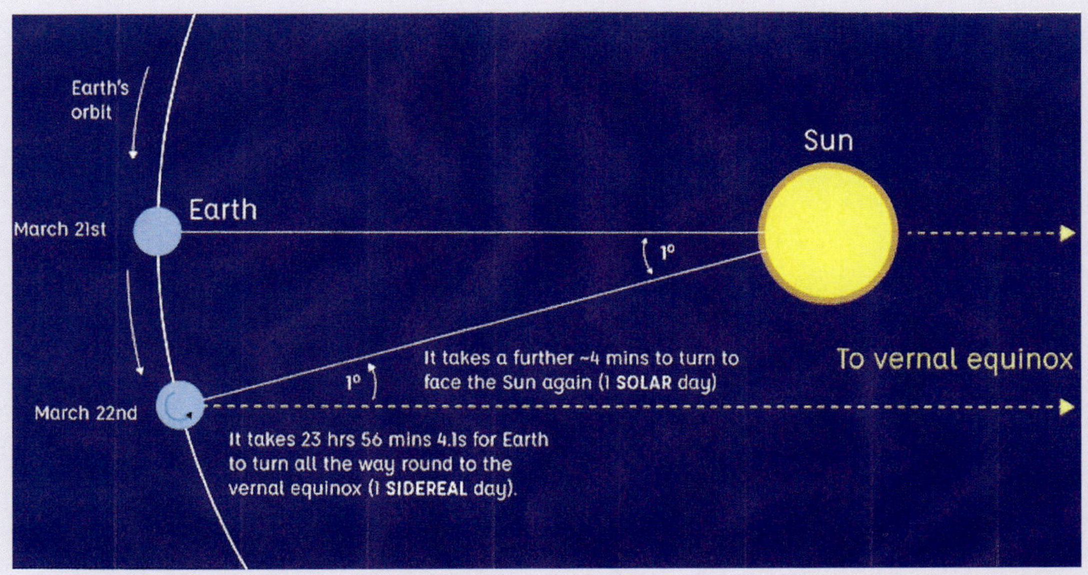

Comparison of a solar and sidereal day at the vernal equinox.

Flamsteed's death in 1719 by his widow and the ones at present in the Observatory are electrically driven. However, in his letters and notes, Flamsteed gives us a good deal of information on Tompion's clocks. They were year-going and the 13ft pendulums would have beat 2 seconds; one pendulum had a spring suspension and the other was suspended 'on the pivots'. They were, unusually, hung above the clock movements behind the wainscot of the Octagon Room and swung fore and aft. Thus, they needed an escapement design that would impulse the pendulums from below.

Flamsteed, in a letter to Townley in 1678, sketched Tompion's design of dead-beat escapement, which would have been suitable for the Great Clocks. Based on this sketch, it has been possible to reconstruct Tompion's lost escapement, which is probably as close as we will get to answering the question of how Tompion impulsed the two 13ft pendulums.

The new Observatory was completed by 29 May 1676 and the inaugural observation was planned for a partial eclipse of the sun, to be graced by the presence of the King. Flamsteed's clock was moved up from the Queen's House and, despite cloudy conditions, Flamsteed, assisted by the twenty-year-old Edmond Halley, managed a successful observation. The King, alas, did not turn up. On 6 July, Flamsteed wrote to Towneley: 'We shall have a pair of watch clocks down here tomorrow with pendulums of 13 foot and pallets partly after your manner.' This is the earliest reference we have for the two clocks shown in the etching by Frances Place.

Octagon Room *by Frances Place.*

Royal Observatory.

Queen's House, Greenwich.

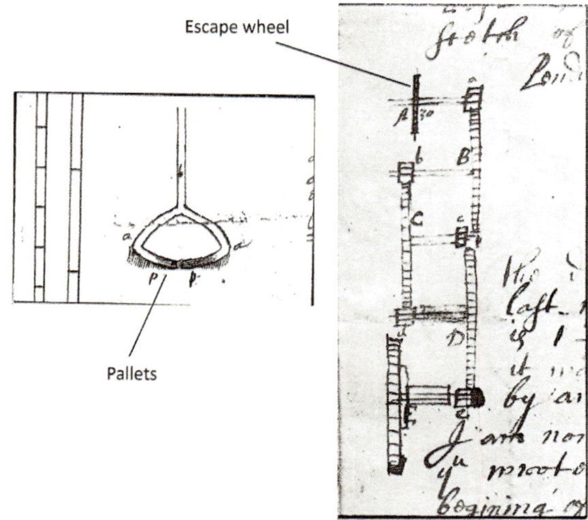

Flamsteed's sketch of Tompion's modified escapement.

The clocks were duly installed and set going; however, in November 1677 Tompion removed the escapement parts to his workshop to be modified. Whether this alteration to the escapement was as radical as the design Flamsteed was to sketch in the 1678 letter, or simply an improvement to the earlier design, we have no information. We must consider that Tompion was breaking new ground with these two Great Clocks, with their two-second pendulums, and it is not surprising that there were many teething troubles to be solved.

Shown here, the two clocks on the left of the door have windows above to display the pendulum bobs; these were clearly the two Great Clocks ordered from Tompion in late 1675. The third clock on the right is somewhat mysterious. It has been suggested that it was made by Towneley, who was asked to make just a movement, 'the face and figures made to be added here . . .', which presumably refers to a dial provided by Tompion to match the two Great Clock dials. This clock, however, does not appear in the observation books, which suggests that it was not a success.

Detail of the Octagon Room *by* Frances Place.

The Great Clock dials are inscribed: '*MOTUS-ANNUS* [year going] *Sr. Jonas Moore Caused this Movement With great Care to be made Å 1676 by Tho. Tompion*'. The clocks must have been ordered from Tompion in late 1675; according to one source he was paid 100 guineas.

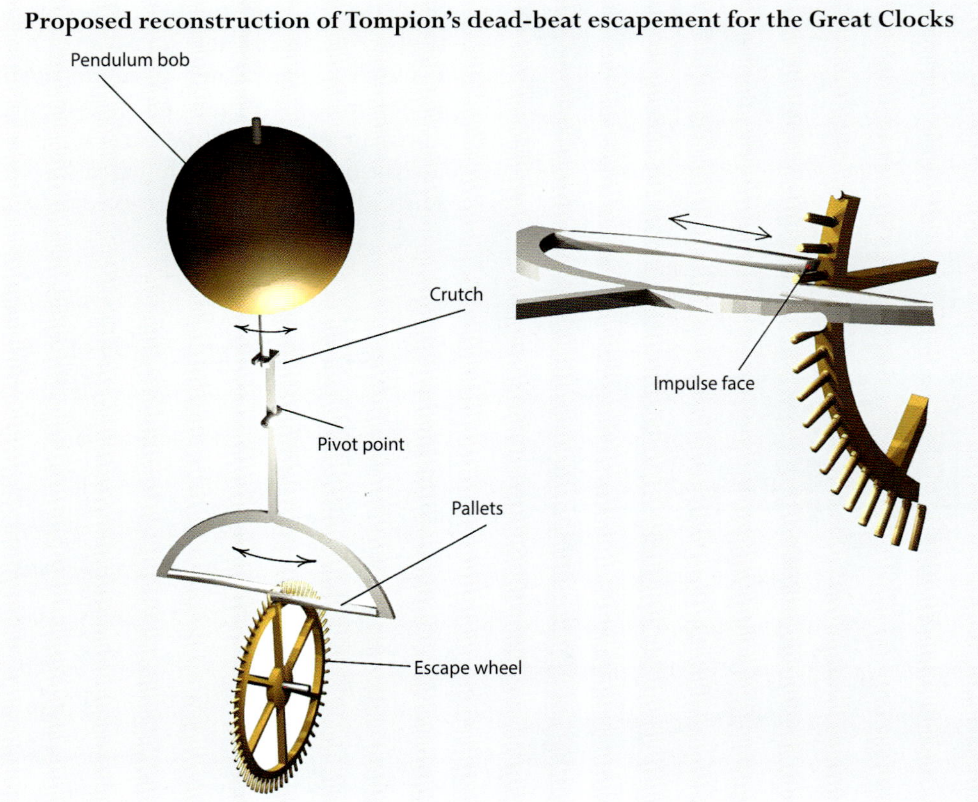

The Great Clocks in the Octagon Room.

The Performance of the Great Clocks

We can see from Flamsteed's notes that the clocks were installed in early July 1676, no doubt supervised by Tompion, who must have made regular journeys from Water Lane to Greenwich to adjust his timepieces until they were 'set together' on 2 September. By 31 October, Flamsteed records one clock gaining 7½ seconds and the other 4½ seconds daily. Bad weather caused problems in November when 'strong winds carried off the whiting from the walls and lodged it on the pendulums'. After Tompion had removed the escapements for further work in December, Flamsteed records that on 30 January 'Both started again. New pallets.' He recorded the following April that: 'One of our clocks goes well, the other may be made to do so if Mr Tompion could be prevailed upon to bestow a little time upon it.' It seems that the clock settled down and Flamsteed was able to report in July 1678 that: 'I have got our clocks now nearer the true mean movement that I had last year ... I hope they will now answer our expectation.'

It seems that the two Great Clocks continued to perform as expected and the observation books record no stoppages until the next cleaning in 1682. These clocks played an essential part in proving that the Earth's rotation is isochronous. Astronomers had assumed that the planet rotated at a constant speed; however, they lacked the means to prove that this was so. One of Flamsteed's priorities at the new Observatory was investigating the 'Equation of Natural Days'. It was necessary to prove that the Earth was indeed isochronous, so that the accurate observations needed to enable longitude to be calculated by the Lunar Difference method could begin. Flamsteed would have relied on the Great Clocks for the preparation of his 3,000-star catalogue, *Catalogus Britannicus*, and his star atlas, *Atlas Coelestis*, which eventually was used for the accurate determination of longitude.

Detail of the Great Clock dial.

TOMPION AT WATER LANE

Water Lane (now called Whitefriars Street) stretched between Fleet Street and the River Thames and it is probable that Tompion rented a property there in 1671 when he first arrived in

ATLAS

COELESTIS.

By the Late Reverend

Mr. JOHN FLAMSTEED,

REGIUS PROFESSOR of ASTRONOMY at Greenwich.

LONDON:

PRINTED in the YEAR M.DCC.LIII.

Flamsteed's Atlas Coelestis.

London. As we can see from the map, the lane was quite narrow and terminated at Dung Wharf. It would have been one of London's less salubrious thoroughfares, busy with traffic including dung carts moving the 'soil' off the streets to barges and dung boats to be transported to farms and gardens as manure. Without street lighting, venturing out at night was a risky business and the few wayfarers would need to carry arms, or hire a linkman, who would escort the traveller with a lighted torch. Despite its drawbacks, Water Lane would have been convenient for busy Fleet Street and the river boats – then the most popular form of transport in London.

Tompion, at the head of a growing business, was in need of better premises, so in 1675 he moved into part of a large house on the corner of Fleet Street and Water Lane. Here, his sign of the 'Dial and Three Crowns' marked what became one of the best-known addresses in London. It seemed that the cost of moving was a serious strain on Tompion's funds and he was obliged to borrow £50 from Sir Jonas Moore to cover his expenses. Tompion was unmarried and his household at that time comprised four apprentices and a female servant. By 1680, he had taken over more of the building and at some stage his widowed sister with her two children moved in to keep house for him.

By 1695, Tompion's establishment had increased considerably; the rating authorities listed his household as containing nineteen individuals, seven of whom were apprentices. Tompion also employed a number of journeymen, including the notable watchmaker Edward Banger, who had just become a freeman of the Worshipful Company of Clockmakers and had recently married Tompion's niece, Margaret. Some of the journeymen lived at the 'Dial and Three Crowns'; other married men, not included in the lists of residents, would have lived nearby, increasing the staff at the corner house. Tompion was by then at the height of his fame, becoming recognised as the leading clock- and watchmaker not only in England, but increasingly to the nobility and crowned heads of Europe. He had his portrait made by the court painter Sir Godfrey Kneller and, in 1697, an engraving was published by John Smith.

Fraudulent copies of Tompion's pieces were becoming increasingly common and a story circulating at the time tells of a customer at the 'Dial and Three Crowns' who brought in such a watch for repair. After a cursory look, Tompion picked up a hammer and smashed the watch to pieces (another version of the story has it that he stamped on the watch). He immediately handed the dismayed owner another watch, saying 'Sir, here is a watch of my making'.

William III was an extravagant patron of Tompion and acquired many of his clocks and watches, not only for himself but as presents for his friends. On the King's death, Tompion had to petition his successor, Queen Anne, for payment of £564.15 shillings owed for watches and clocks William had ordered for presentation to the Duke of Florence. Anne, unfortunately, declined to honour her brother-in-law's debt.

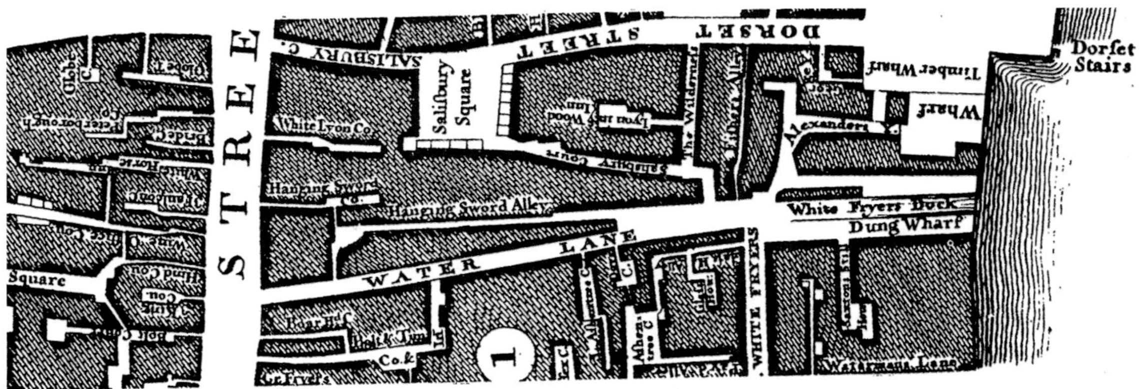

Water Lane from John Rocque's Map of London, 1746.

Map of Water Lane.

The photograph shows one of the earliest surviving Tompion longcase clocks, *c.* 1680, the 'Graves Tompion', now in the Metropolitan Museum of Art, New York. The dial indicates hours and minutes, subdivided into ten-second intervals (on the silvered chapter ring), with a calendar. The central ring shows the age of the Moon (0 to 29½ days) and the phases of the Moon. The inner dial shows the time of high tide at London Bridge. The eight-day, weight-driven movement, with anchor escapement and long pendulum, strikes in an unusually complicated way: full and half hours are struck respectively on large and small vertically mounted bells; and the first and fourth quarters, once and twice respectively, as double blows on small horizontally mounted bells. The beautifully proportioned case, standing at 77in, is attributed to Jasper Braem. It has panels of floral marquetry and oyster-shell cut veneer and Baroque columns supporting fine Corinthian capitals.

We can picture Tompion's house as the forerunner of the clock manufactories of a century later. Customers would be welcomed in the ground-floor shop, which would have had a number of clocks and watches on display. Living accommodation would have occupied the top floors, while the rest of the building was taken up with workshops, busy with journeymen and apprentices at benches arranged near large windows. We know that such workshops had a good deal of machinery for cutting wheel teeth and fusees, as well as throws – an early form of lathe. As we have seen in Chapter 4, there is evidence of a wheel-cutting machine that was too large to be transported from the workshop. With Hooke's advice, Tompion was clearly developing new tools and machinery throughout his career.

In his declining years, Tompion suffered from poor health and was a regular visitor to Bath to take the waters. He was made an Honorary Freeman of the City in 1707 and presented an impressive equation clock to the Pump Room, where it still stands. Such was his renown that on his death in 1713, Tompion was buried in Westminster Abbey.

The 'Graves Tompion'.

Early eighteenth-century wheel cutter.

GEORGE GRAHAM

In the first half of the eighteenth century, the outstanding figure in both clock- and watchmaking was George Graham (1673–1751). He came from his native Cumberland to London in 1688 to begin an apprenticeship with Henry Aske and in 1695 went to work with Thomas Tompion, who appears to have treated him like a son. He married Tompion's niece, Elizabeth, in 1704 and became a partner in the business in 1708. On the death of Tompion in 1713, the following notice was printed in the London Gazette:

> George Graham, nephew of the late Mr Thomas Tompion, who lived with him upwards of 17 years, and managed his trade for several years past, whose name was joined with Mr Tompion for some time before his death, and to whom he left all his stock and work, finished and unfinished, continues to carry on the said trade at the dwelling house of the said Mr Tompion at the sign of the Dial and the Three Crowns, at the corner of Water Lane and Fleet street, London, where persons may be accommodated as formerly.

Graham was clearly a man of exceptional talent and intelligence. His interest in astronomy led to his appointment as a Member of the Royal Society in 1721 and he became Master of the Worshipful Company of Clockmakers in 1722. Graham developed a number of instruments for the Royal Observatory, the most important being a new, highly accurate type of clock – later known as a regulator and capable of keeping time to a few seconds per month.

In order to achieve such accuracy, Graham had to develop a new form of pendulum that was not affected by a change in temperature. Normally in a rising temperature, a pendulum rod expands, lengthening the rod and causing a losing rate; a falling temperature results in a gaining rate. The mercury thermometer was invented by physicist Daniel Gabriel Fahrenheit in Amsterdam in 1714 and Graham adapted the idea of using the change in the volume of mercury in rising and falling temperatures to create a new form of pendulum.

For the new pendulum, Graham used a jar of mercury in place of the pendulum bob. In a rising temperature, mercury expands upwards, effectively shortening the pendulum to compensate for the losing rate caused by the expansion of the rod; vice versa in a falling temperature. This method of compensation became the norm in English regulator clocks for over a century.

Portrait of George Graham with his regulator clock.

Graham also revived the idea of a dead-beat escapement, which eliminated the recoil of the anchor escapement and interfered less with the impulsing of the pendulum. His form of dead-beat escapement was very successful and became the standard for English precision clocks for over a century. In the diagram, note how the crutch transfers the impulses from the pallets to the pendulum rod. The operation is as follows:

1. The escape wheel is locked on the exit pallet; as the pendulum swings, the point of the wheel tooth slides along the inner curve of the pallet without moving the pallets.
2. The pendulum swings anticlockwise until the tooth pushes on the impulse face, giving the impulse to the pendulum.
3. The pendulum continues and the escape wheel locks on the entry pallet, sliding along the curved pallet face.
4. The pendulum reverses direction and receives its impulse from the entry pallet.

Graham's regulator, 1740–50.

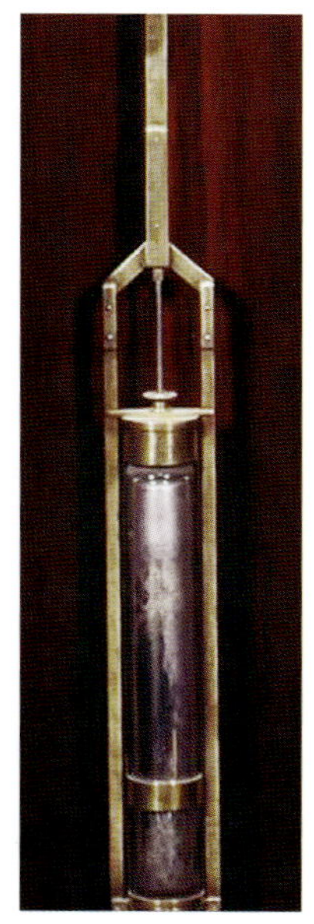

George Graham's mercurial pendulum.

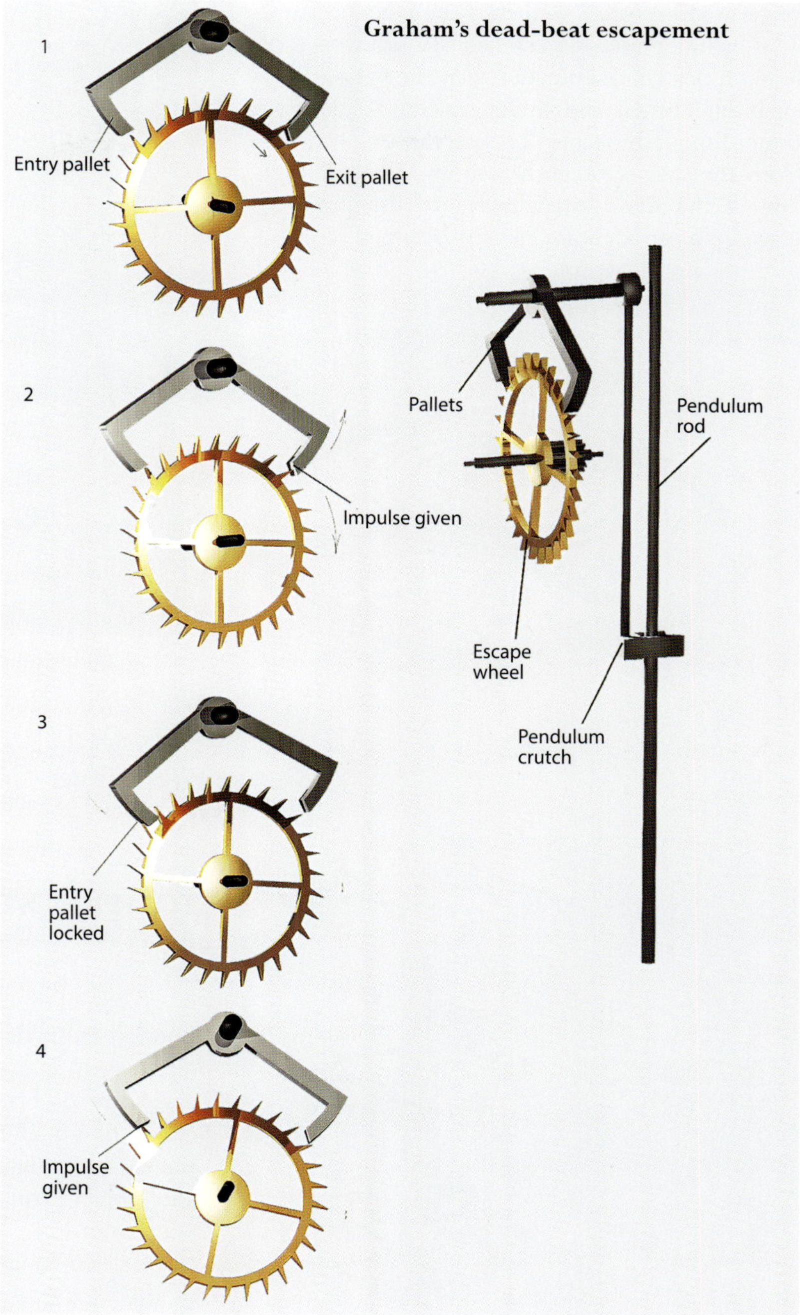

Graham's dead-beat escapement

1
Entry pallet
Exit pallet

2
Impulse given

3
Entry pallet locked

4
Impulse given

Pallets
Pendulum rod
Escape wheel
Pendulum crutch

Graham's most important contribution to watch technology was the development of the cylinder escapement in 1726. It was an improvement on the earlier verge escapement and probably originated with experiments in Tompion's workshop. He used the escapement in all of his later watches, although most makers continued producing verge watches until well into the next century. The cylinder escapement had the advantage of being much more compact than the verge, later enabling French and Swiss makers to develop their slim, fashionable 'Lépine calibre' watches from the late eighteenth century. Graham was one of the first watchmakers to use jewelled bearings after Nicholas Facio's patent in 1704.

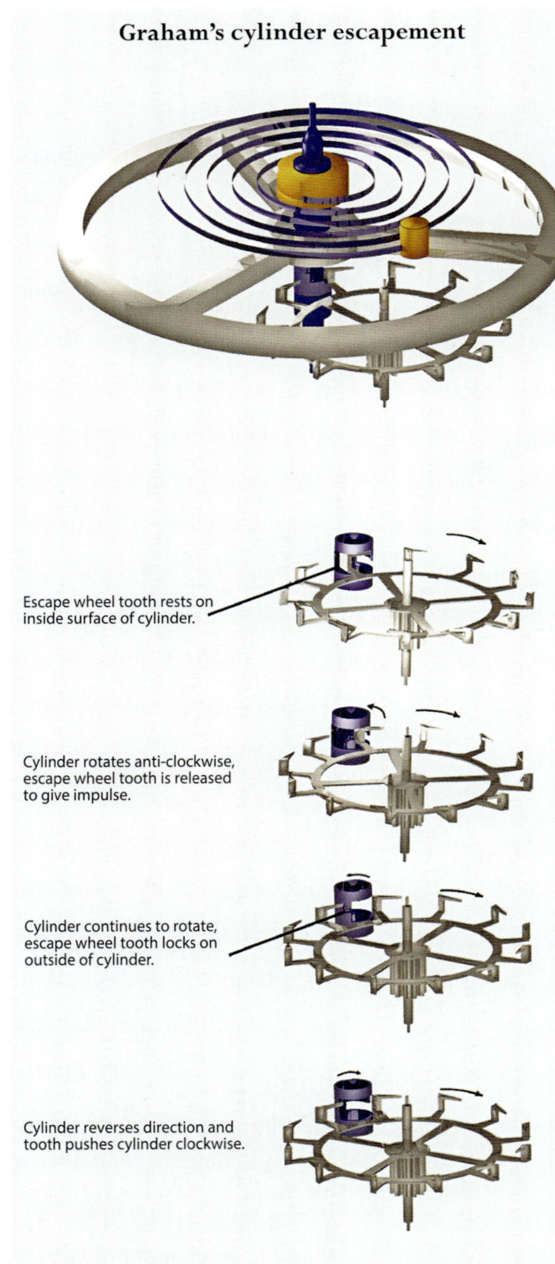

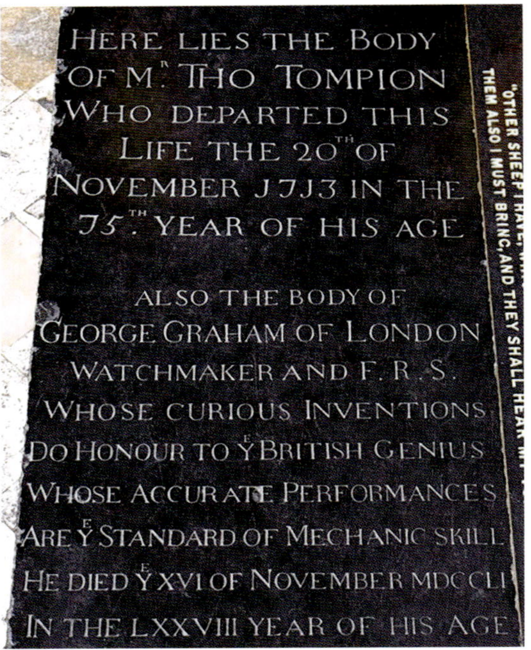

Tompion and Graham Memorial in Westminster Abbey.

On his death in 1751, Graham was buried in Westminster Abbey next to his old friend and partner, Thomas Tompion.

TOMPION'S CONTEMPORARIES AND NEW DESIGNS

A group of notable clockmakers working in London from the late seventeenth to the early eighteenth century contributed to the pre-eminence of English horology. They produced clocks of a quality and elegance rarely matched since. Important names include Ahasuerus and John Fromanteel, who introduced the pendulum in England; Edward East, the clockmaker to Charles I and a founding member of the Worshipful Company of Clockmakers; and Joseph Knibb, who probably introduced the anchor escapement.

Longcase Clocks

From the mid-seventeenth century, a new design of clock evolved to incorporate the new Royal Pendulum, around 3ft long and beating seconds.

Beginning as wall clocks with the pendulum and weights exposed, they evolved into floor-standing timepieces with the pendulum and weights enclosed in a case. Apart from some early examples with verge escapements and short pendulums, they were associated with the more advanced anchor escapement, which improved timekeeping considerably. These clocks, which began at a height of around 6ft, grew to over 7ft to suit the great houses of the nobility. The illustration shows how Daniel Quare's clocks evolved from the smaller eight-day clocks of the 1680s to larger, more impressive month-going clocks of the early 1700s, which would suit the new larger houses of the period.

The cases of early longcase clocks were mostly made from native woods; burr walnut was much used due to its attractive figuring. Marquetry and japanned cases were introduced after the restoration of Charles II, who brought the style to England from the Low Countries. The Joseph Knibb longcase shown here has a walnut case with the twisted pillars popular in the period. The movement has the earlier form of count-wheel striking.

Revolution in Movement Design

The earliest English clocks we know of used a construction called 'bird cage'. At a time when iron was the main material used, a forged iron framework was the obvious way of holding the working parts in place. This method of construction persisted well into the seventeenth century, when brass was increasingly used for smaller domestic clocks.

The components were arranged from front to back and the case pillars formed part of the framework. This was a very economical form of construction, using a minimum of expensive brass. However, as clocks became more complex, this layout was abandoned and the components were laid out sideways between two brass plates separated by turned pillars. In the illustration, note that the movement on the right has six pillars, typical of London work and giving great stability. A tribute to the skill of clockmakers of this period is that many such clocks are still working well after more than 300 years of service, with little sign of wear. Later, more modest clocks made do with four pillars.

Two longcase clocks by Daniel Quare.

Joseph Knibb longcase, 1680–85.

Typical seventeenth-century lantern clock movement.

Two longcase movements by Joseph Knibb, c. *1680.*

Table or Bracket Clocks

These free-standing spring-driven clocks had many advantages over weight-driven clocks, which were either fixed to a wall or the longcase type that was difficult to move. The flat movement design could be used in compact wooden cases; they are correctly known as table clocks, or bracket clocks when placed on a wall bracket. This freed clockmakers from the restrictions of the older lantern style and gave them new opportunities to design and decorate cases. In some ways, they were a step backwards in the evolution of clock technology, as they retained the old verge escapement and short pendulum. However, the advantages of portability outweighed the improved accuracy of longcase clocks with anchor escapements and long pendulums.

The timekeeping of a well-made table clock would be in the region of a minute or so per day, which was quite adequate for most owners, who would not have access to an accurate time standard. In the absence of an observatory, clocks had to be set by sundials and local time would differ from east to west, 4 minutes for each degree of longitude. Thus, as Bristol is about 2½ degrees west of London, the time difference would be around 10 minutes.

The illustration shows one of the earliest table clocks by Edward East from around 1665. The simple ebonised wood case stands 37cm high and the dial is of matted and engraved brass (matting is a form of decoration made with a special punch), with a silvered brass chapter ring. East was one of the pioneers of this new elegant form of dial, which was also used in longcase clocks. The figures are engraved into the brass and filled with black wax before coating the surface with a thin silver layer, lacquered to prevent tarnish. The clock runs for 30 hours and strikes the hours on a bell. Note that the bob pendulum is fastened to a hook on the back plate; this makes the clock very easy to move. The side view of the movement illustrates East's exemplary workmanship, particularly the beautifully turned pillars.

The style of table clock became more elaborate later in the seventeenth century; the example here is from about 1700 and is by Joseph Windmills (*c.* 1640–1724), one of the finest clockmakers of his time. The case is of walnut veneer with gilded bronze decorative castings. The dial includes a calendar and a dummy pendulum, a device that is attached to the front of the pallet arbor behind the dial. A silvered disc moves with the pendulum to and fro in the dial aperture, a popular feature at the time. The corners of the dial are decorated with spandrels in the form of cherubs. The movement has a finely engraved back plate, visible through the door's glass window – the clocks were often placed on mantles in front of a mirror to display the back plate. The clock is of eight-day duration and uses the new rack striking system with a repeating cord (you can see this coming from the side of the movement behind the pendulum and through a hole in the bottom of the case). The repeating feature would cause the last hour to be struck when the cord was pulled – very useful after dark.

The Richard Carrington clock is an example of a table clock from the late eighteenth century. This clock has a mahogany case – mahogany became popular for all kinds of furniture from the mid-century. It was imported in large quantities from the West Indies after the removal of import duties in 1721. The case features a caddy top with acorn finials and a break-arch dial, which extended the dial upwards to include devices such as the strike/silent feature here. The movement has a less elaborately engraved back than earlier clocks, but it was still a feature of high-quality work. This clock has rack striking with a repeating function and an anchor escapement. The pendulum was hung from a bracket and could be locked into the central bracket on the back plate for transportation; the screw that secured the pendulum can be seen attached to the back plate on the left.

Table clock by Joseph Windmills, c. 1700.

Table clock by Edward East, c. 1665.

Table clock by Richard Carrington, London 1790.

Chapter 6
Finding the Longitude

One of the most pressing needs of the seventeenth and eighteenth centuries was to avoid maritime losses due to faulty navigation. With growing overseas empires, long-distance shipping was expanding rapidly and European governments and individuals offered rich rewards for anyone who could come up with an improved method of navigation.

PROBLEMS WITH NAVIGATION

In 1707, Admiral Sir Cloudesley Shovell was sailing home with his fleet from Gibraltar. The weather had been cloudy and the navigators, as usual, relied on dead reckoning (estimating the speed of a ship). The consensus of their calculations put their position safely to the west of Ushant. Examination of the 44 surviving logbooks from the fleet show errors in longitude between 1 and 3 degrees; combine this with inaccurate charts and you have a recipe for disaster. The fleet was heading for the rocky shores of the Scillies. On the night of 22 October, four ships were lost, with close to 2,000 men, including the Admiral. A story later surfaced that he made it alive to the shore, where a local woman killed him for the rings on his fingers.

Due to similar mistakes in calculating longitude, such tragic losses continued to mount year by year. A particularly woeful example was the error on an Atlantic voyage in 1711, when a mistake of just half a degree within 24 hours of the mouth of the St Lawrence River resulted in the disastrous loss of several naval transport vessels.

Admiral Sir Cloudesley Shovell *by Michael Dahl.*

A contemporary woodcut of the Scillies shipwreck.

THE BOARD OF LONGITUDE

The great maritime powers urgently needed a practical solution to the longitude problem and decided that offering a cash prize to anyone who could contribute to finding the answer might concentrate minds. As far back as 1598, Phillip III of Spain, at a time when memories of the disaster of the Armada were still fresh, offered a generous pension and large cash payment to 'the discoverer of longitude'. Considerable sums were advanced to encourage anyone who showed promise of making progress. It is hardly surprising that the Escorial was besieged by a stream of con artists and lunatics, as well as serious inventors. However, after many years of fruitless investigation and considerable expenditure, the Spanish government lost interest and the search was abandoned.

Holland, France, Venice and Great Britain all followed the same route, together with private individuals offering generous prizes for the elusive solution. The largest and best-known was the British scheme. In 1714, Parliament set up a committee, which consulted a number of eminent men, including Newton and Halley. Newton's evidence is worth quoting:

> ... for determining the Longitude at sea, there have been Projects, true in theory but difficult to execute... One is by a Watch to keep time exactly. But by reason of the motion of the ship, the variation of Heat and Cold, Wet and Dry, and the difference of Gravity in different Latitudes, such a watch hath not yet been made.

Newton discounted the lunar method and the eclipses of Jupiter as impractical.

Eventually, a bill was put before Parliament 'for providing a publick reward for such person or persons as shall discover the Longitude'. The act offered the following scale of rewards:

- £10,000 for any method capable of determining the ship's Longitude to within one degree
- £15,000 if it is determined to within 40 minutes
- £20,000 if it is determined to within half of a degree.

Provision was also made for reduced awards to be granted for promising experiments.

The method would be tested by a vessel sailing from a British port to the West Indies and arriving after calculating the longitude within the specified limit. A commission, later known as the Board of Longitude, was established to investigate claims. Its importance was reflected in the eminence of its ex officio members:

- Lord High Admiral or First Lord of the Admiralty
- Speaker of the House of Commons
- First Commissioner of the Navy
- First Commissioner of Trade
- Admirals of the Red, White and Blue Squadrons
- Master of Trinity House
- President of the Royal Society
- Astronomer Royal
- Savilian, Lucasian and Plumian Professors of Mathematics.

Sir Isaac Newton *by Sir Godfrey Kneller.*

CELESTIAL NAVIGATION

Accurate navigation depends on the fixing of two coordinates: latitude and longitude. Latitude – the ship's north/south position – could be easily found by measuring the angle above the horizon of a known star such as Polaris, or the sun at noon.

By the seventeenth century, the size of the Earth was known with reasonable accuracy and the ship's distance from the equator could be found by simple observation. Constant improvement in optical devices, such as the invention of the sextant in the 1730s, made observation of the angle much more straightforward than with earlier tools, such as the quadrant or the backstaff.

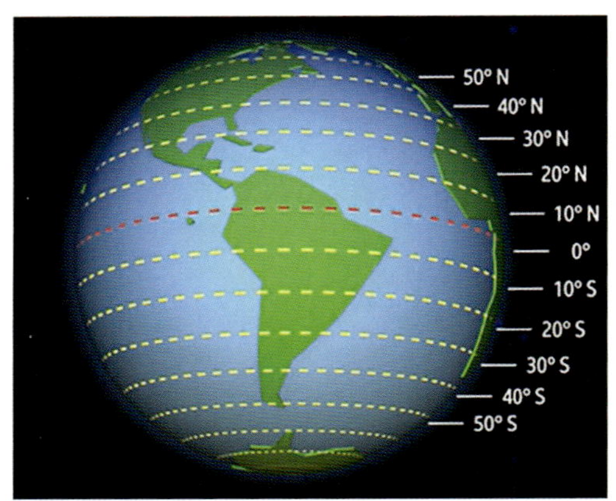

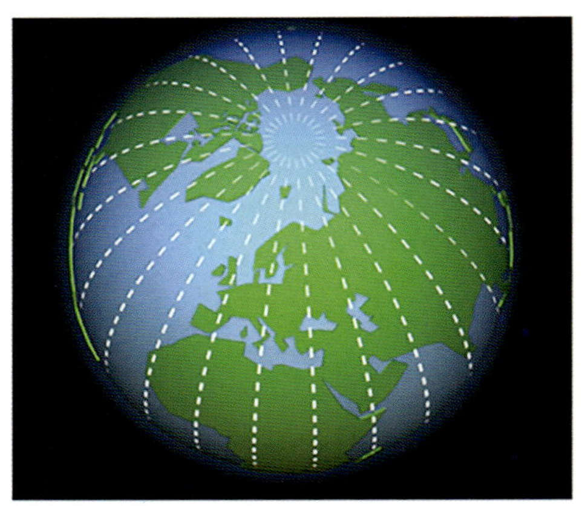

Lines of latitude and longitude.

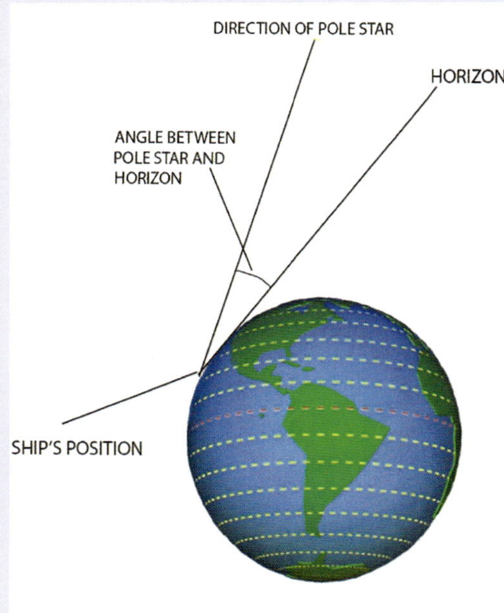

Working out latitude.

A navigator could sail north or south until he reached the latitude of his destination, then turn east or west and, using his compass, sail along that line of latitude until he reached his goal. Finding longitude, the east/west position, was a much tougher problem; he needed to know how far the ship had travelled each day along the line of latitude. The only way to do this was by dead reckoning – estimating the vessel's speed and attempting to allow for ocean currents, which could increase or slow down the ship's progress. Over a long voyage, even minor errors could result in the ship's estimated position being hundreds of miles out – with the inevitable consequences.

The most obvious solution to the problem was to take an accurate clock on board ship to show the time at a fixed location, for example Greenwich, then compare the time at Greenwich

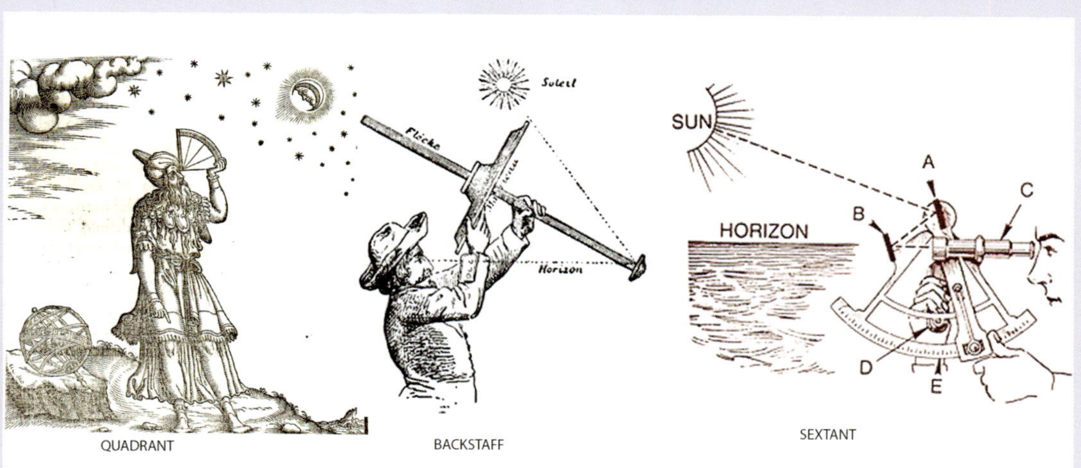

Quadrant, backstaff and sextant.

with the time on the ship. This could be found by observing the highest point of the sun to give noon, or at night using the position of a known star. The time difference between the ship and Greenwich could easily be converted into degrees of longitude on a chart. The only problem was that no such clock existed and would not be developed until the 1770s.

The other solution was to forecast the moon's position accurately against the background of known fixed stars from any point on the globe on any particular day. Tables would need to be published, giving a navigator the information he needed to calculate his longitude by measuring these positions. This became known as the Lunar Difference method of finding longitude. The arduous task of making the thousands of accurate observations required to create the tables led to the construction of observatories such as the Royal Observatory at Greenwich.

LONGITUDE LUNACY

At this time, an unusual form of insanity was observed; the first manifestations of the condition appeared soon after the 1714 Act of Parliament. One of the earliest comments appears in a letter in the *Post Boy* from a correspondent in the Hague in 1717:

> To convince you that we have Lunaticks among us, as well as other Nations, one Mr. John Rascher, who lodges at Leithauseh's Coffee-House in the Square here, advertises to Mathematicians, and Virtuoso's of whatever Denomination, that he is to make sundry Experiments … of his Discovery of the Longitude … and invites all the Lovers of Navigation, who fancy they know something in that way, to come and try their Experiments at the same Time and Place, if they please. A fair Challenge!

The huge prize attracted not only some of the best minds of the age, but also all manner of cranks and chancers with crazy schemes.

One of the most unlikely solutions, although not altogether serious, was an anonymously published method based on a quack cure known as 'the powder of sympathy'. This substance, invented by Sir Kenelm Digby, was supposed to cure wounds – not by application to the actual wound, but to the weapon that caused it. One of the numerous properties claimed for this miraculous powder was that if a bandage was taken from a wound and immersed in water, together with some of the powder, the patient, some distance away, would feel pain. Finding a standard time at sea would now be simple. All you had to do was to inflict a wound on a dog; the unfortunate animal would then be sent aboard ship. Meanwhile, a trusted assistant at the home port, equipped with a powdered bandage from the animal's wound and an accurate clock, would dip the bandage in water exactly at noon each day. The dog on the ship at the same instant would yelp, giving the navigator the exact time ashore.

Two mathematicians, William Whiston and Humphrey Ditton, advocated a slightly less improbable solution. They proposed that chains of stationary ships should be moored in the oceans. On board these vessels would be cannon capable of firing shells or rockets that would explode at precisely 6,440ft high. They calculated that the flashes and reports of the shells would be visible up 100 miles away. A navigator would simply look out for the flash and time the interval until he heard the explosion of the shell; the difference, allowing for the speed of sound, would give him his distance from the signal vessel and thus his position.

It was soon pointed out that the scheme suffered from several insurmountable drawbacks, including the impossibility of anchoring ships in the deep oceans, the vast expense of the undertaking and the plight of the unfortunate crews of these vessels, marooned in mid-ocean at the mercy of the elements and the temptations of strong drink. Dr Arbuthnot wrote to his friend

A Rake's Progress: Tom Rakewell in Bedlam *by William Hogarth.*

Jonathan Swift: 'Whiston has at last published his project on the longitude; the most ridiculous thing that was ever thought on ... a pox on him!' Despite these objections, Whiston and Ditton doggedly pursued their plan and published it in book form in 1714. Their method was inevitably doomed to failure; however, the publicity it achieved galvanised the London shipping interests into united action. Within a few months, a petition signed by 'Captains of Her Majesties Ships, Merchants of London and Commanders of Merchant Men' was presented to Parliament. It was this petition that spurred the government into action and resulted in the Longitude Act.

The seemingly impossible task of finding a solution to the longitude problem as the years passed led to 'Longitudinarians' being satirised as suffering from a form of madness. The artist William Hogarth portrayed a pair of 'longitude lunatics' in the eighth scene of his 1733 work *A Rake's Progress*. He depicts the inhabitants of Bedlam, London's notorious insane asylum. The scene includes two longitude lunatics, one gazing at the stars through a paper telescope, while the other covers the wall with fantastical drawings.

Serving on the Board of Longitude must have been a most frustrating task. A few extracts from the minutes of their meetings give a glimpse into the obsessive world of longitude enthusiasts:

> Mr Robert Davidson hath invented a machine that keeps perpetually going, and may be completed to work the largest mill, or keep a clock constantly going.
>
> A person who calls himself John Baptist desiring to speak with the Board, he was called in and showed them some schemes and drawings of figures which he desired they would enable him to publish; he was informed that it was not in their power. He was then asked to withdraw.
>
> A memorial from Mr Owen Stratton was read, proposing a method of finding out the longitude by an instrument of his invention, and the said Mr Stratton, who was attending, was called in, and it appearing that the instrument proposed is a sun dial, he was told that it could not be of any service, and then withdrew.

JOHN HARRISON AND THE FIRST SUCCESSFUL SEA CLOCK

John Harrison was born at Foulby in the parish of Wragby, Yorkshire, in 1693. His father was a carpenter and joiner employed by a large landowner, Sir Robert Winn. He was the eldest of five children and was naturally destined to work with his father on Winn's estate at Nostel Priory. When John was six or seven years old, the family moved to Barrow upon Humber in Lincolnshire, where his training began in his father's workshop. It is not clear how young John acquired his education. Still, we know that a local clergyman had spotted the boy's talent for mathematics and lent him his copy of a series of lectures on natural philosophy at Cambridge by the mathematician Nicholas Saunderson. Harrison made his own copy of the manuscript and we can see from his copious notes that he spent many years developing his understanding of the principles of mechanics, including Newton's laws of motion. His interests ranged widely and included music; he played the

John Harrison *by Thomas King.*

Early clock movement by John Harrison.

viol and took an active interest in the tuning of church bells. His mathematical bent led him to an interest in the theory of the musical scale and he later published his own theory on the subject.

Where Harrison's interest in clocks came from is a mystery; we know of no clockmaker in his locality, but perhaps his studies of mechanics led him in that direction. We do know that he built his first clock in 1713, before his twentieth year. The clock's design is unremarkable except for the construction of most of the wheels made from the material Harrison knew best – wood. The wheels were turned mainly from oak and boxwood, with individual oak teeth let into the rims and the grain of the wood oriented to give maximum strength. He also used lignum vitae, a naturally oily tropical hardwood; the lack of wear on these wheels testifies to the quality of his craftsmanship.

Two similar clocks were built over the next four years. The movements of these have survived and one is on display at the London Science Museum; the other at Nostell Priory. An interesting document pasted to the inside of the door of the last of these clocks was Harrison's own time-table equation, which he entitled, 'A Table of the Sun rising and setting in the Latitude of Barrow 53 degrees 18 minutes; also of difference that should & will be betwixt ye Longpendillom & ye Sun if ye clock goes true.' Harrison appears to have based the table on his own observations and calculations.

Being isolated from the influence of other clockmakers surely contributed to Harrison's originality. He quickly identified the problems that needed to be overcome and devised his own solutions. His ability as a clockmaker reached the notice of Sir Charles Pelham, who, around 1720, commissioned him to build a clock for the tower of his new stable block at Brocklesby Park, a few miles south of Barrow. This remarkable clock, again constructed mainly of wood, has the huge advantage of running without oil.

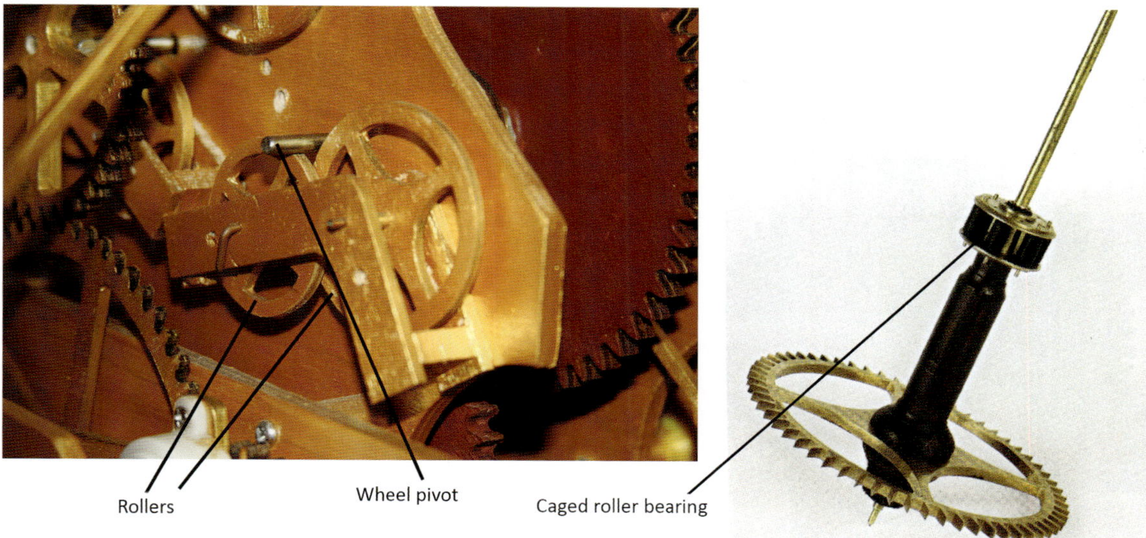

Roller bearings.

Characteristically, Harrison had homed in on one of the main drawbacks of trying to build accurate timepieces – lubrication. The primitive oils of the period were made from animal fat and soon turned into a sticky mess, which clogged working parts and played havoc with timekeeping. He also avoided using iron or steel, which would be prone to rust, and used brass where metal parts were needed. The clock was finished in 1722 and has run continuously since then, apart from a short period of refurbishment in 1884.

Was Harrison consciously working towards the construction of a marine timekeeper in the mid-1720s? At what point he decided to throw his hat into the ring and compete for the award we do not know, but he must have been aware of the fortune (at least two million pounds in today's money) on offer for the solution to the longitude problem. The logical start in the quest to build an accurate marine timekeeper would be to construct a stationary clock of great accuracy, surpassing the best pendulum clocks of the time, which had reached an accuracy of a few seconds per week, and this is precisely what Harrison did.

During two years from 1725, Harrison, working in isolation away from the London trade with the assistance of his younger brother James, another fine craftsman, produced three extraordinary longcase clocks. These regulators, as clocks built for accuracy became known, were entirely original. Harrison had taken a quite different direction to the London horologists, the greatest of whom, George Graham, was also working on precision regulators.

These clocks once again used Harrison's pioneering wood technology to eliminate the need for lubrication. He was also determined to reduce friction as much as possible, which he realised was one of the drawbacks of earlier timepieces. The gear wheels of a clock transfer the energy from the power source – a falling weight – to the escapement, which gives regular impulses to the pendulum. Friction, particularly in the wheel bearings, absorbs energy, resulting in uneven transmission of power and impulses to the pendulum. Harrison developed a new type of bearing, a forerunner of the roller bearings found in modern machinery; the wheels of his clocks turned in these bearings with hardly any resistance.

Harrison's gear train, with its low friction bearings, avoided the problems of lubrication and gave a very even power supply to the escapement. Harrison was not happy with the normal anchor type escapements that he had used in his first clocks, as the sliding components needed lubrication and were prone to wear. Typically, he took a completely new approach to escapement design and developed the 'grasshopper' escapement for his regulator clocks. Although this revolutionary design was never adopted generally in clockmaking, enthusiasts have been fascinated by its unique action. The best way to appreciate this is to find one of the many online animations.

The pendulums of these clocks had a very large arc of vibration and needed cycloidal cheeks (*see* Chapter 4). To solve the problem of temperature variations on the length of the pendulum, Harrison devised his own unique solution – the gridiron design.

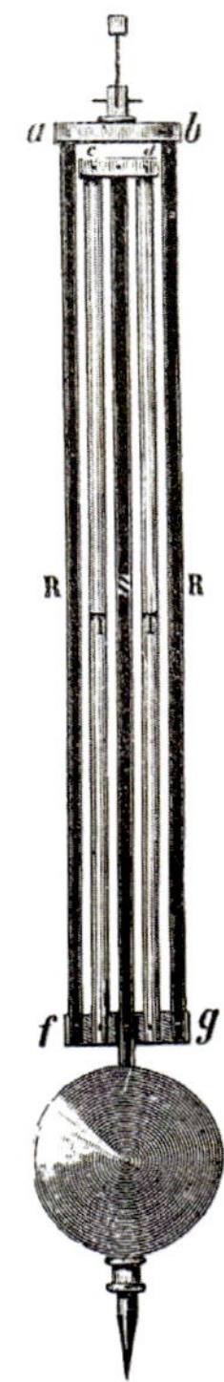

Gridiron pendulum.

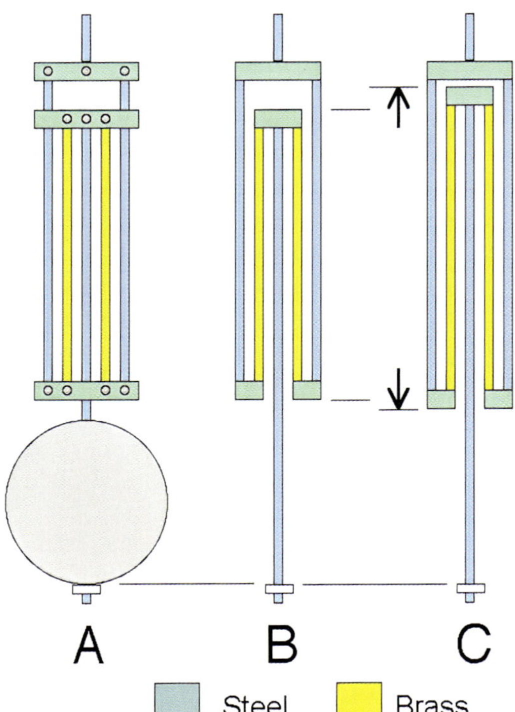

Principle of the gridiron design.

Harrison's regulator no. 2.

Harrison used the different expansion rates of steel and brass rods to keep the pendulum length the same in changing temperatures. The inner brass rods expand upwards in rising temperatures, raising the pendulum bob to compensate for the downward expansion of the steel rod. The reverse occurs during lowering temperatures, providing automatic compensation. This type of pendulum supplied a very good alternative to Graham's mercury compensation (*see* Chapter 5) and although English makers did not generally take it up, it was used extensively in European precision clocks. Yet another innovation in these remarkable clocks was a new type of maintaining power – a device to keep the clock working whilst it was being wound. Harrison's maintaining power soon became an essential component in precision timepieces until the present day.

To check the timekeeping of their regulators, the Harrison brothers set up their own 'observatory' using a corner of one of their house windows to sight stars passing behind a neighbour's chimney stack. A selected star transits a given point 3 minutes 56 seconds earlier (Solar Time). Each night, using his own equation of time tables, Harrison converted this to mean time in order to regulate his clocks. The result was a triumph; the regulators showed no more than one second per month error and over the next fourteen years the clocks kept time to within 30 seconds.

It is now accepted that these experimental regulator clocks were far superior to Graham's observatory clocks in terms of accuracy. However, Harrison soon became fully occupied in the development of his sea clocks and he did not pursue his work on weight-driven clocks. The simpler Graham type of regulator became the standard model for English makers for over a century.

Having solved many of the problems, Harrison now began in earnest to design a sea clock. His gridiron pendulum was, of course, useless at sea and a new time controller was needed. Once again, Harrison proved his ingenuity by producing more groundbreaking designs. By 1728, he had completed his plans and set out on his first journey to London with drawings of his proposed timepiece.

Harrison Visits London

Harrison's first port of call was the Royal Observatory, where he sought the advice of the Astronomer Royal, the eminent Dr Edmond Halley. Harrison was fortunate that Halley had succeeded the puritanical and prickly Flamsteed, a man who had once denounced Halley for his drinking and swearing. Halley realised too well that the Board of Longitude, top-heavy with astronomers and mathematicians, would be unlikely to favour a mechanical device over the lunar method, which would naturally seem more promising to them. Halley, to his credit, gave Harrison a fair hearing and told him that he was impressed with his ideas. He advised him not to approach the Board directly, but to take his ideas to George Graham, the most eminent horologist of his time and Fellow of the Royal Society. This suggestion must have worried Harrison, as Graham was in many senses a rival in the sphere of precision timekeeping. Should he disclose his secrets to a possible rival for the longitude prize? As it happened, Halley's advice was sound; 'Honest' George Graham, a Quaker and a man renowned for his generosity and probity, was the one person who might help Harrison.

Edmond Halley *by Thomas Murray,* c. *1690.*

The meeting apparently began badly. Harrison later wrote (in his inimitable prose style) that: 'Mr Graham began as I thought very roughly with me, and the which had like to have occasioned me to become rough too; but however we got the ice broke ... and indeed he became at last vastly surprised at the thoughts or methods I had taken.' They apparently spent the whole day deep in discussion, at the end of which Graham invited the younger man to stay for dinner. By the end of the evening, Graham had become Harrison's patron and generously provided him with an interest-free loan of £200, enough to return home and start work on his timekeeper. They agreed that the time to approach the Board was when its members could be shown a completed device.

The First Sea Clock

For the next six years, Harrison laboured on his marine timekeeper. The finished sea clock was not only remarkable in appearance, but was totally original in concept and a work of extraordinary ingenuity

In this first sea clock, later known as H1, Harrison developed many ideas from his regulators. Instead of a pendulum, which would be useless at sea, he used two dumbbell-shaped bar balances, each weighing about 2.3kg; they oscillate in opposing directions linked by an ingenious system of wires that gear the balances together. The balances rotate, almost friction-free, on a form of roller bearing. The four weighted arms protruding from each side of the clock are the counterbalances for the bearing arms.

The balances are impulsed by an adapted form of the grasshopper escapement used in his regulators. Four helical springs at the upper and lower ends of the balances control the timekeeping. To compensate for the varying elasticity due to temperature change, Harrison used a version of his gridiron compensation to automatically vary the strength of the springs. Although the clock is mostly constructed from brass and steel, Harrison continued to use wood for many of the wheels, which all run on his anti-friction bearings. Two mainsprings linked to a central fusee give the clock a going time of about 38 hours on one winding.

In all, H1 weighs in at a massive 34kg. It has four dials, reading seconds, minutes, hours and the day of the month. The clock was suspended in gimbals, which kept it level as the ship pitched and rolled, while the wooden case that enclosed the instrument was in turn suspended from springs at its corners

The machine was finished in 1735 and after successful testing on a barge on the Humber, Harrison was ready to transport it to London and make a formal application to the Board of Longitude to arrange a sea trial. George Graham must have been delighted to see his protégé and his masterpiece after seven years and he immediately arranged a presentation of the clock to the Royal Society, where Harrison was given an enthusiastic welcome. Graham had a certificate of endorsement signed by Halley and three other prominent members of the Society:

> John Harrison, having with great labour and expense, contrived and executed a Machine for measuring time at sea, upon such Principle, as seem to us to Promise a very great and sufficient degree of Exactness. We are of the Opinion, it highly deserves the Public Encouragement, In order to a thorough Tryal and Improvement, of the severall Contrivances, for preventing those irregularities in the time, that naturally arise from the different degrees of Heat and Cold, a moist and drye Temperature of the Air, and the Various Agitations of the ship.

Despite this ringing endorsement, Harrison had to wait until May the following year until he could depart on the sea trial of his clock. Even then, the Admiralty did not arrange to send the sea clock to the West Indies as stipulated in the Act, but instructed Harrison to take his clock to Spithead to board HMS *Centurion* bound for Lisbon. Sir Charles Wager, First Lord of the Admiralty, sent the following letter to Captain Proctor of the *Centurion*:

> Admiralty 14th May 1736
> Sir,
> The Instrument which is put on Board your Ship, has been approved by all the Mathematicians in

HMS Centurion *by Samuel Scott, 1743.*

> Town that have seen it (and a few that have not) to be the Best that has been made for measuring Time; how it will succeed at Sea, you will be a Judge; I have writ to Sir John Norris, to desire him to send home the Instrument and the Maker of it (who I think you have with you) by the first ship that comes ...The Man is said by those who know him best, to be a very ingenious and sober Man, and capable of finding out something more than he has already, if he can find Encouragement; I desire you therefore, that you will let the Man be used civilly, and that you will be as kindly to him as you can.

Proctor replied:

> *Centurion*, at Spithead, seventeenth May, 1736
> I am very much honoured with yours of the 14th, in relation to the Instrument I carried out, and its Maker: the Instrument is placed in my Cabbin, for giving the Man all the Advantage that is possible for making his Observations, and I find him a very sober, a very industrious, and withal a very modest Man, so that my good wishes can't but attend him; but the difficulty of measuring Time truly, where so many unequal Shocks, and Motions, stand in Opposition to it, gives me concern for the honest Man, and makes me fear he has attempted impossibilities; but Sir, I will do him all the Good, and give him all the Help, that is in my Power, and acquaint him with your Concern for his Success, and your Care that he shall be well treated ...'

Proctor was as good as his word and Harrison and his clock were installed in his cabin. The voyage to Lisbon was swift by eighteenth-century standards, taking just a week. However, the strong winds and rough seas that the *Centurion* encountered did not suit a landsman like Harrison. Proctor recorded in his log that the clock fared better than his passenger, who 'was sick withal, but seems satisfied that the motion of the ship was not in the least detrimental to its keeping true time'. However, the ship's log indicates that the clock did not perform as well as Harrison had hoped on the outward voyage. Unfortunately, Proctor, a sick man before the voyage, died in Lisbon, and Harrison was transferred to HMS *Orford* for the return voyage. The *Orford*'s Master, Roger Wills, recorded that the return voyage, which took a full month, was 'very mixed with gales and calms'. The clock performed much better during this voyage and gave Harrison a notable triumph when he used it to correct a significant error in the position of the vessel as they sighted land. Wills and all his officers believed that they had reached Start Point near Dartmouth; Harrison insisted that it was in fact the Lizard, 60 miles from the Start. Fortunately, Wills had the good sense to take evasive action and avoid putting his ship in dire peril; later, he presented Harrison with a certificate recording the event.

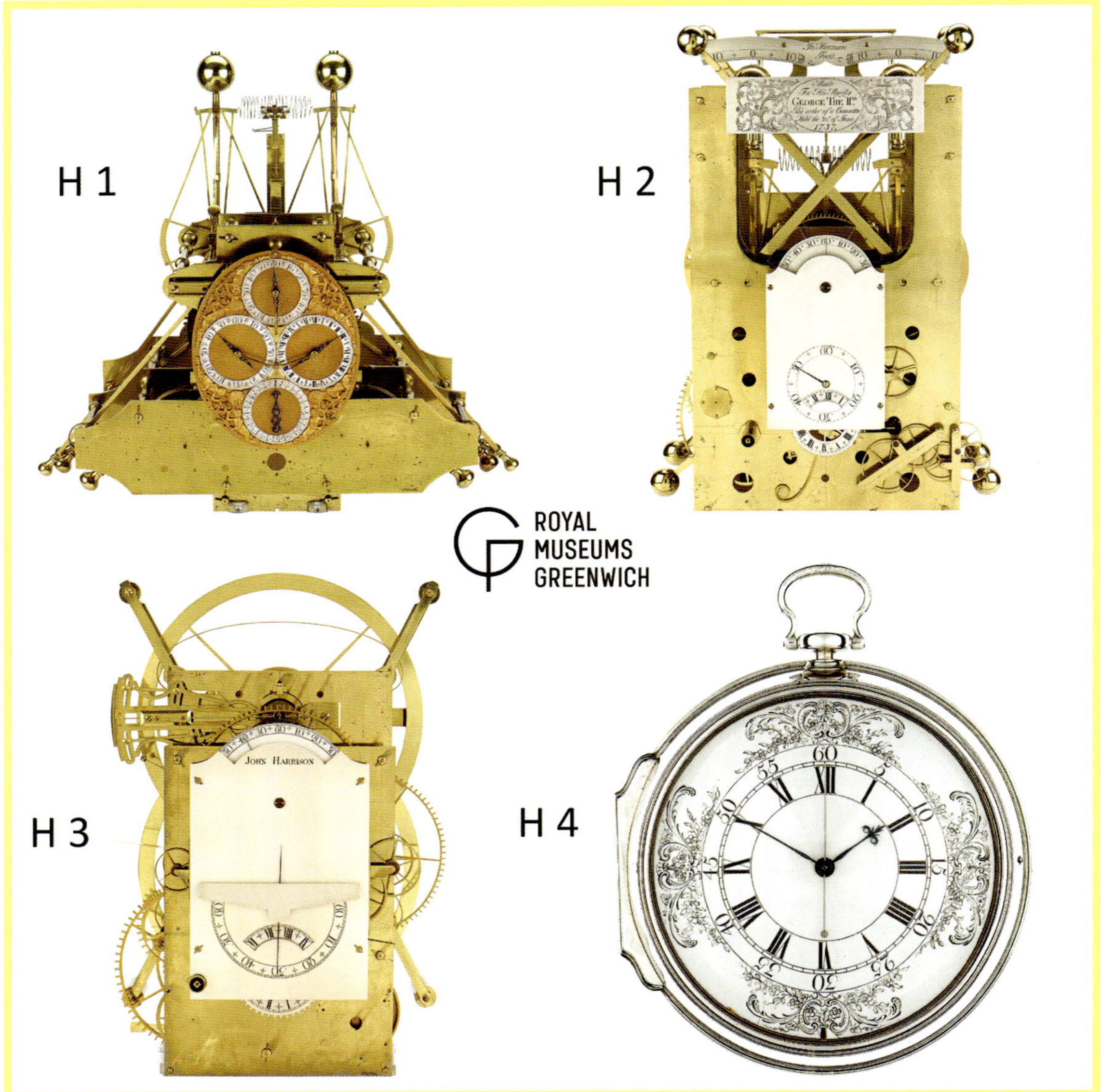

Harrison's four sea clocks, spanning the period 1736 to 1759.

On 30 June 1737, the Board of Longitude convened to consider the results of the trial and inspect the revolutionary sea clock. The minutes of the meeting record that:

> Mr John Harrison produced a new invented machine, in the nature of clockwork, whereby he proposes to keep time at sea with more exactness than by any other instrument hitherto contrived … and proposes to make another machine of smaller dimensions within the space of two years, whereby he will endeavour to correct some defects which he hath found in that already prepared, so as to render the same more perfect …

Despite the admitted imperfections in the timekeeper, the Board was sufficiently impressed with Harrison and his invention to award him a grant of £250 to carry on his experiments, with a promise of a further £250 on completion of a second approved machine. Harrison promised that within two years he would present the Board with a more compact and accurate machine, which would be submitted for trial on a voyage to the West Indies. Meanwhile, Harrison lent the now famous machine to his friend George Graham, who kept it going in his shop for the general public to wonder at.

Thus, H1 was consigned to history. It was like most prototypes – a work in progress, a first step in Harrison's lifelong quest to find an answer to the longitude problem. Despite its lack of ultimate success, H1 has attained an iconic status and it is rightly the star turn in the splendid exhibition of Harrison's machines in the National Maritime Museum at Greenwich.

Harrison's London Period

Harrison moved to London in 1736 and took a house in Leather Lane, Holborn. Three years later, he moved west to Red Lion Square, where he remained for the rest of his life. For the next two years he laboured on the second timekeeper, H2. He did not succeed in producing a more compact timepiece – it was larger than H1 and even heavier, at 39kg. It follows the same basic design as H1, but shows the influence of the London craftsmen who would have contributed to its construction and finishing. Very little wood is used in its construction and it boasts a prominent engraved plate bearing the inscription 'Made for His Majesty George The IInd, By order of a Committee Held on 30th of June 1737'.

Harrison's improvements included simplified and more efficient temperature compensation and a remontoir, a device designed to avoid the power variations that inevitably occur as the large mainsprings of his earlier clock unwound. The mainspring of H2 is used to wind a small spring every 3 minutes 45 seconds; this spring drives the escapement directly, resulting in much more even impulses to the two bar balances. Despite these improvements, Harrison was not satisfied with the performance of H2. He came to recognise that his original idea of using two heavy bar balances as his time controllers was the main problem. Although they were linked together and rotated in opposing directions,

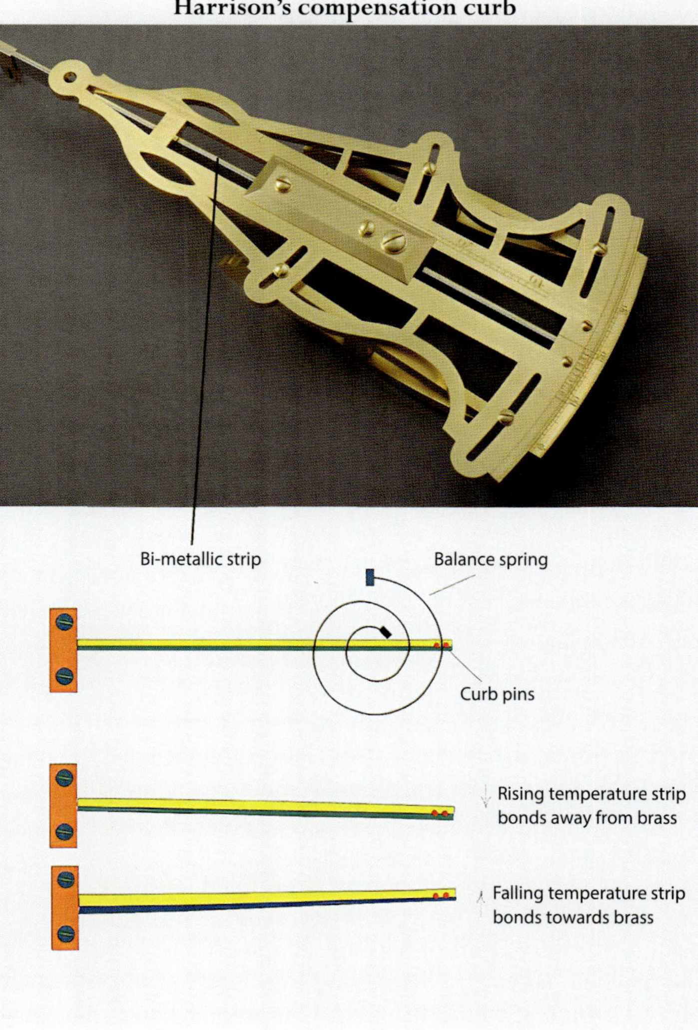

this did not fully cancel out the motions of the ship as he had hoped. The centrifugal force of the rotations of the ship in different planes affected the balances and caused unpredictable timekeeping errors.

Harrison seems to have concluded that the solution to H2's problems was to dispense with the dumbbell balances and replace them with rotating wheel balances. It was not possible to adapt H2, so rather than submit what he considered a defective design to the Board, he petitioned for a further grant of £500 to complete a third timekeeper, which, he assured the Board, would be far in advance of the first two machines. To its credit, the Board continued to support Harrison and he returned to his labours on what would become H3.

H3 was to occupy the inventor for almost twenty years. He did not realise it, but in continuing to develop the ideas he had used in the two earlier timekeepers he was fundamentally on the wrong track. However, his time was not altogether wasted, as it was from this machine that the two inventions came that would have a lasting contribution to future technology – the bimetallic strip, used to compensate for changing temperature, and the caged roller bearing.

The compensation curb was an extension of Harrison's gridiron pendulum principle. He realised that the differential coefficient of expansion of brass and steel could be used to cause a bimetallic strip, consisting of a length of brass welded to a length of steel, to bend with changing temperatures. This bending action could be used to move a pair of curb pins along a balance spring to speed up and slow down a balance to compensate for the changes in elasticity of the spring in changing temperatures. This automatic compensating device was one of Harrison's most important inventions, not only used in watch and chronometer design for the next 200 years, but in later thermostats.

The first testing of H3 after five years of development work was disappointing; nevertheless, Harrison stubbornly continued to persevere with his basic concept. The years passed, yet despite all of his painstaking efforts the machine failed to perform well enough for him to submit it to the Board of Longitude for testing. Harrison's supporters kept faith in him and the Board continued to supply the funds for his work on H3, giving him over £3,000 during this period, an unprecedented example of government support for this kind of scientific research. The Royal Society honoured him with its highest award, the Copley Medal. Yet despite his fame, it is not difficult to imagine Harrison's state of mind at this time, as the early promise of the success of H1 was years in the past and all of his efforts with the two subsequent timekeepers seemed doomed to failure. At some period in the early 1750s, he seems to have come to the realisation that large machines with slow-moving, heavy balances were too prone to the influence of the violent movements of a ship and that he must change direction.

The Jefferys Watch

Harrison now turned his inventive talents to watch technology, which had essentially remained unchanged since the introduction of the balance wheel controlled by a spiral spring around 1675. The best watches were capable of no better timekeeping than a minute or so per day; perhaps this could be improved?

Harrison thought the way forward was to make a watch with a balance wheel that beat faster and swung through a greater arc than the standard watch. He redesigned the verge escapement

The Jefferys watch.

to allow the balance wheel's amplitude (angle of rotation) to be much greater than a normal watch. A larger and heavier balance than normal would be fitted with a spring strong enough to drive the wheel to 'vibrate' five times per second. The only disadvantage with this arrangement was that if the watch stopped it would not self-start, but would need a shake to get it going. This would have been considered a fatal flaw by any professional watchmaker. What use was a watch that needed shaking to get it started? However, Harrison believed that his fast-moving, high-energy balance would improve the performance of the watch he had in mind. Rather than attempting to construct it himself he commissioned a London watchmaker, John Jefferys, to build a watch to his new design between 1751 and 1752.

Evidently Harrison expected that the experimental watch would show a modest improvement in timekeeping; however, the new design was far more successful than he could have hoped. At last, he seemed to be on the right track and although he did not altogether abandon his work on H3, he saw the potential of a new approach based on improving the performance of the Jefferys watch (it is this watch that Harrison is shown holding in the Thomas King portrait).

At Harrison's next appearance before the Board in June 1755 to request a further grant to continue his work on H3, he asked for support to make two watches:

> one of such a size as may be worn in the pocket & the other bigger ... having good reason to think from the performance of one already executed in that direction ... that such small machines may be rendered capable of being of great service with respect to Longitude at sea.

The Board duly gave him the grant he requested and over the next four years he laboured on his magnum opus, the large watch in the modest silver case now known as H4, the first successful marine timekeeper.

H4 was the logical development of the Jefferys watch; Harrison used the same design of escapement to drive a large plain steel balance wheel 55mm in diameter. Like

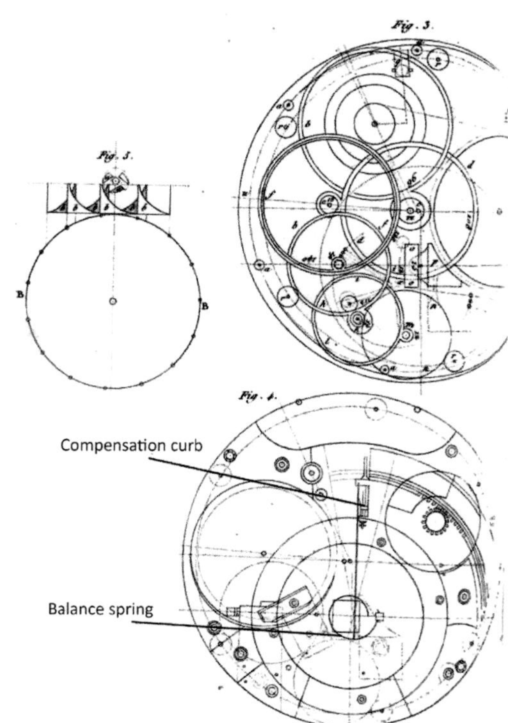

Harrison's drawing.

the earlier watch, the balance oscillates at a frequency of five times per second and has a spiral steel balance spring of a little over three turns. In addition to its high frequency, the balance turns through a much greater arc than a normal watch of the time, up to 145 degrees in each direction from its rest point, where it receives an impulse from the escapement. To smooth out the uneven power delivered from the mainspring, he again used a remontoir, which rewound every 7½ seconds. Compensation for changing temperatures was achieved with a miniature version of the compensation curb developed for H3, which can be seen on Harrison's own drawing.

The use of watch technology meant that Harrison had to abandon his low-friction bearings. This timekeeper would need to be oiled – something he had taken great pains to avoid in his earlier machines. He adopted an improvement that had been developed by London craftsmen earlier in the century – jewel bearings. The pivots of wheels in watches and clocks had always turned in holes drilled in the brass plates, but these were subject to wear, resulting in poor engagement of the gear teeth. It was realised that ruby or sapphire (the same mineral – corundum, the next hardest substance to diamond) could be shaped and drilled to make bearings that were set in the watch plates. The combination of hardened steel pivots turning in even harder jewel bearings greatly improved the running and longevity of watches. This technology soon became standard practice in quality watchmaking.

In addition to the use of ruby jewels wherever possible, Harrison went a step further and made the two acting faces of his escapement – the pallets – out of diamond. He later admitted that he had found the making of these pallets a great problem, which is not surprising; indeed, it is still something of a mystery how he managed it. One face of each tiny pallet is a curve in the form of a cycloid. Shaping them out of ruby would be difficult enough, but to make them of diamond, many times harder than ruby, was a great achievement.

It had taken 30 years of painstaking work, most of this time spent on H3, which he later called his 'curious machine', to realise that he was on the wrong track. His dogged perseverance and single-minded determination have to be admired, as is the decision to abandon his large sea clocks and devote his genius to developing the common watch. H4 is just 13cm in diameter and is enclosed in a plain silver 'pair case', a large version of the type used for the standard pocket watch of the day. An inner case allows access for winding and setting the hands and this is enclosed in an outer protective case. The case has the London Hallmark for 1760/61 and was probably made by Henry Thompson, a 'small worker', who lived close to Harrison in Silver Street.

New Trials

The first tests of H4 were very encouraging and at the 1760 meeting of the Board of Longitude Harrison asked that a sea trial for H3 should also include the new watch. He asked for another winter to test its temperature compensation. In the meantime, John's son, William Harrison, was given a grant of £250 to equip himself for a sea trial of both timekeepers to Jamaica the following year. However, they now had to face serious competition from the astronomers. Considerable progress had been made during the 1750s in mapping the stars and producing data that could be used for the Lunar Distance method of finding longitude.

New instruments had been developed for measuring the angles of heavenly bodies at sea, which made the Lunar method a serious competitor for the longitude prize.

The third Astronomer Royal, James Bradley, had put his weight firmly behind the Lunar method and, since 1755, had been carrying out a laborious series of observations in testing tables that had been produced by Tobias Mayer of Nuremberg, which promised to be the basis of a set of lunar tables. Bradley was, of course, a member of the Board of Longitude and, as a possible competitor for the prize, would today be accused of a conflict of interest. He was assisted by a man who, with good reason, was to become a bitter opponent of the Harrisons – Nevil Maskelyne.

In January 1761, Maskelyne set sail for St Helena in the South Atlantic, one of a number of international expeditions to observe the transit of Venus, an event that occurs just twice each century when the planet passes across the face of the sun. By comparing observations from different parts of the Earth, it would be possible to calculate the true distance from the Earth to the sun. Unfortunately, bad weather spoilt the observation. However, Maskelyne successfully used the Lunar method to calculate the longitude during the voyage and to fix the precise longitude of St Helena, which had not been known before.

Meanwhile, in May 1761, William Harrison arrived in Portsmouth with H3, ready to depart on the trial. His father was due to meet him there with H4 after last-minute adjustments had been made. In the event, he was forced to kick his heels at the dockyard town for the next seven months until the Board allowed the trial to begin. William suspected that Bradley had used his influence with the Board to delay the voyage while Maskelyne was gathering evidence for the rival Lunar method. He might be accused of paranoia if it was not for the record in his diary of a chance encounter between his father and Bradley. According to William, 'the doctor seemed very much out of temper and in the greatest passion told Mr Harrison that if it had not been for him and his plaguey watch, Mr Mayer and he should have shared Ten Thousand Pounds before now'.

At last, on 18 November 1761, William set sail for the West Indies on the *Deptford,* a 60-gun frigate, with just one timekeeper on board – H4 – which was accurately set to local time at Portsmouth. The Harrisons had decided to put all their eggs in the one basket and rely on the smaller instrument for their claim to the prize. There were probably still doubts about the effects of violent motion on the performance of H3 and the decision underlines the confidence they had in the new machine. As a precaution against tampering, H4 was enclosed in a box with four locks, one key held by William Harrison, the other three by William Lyttleton, the governor-designate of Jamaica, the ship's captain Dudley Digges and his first lieutenant. Thus, all four had to be present when H4 was removed for its daily winding.

The first port of call was to be Madeira, where ships making the Atlantic crossing routinely put in for supplies. This was a matter of urgency for the crew of the *Deptford*, as, by the ninth day out, their supplies of beer and cheese had become tainted. On that day, the last drinkable beer ran out and the crew were forced to drink the remaining foul water, but William, who was carefully plotting the ship's position using H4, predicted that they would make Madeira within a day. Captain Digges disagreed; by his reckoning they were over 100 miles from Harrison's position and he offered to bet him five to one that his own position was correct. The whole ship's company was delighted when, as William had predicted, they sighted the Porto Santo at 6am the following morning. Digges was so impressed that he offered to purchase the first Harrison timekeeper that would be put up for sale. Whilst in Madeira, Digges despatched a hurried message to John Harrison:

> Dear Sir, I have just time to acquaint you … of the great perfection of your watch on making the island on the Meridian; according to our Log we were 1 degree 27 minutes to the Eastward, this I made by a French map which lays down the longitude of Teneriffe, therefore I think your watch must be right. Adieu.

During the rest of the three-month voyage, the timekeeper appeared to be performing equally well and correctly predicted their arrival at Port Royal, Jamaica, on 19 January 1762, whilst the *Deptford*'s log showed their position to be well over 100 miles away. When the Board's representative, John Robison, set up his observatory and instruments to establish the exact local time, it was apparent that H4 had lost just 5 seconds during the whole voyage of 81 days, an almost unbelievable achievement. As a commemoration of the triumph, Captain Digges presented William with an octant, the latest instrument for measuring the angle of heavenly bodies above the horizon.

This was the official end of the trial and it must have seemed to William that the prize was in the bag. The Act stipulated that £20,000 would be paid if the position at the end of the voyage could be measured within 1 degree of longitude. William had calculated the ship's position to be within 1¼ seconds of longitude! All the Harrisons needed to do now was to show that their method was 'generally practicable and useful'.

After the fair weather of the outward journey, the return voyage aboard the small sloop of war, the *Merlin,* was cursed with violent storms; with high seas crashing over the decks, nothing in the ship was dry. Even the captain's cabin was at times awash with 6in of water and poor William, running a high fever and prostrate with sea sickness, was forced to cradle the timekeeper, which was wrapped in blankets for protection. He succeeded in keeping it running and on return to Portsmouth it was found that H4, despite its pounding at sea, showed an error of 1 minute 54.5 seconds over the whole 147 days since it was set on leaving England. This was the equivalent of just 28.5 minutes of longitude, a fantastic achievement that far exceeded the stipulation of the Act, which had set the payment of the full £20,000 for a method of finding longitude on a single voyage to the West Indies within 30 minutes of longitude (half a degree).

If the Harrisons celebrated their success, they were to be sorely disappointed. The Board of Longitude, which had given John Harrison every support he could have expected over a quarter of a century, refused to authorise payment of the full award. The membership of the Board had changed over the years and George Graham, Harrison's staunch supporter, had died. The members were now more than ever inclined to favour the Lunar method and it is perhaps understandable that before such a large amount of public money should be disbursed, every objection should be fully considered.

A long list of problems was raised with the conduct of the trial, which admittedly had been badly organised both from the point of view of the Board and the Harrisons. The principal objection was that the Harrisons had not declared a 'rate' for the timekeeper before setting out. No timepiece keeps exact time and in the case of chronometers a known daily error would be allowed for when the time was read; thus, if the rate was minus 5 seconds, then after 10 days, 50 seconds would be added to the time shown. William's calculations allowed for the estimated rate of H4 and although he had shown that he could correctly predict the ship's longitude, he needed to declare a rate to provide proof of H4's performance. Another legitimate objection was that the exact longitude of Jamaica had not yet been properly measured, throwing doubt on William's calculations on the outward voyage. One member of the Board even argued that if someone took a gross of ordinary watches to the West Indies and one of them happened by chance to keep the correct time, then he would also be entitled to the prize.

The Board finally concluded in August 1762 that 'the Experiments already made of the Watch have not been sufficient to determine the Longitude at Sea'. The Harrisons were obliged to submit H4 for a second trial. They were, however, awarded an immediate payment of £1,500 with a further £1,000 promised on completion of the trial. To add to their woes, Maskelyne had returned from his voyage to St Helena flushed with the success of his calculations using the Lunar method. He quickly staked his claim to the prize by publishing *The British Mariner's Guide*, which contained the latest lunar tables and directions on how to use them to calculate longitude.

The death of their old adversary, Bradley, the Astronomer Royal, gave the Harrisons no respite. When his replacement, Nathaniel Bliss, took his seat on the Board, he immediately attacked the Harrisons, asserting that the claimed performance of the watch was a chance occurrence and putting his weight behind the Lunar method. John Harrison, a self-educated, plain-speaking northerner who cared little for the niceties of social graces, would always be at a disadvantage facing the largely aristocratic commissioners. His decision to leave negotiations with the Board to his son turned out to be a mistake, as William was not a good advocate and came over as arrogant and bad-tempered in his dealings with the Board.

Part of the agreement to the second trial was that the details of H4 should be disclosed. The Board insisted that the design should be widely disseminated for the benefit of the scientific community as a whole. However, the Harrisons were reluctant to comply, having understood that the construction of the machine should be kept secret in the national interest. In April 1763, the Board gave leave to the French astronomer Jérôme Lalande to inspect the timekeeper, but Harrison only showed him the outside of H4. Lalande persevered and on a second visit in May, accompanied by the clockmaker Ferdinand Berthoud and the mathematician Charles Étienne Camus, Harrison refused them even an external glimpse of the machine.

Under increasing pressure by the Board for the disclosure of H4's design before a second trial could take place, John Harrison petitioned Parliament for formal clarification of his position. Parliament eventually confirmed that no one else could be awarded the prize until his timekeeper had been properly tried. The strained relations with the Board now had reached breaking point. Harrison refused to accept their new demand that as part of the 'disclosure' stipulated in the original Act, he must prove that the timekeeper was a practicable solution to the longitude problem by overseeing the construction of two copies of H4. This and other demands by a largely hostile Board resulted in an impasse, which was eventually resolved by the First Lord of the Admiralty, the Earl of Sandwich. One of the most talented and forward-looking politicians of his day, Sandwich (who sponsored James Cook on his great voyages of exploration) declared that Harrison should have his second trial 'when he pleased and as soon as he pleased'.

A Second Sea Trial for H4

It was agreed that the new trial should take place after allowing Harrison four or five months for further improvements and adjustments to the timekeeper, provided that he submitted it for testing at Greenwich to establish the machine's rate. When the time came, Harrison stubbornly refused to allow H4 to be tested at the Observatory (he was rightly suspicious of the treatment it might receive there, as we shall see later). He declared that 'he did not chuse to part with it out of his hands till he shall have reaped some advantage from it'. A compromise was reached over the vexed question of the rate, whereby Harrison should send a sealed letter to the Secretary of the Admiralty before the ship sailed containing his own declared rate, which would be used during the trial to allow for the known error in H4's timekeeping.

John Montagu, Fourth Earl of Sandwich *by Thomas Gainsborough.*

While Harrison was working on H4, the Board sent two astronomers to set up an observatory in Barbados to confirm its exact longitude and judge the performance of the timekeeper on its arrival the following year. Charles Green was accompanied by none other than the Astronomer Royal's henchman Nevil Maskelyne, who believed that his Lunar method would soon win the longitude prize. William and a companion, Thomas Wyatt, set sail aboard the *Tartar* on 24 March 1764 with H4. John Harrison officially rated it; he gave a series of corrections to be made at different temperatures ranging from a gain of 3 seconds per day at 42 degrees to a loss of 1 second at 82 degrees. He stated that he would settle for an overall rate of 1 second per day gain. The voyage went well and William again calculated the landfall at Madeira with impressive accuracy, confirmed in writing by Captain Sir John Lindsay.

On reaching Barbados, William was furious to hear from the local residents that Maskelyne was claiming that his Lunar method was far superior to Harrison's watch. He understandably objected to H4 being checked by Maskelyne, who, as a competitor for the prize, clearly had an interest in the result; Sir John Lindsay supported William. After much wrangling, William reluctantly accepted that observations should be made alternately by Maskelyne and Green. It was reported that Maskelyne was so discomposed that he could hardly make his observations.

William need not have worried, as the results of the observations confirmed that the timekeeper was just 39.2 seconds out over the seven weeks of the voyage, an error of less than 1 second per day, an incredible performance. On their return to Portsmouth, H4 was found to have gained just 54 seconds during the 156 days since they had set out. This was using the 1 second per day correction John had agreed to; if the declared corrections for the various temperature changes were allowed for, the timekeeper would have showed an overall error of less than one-tenth of a second per day, a truly remarkable achievement.

Surely, there would be no further delay in awarding the prize Harrison had proved so convincingly that he had earnt. Incredibly, his enemies on the Board, who now included the new Astronomer Royal, none other than Nevil Maskelyne, found reasons to delay further. They insisted that to be awarded half of the prize, Harrison must disclose the details of the mechanism on oath to a specially appointed committee; furthermore, he must produce two copies of the timekeeper to prove that H4 was not a fluke. He must also hand all four timekeepers over to the Board. Understandably, Harrison was furious and refused to negotiate on any of the Board's demands. A letter he wrote to them complained that: 'I cannot help thinking that I am extremely ill used by Gentlemen who I might have expected better treatment from'. At a fraught meeting with the Board, Harrison lost his temper and stormed out, declaring: 'that he would never consent to it as long has he had a drop of English blood in his body'. The commissioners dug their heels in and refused to have any further dealings with him 'until he alters his present sentiments'. After a four-week stand-off, Harrison finally agreed to disclose the secrets of his machine.

The committee appointed by the Board who were to meet Harrison included three established London watchmakers: Thomas Mudge, William Matthews and Larcum Kendall. The latter had been apprenticed to John Jefferys and may well have been employed by Harrison to make some of the parts of H4. The disclosure took place at Harrison's house in Red Lion Square on 14 August 1765. It must have been a tense occasion, given that it was conducted under the supervision of Maskelyne himself. Harrison complied and duly dismantled the timepiece, explaining all its workings. He also provided detailed drawings and gave full answers to their questions.

Harrison's Award

Having satisfied the board on the question of disclosure, Harrison was awarded the agreed sum of £7,500, which, with the £2,500 already received, made up the first half of the total prize money. In return, the Board insisted that H4 be handed over so that a copy could be made by Larcum Kendall. Now that the Board was preparing to publish details of H4, Harrison felt free to negotiate with the French for an award for disclosing to them details of the timekeeper. He agreed to receive Ferdinand Berthoud and reveal his secrets to him for an award of £4,000. However, when he turned up with just £500 Harrison sent him packing. The resourceful Berthoud did not give up. He simply went to see Thomas Mudge, who had been present at the disclosure and was happy to freely pass on the details, no doubt believing that he was carrying out the will of the Board in disseminating the information.

Within a year, the Board published *The Principles of Mr. Harrison's Time Keeper*, which was rapidly translated into French. The book, in fact, was not of much practical use to anyone wanting to construct a timekeeper. However, the principles it contained turned out to be very influential in the future development of the chronometer. In Paris, Ferdinand Berthoud and Pierre Le Roy later produced their own *montres marines*, but they were more interested in producing luxury clocks for the French aristocracy and did not achieve the all-important objective of producing a reliable and affordable chronometer.

Meanwhile, the already strained relations between Harrison and the Board of Longitude took a further turn for the worse when they decided to submit H4 for rigorous testing to none other than Nevil Maskelyne at the Royal Observatory. This was at a time when Maskelyne was advocating his Lunar method for a share of the prize money. To make matters worse, Maskelyne turned up unannounced at Harrison's door with a warrant which read:

> Mr John Harrison
> We the ... Commissioners appointed by the Acts of Parliament for the discovery of Longitude

> at Sea, do herby require you to deliver up to the Rev. Nevil Maskelyne, Astronomer Royal at Greenwich, the three several Machines or Timekeepers, now remaining in your hands, which are become the property of the public ...

After a long altercation, Harrison had no option but to surrender the three timekeepers to Maskelyne's servants, who roughly manhandled them to a waiting cart in the street outside, on the way 'accidentally' dropping H1 in the process. We shudder to imagine the damage done to these precious and delicate timepieces during their process through the rough London streets in a common, unsprung cart. It must have been utterly heartbreaking for Harrison.

The new trial of H4 went badly from the outset. Harrison had not been given the opportunity to clean or adjust the timekeeper since it had been dismantled for the disclosure. Maskelyne seems to have given it the most severe testing he could devise short of resorting to blatant trickery. H4 was left in a glass-topped box in direct sunlight in an unheated room where it was by turn roasted and frozen as the seasons progressed. At the end of the ten-month trial the timekeeper had gained 1 hour 10 minutes 27.5 seconds. Based on this performance, Maskelyne gleefully reported to the Board that: 'Mr Harrison's Watch cannot be depended upon to keep the Longitude within a degree in a West India Voyage of six weeks ...', despite the fact that H4 had already proved itself more than capable of that feat on two voyages.

Harrison immediately responded by publishing a pamphlet refuting Maskelyne's results, although this did nothing to improve his relationship with the Board. They insisted that Harrison, despite his advanced age (he was now 73) must produce two more timepieces before he could be considered for the award of the second half of the prize money. In fact, Harrison, with the assistance of his son William, was already working a second version of H4. His last timekeeper, H5, was completed in 1772. Meanwhile, Larcum Kendall had finished, for a fee of £500, his copy of H4 (now known as K1) in 1769; Harrison was given leave to examine it and confirmed that it was of exceptional quality.

By this time, it seems that the Board had lost interest in timekeepers as a viable solution to the longitude problem, as most of the commissioners believed that the Lunar method was more practical now that tables were being published regularly. They continued to insist that Harrison must produce a second copy of H4 to qualify for the full award, despite the success of K1. John Harrison was now 79 years old and in poor health; he could not possibly contemplate starting work on yet another copy of his timekeeper. In desperation, the Harrisons decided to appeal to the King for help in their claim for justice, as they had heard that George III, who had a keen interest in scientific matters, had taken an interest in their timekeepers.

In February 1772, William Harrison was granted an interview with the King, who agreed to put H5 (Harrison's second version of H4) on trial at his private observatory at Richmond. After listening to William's story, the King was said to have remarked, 'these people have been cruelly treated – by God Harrison, I will see you righted'.

The King was as good as his word and H5 was set up at the observatory under the supervision of the resident astronomer, Dr Demainbury, and the King himself, who attended the daily checks. Much to William's alarm and embarrassment, the timekeeper at first performed very erratically. Luckily, the cause was soon found. It seemed that the King had stored a number of lode stones in a cupboard next to where H4 was set up and the strong magnetic field they generated was interfering with the timekeeper. After the offending items were removed, H5 settled down and performed immaculately; over a two-month trial it was found to be just 4½ seconds astray. Harrison advised the Board of the results of the trial in the hope that they would reconsider their position. However, the Board refused to make any compromise and Harrison finally gave up any hope of justice from that quarter.

Taking the King's advice, Harrison petitioned Parliament for justice. Backed by several influential members and with the powerful support of Fox, a bill was drawn up to award Harrison a further sum of £8,750, which made up more than the balance of the £20,000 owing to him. It should be noted that this was a bounty awarded by Parliament and not the actual longitude prize, which was still open to competition, with even more stringent conditions; the prize was, in fact, never awarded.

Meanwhile, K1 had been entrusted to Captain James Cook for testing on his second great voyage to the Antipodes. Cook had relied on the Lunar method on his earlier voyage to the South Seas and on this voyage he compared the results of this method with those obtained using the chronometer. He was soon converted to the new mode of navigation using 'our trusty friend the watch', which he praised in his log as 'our never failing guide'. This, coming from one of the greatest navigators of the age, was praise indeed. It must have been a great consolation to the aged Harrison to hear of the success of his invention on Cook's return in 1775. Cook reported that Mr Kendall's watch (which cost £450) exceeded the expectations of its most zealous advocate. He had no hesitation in taking K1 on his next voyage, which sadly he did not survive. Luckily, the timekeeper did return to England and can now be seen together with the Harrison timepieces at the Royal Observatory.

John Harrison died on 24 March 1776 at the advanced age of 83. For all his 'ill use' at the hands of the Board of Longitude, he succeeded in dying a famous and wealthy man. Although his design for marine timekeepers did not reach quantity production, as it was far too complicated and expensive, he did solve the problems associated with accurate timekeeping at sea. The four sea clocks were stored at the Royal Observatory and, apart from some cleaning in 1830, were left partially dismantled and decaying until 1920.

Captain James Cook.

They were discovered by Lieutenant-Commander Rupert Gould, a talented amateur horologist, who persuaded the authorities to allow him to attempt their cleaning and reconstruction. His interest became an obsession that occupied much of the rest of his life; not only restoring the timepieces, but publishing the definitive book on chronometers and tirelessly promoting Harrison and his great achievement. It is largely due to Gould that we can see the four marine clocks magnificently restored and displayed at the Royal Observatory. Due to their robust construction, it is possible to keep the three large timekeepers running, but H4 is considered too delicate to risk daily winding. H5 came to light in 1891 and was purchased by the Worshipful Company of Clockmakers; it can now be seen as part of its collection at the London Science Museum.

Harrison has at last taken his rightful place as one of the nation's greatest innovators, his discoveries leading to the transformation of marine navigation and the saving of countless lives. After many petitions, his achievements have been recognised with a memorial in Westminster Abbey. In 2006, the plaque bearing the simple inscription: 'JOHN 'LONGITUDE' HARRISON CLOCKMAKER 1693 1776' engraved across a bimetallic strip, was unveiled, appropriately next to the grave that contains the remains of both George Graham and Thomas Tompion.

Harrison's memorial in Westminster Abbey.

Chapter 7
Navigation Transformed

Newton's assessment of the problems to be solved for finding longitude, given to the Board of Longitude in 1714, was correct. His favoured option of using a timekeeper rather than astronomical observation was discounted as impractical, as no such timepiece then existed. However, as Harrison had proved it was possible to make a successful sea clock, this option was now on the table alongside the Lunar Difference method, which, despite its difficulty, was the one advocated by many astronomers. Harrison's design worked well, but was highly complex and prohibitively expensive to make. Other talented horologists decided that it might be worthwhile putting their energies into taking Harrison's ideas forward. The goal was to produce accurate, reliable timepieces at a price that would make them available to the ordinary sea captain.

NEW CHRONOMETER DESIGNS

Larcum Kendall

Kendall was born at Charlbury, Oxfordshire, in 1721 and was apprenticed to John Jefferys in 1735. After serving his time, he set up in business for himself and by 1765 had reached a degree of eminence in the trade to qualify him to serve on the committee that received Harrison's 'disclosure' of the mechanism of H4. He was selected by the Board of Longitude to produce a copy of Harrison's timekeeper for a fee of £450; a bonus of £50 was added to his fee in recognition of the work he had done in dismantling H4. The duplicate timekeeper (K1) took two years to complete after instruction from Harrison himself. It was completed in 1769 and finally delivered after further adjustment in January 1770. As we have seen, K1 performed well and accompanied Cook on his second and third voyages to the South Seas.

The Board asked Kendall to train workmen to make further copies of H4, but he declined the offer, giving as his reasons that due to the complicated construction of Harrison's timekeeper it would take many years before it would be possible to produce timekeepers to Harrison's design and the cost could not be reduced to below £200. He later agreed to produce an experimental timekeeper of a simplified design, omitting aspects of H4 that he considered non-essential. In the event, he produced two almost identical timekeepers (K2 and K3), which retained Harrison's temperature compensations but left out the remontoir. Neither timekeeper performed as well as H4 or K1 and he appears to have lost interest in marine timekeeping after delivering them; perhaps the niggardly fees he obtained from the Board had some influence on his decision. However, K2 had a remarkable history – it accompanied Captain Phipps on a North Polar expedition, but after some years on the North American station was returned to England and sent out with Captain William Bligh on the *Bounty* in 1787.

Thomas Mudge

Born in Exeter in 1715, Mudge was apprenticed to George Graham and continued to work with Graham as one of his most trusted assistants until his master's death in 1751. He was a supreme craftsman, producing exquisite and complex watches for several of Europe's royal houses. He invented the lever escapement around 1754, which in the next century became

Thomas Mudge *by Nathaniel Dance.*

the standard watch escapement and is still used today in practically all mechanical watches.

As one of the members of the committee appointed by the Board of Longitude in 1765 to examine H4, Mudge was most impressed by Harrison's inventions. He soon formed the opinion that he could improve on Harrison's timekeeper and published a short tract with suggestions for improving marine timekeepers; his principal thoughts concerned improvements to the escapement. In 1771, he left his business in London under the control of his partner William Dutton and moved to Plymouth where his brother lived, in order to pursue his experiments and compete for the longitude prize. His first timekeeper was completed in 1774 and is of the most exquisite workmanship. In essence, it is very similar to H4, with the exception of his 'constant force' escapement. This is most ingenious and delivers each impulse to the balance wheel through two small springs, which are rewound with every oscillation of the balance. Unfortunately, it is also extremely complicated and needed the almost unrivalled skills of Mudge himself to produce it.

Mudge presented his timekeeper to the Board for trials and it was sent to the Royal Observatory under the supervision of Nevil Maskelyne. It appears that Mudge's timekeeper suffered as much as H4 from rough treatment at the Observatory, where it was carried daily in and out of the Transit Room by Maskelyne's assistant for checking. The machine suffered stoppages and a broken mainspring, so the trial had to be abandoned. The timekeeper was again submitted for trial in 1776; this time it was agreed to keep it in the Transit Room. It performed well at first and achieved a rate of better than 1 second per day, but suffered a broken mainspring again. Meanwhile, despite failing eyesight, Mudge was completing two further similar timekeepers, known as the 'Blue' and the 'Green' from the colour of their cases.

They were submitted for trial three times between 1779 and 1790, but both suffered problems with temperature compensation. Maskelyne reported to the Board that neither machine had gone within the limits set by the Act. By 1790, Mudge was unable to carry on working on his timekeepers and an attempt made to set up a workshop to produce further marine clocks failed. It has to be said that despite his ingenuity and incredible craftsmanship, Mudge's efforts had led to a dead end. He had failed to meet the essential requirement that a successful marine timekeeper must be relatively simple and reliable, as well as being capable of production at an affordable price.

Further Developments

The key problems that beset the pioneers of marine timekeeping were the same ones that had held back progress in all precision time-pieces. Two elements must come together:

1. **Time controller**: a device that divides time into small, equal intervals.
2. **Escapement**: a way of keeping that device going and counting those intervals without disturbing its timekeeping qualities.

THE STORY OF CAPTAIN BLIGH'S CHRONOMETER

William Bligh.

Bligh notes in his published Journal:

> ... from the board of Longitude I received a time-keeper, made by Mr. Kendal ... During our stay at Spithead, the rate of the time-piece was several times examined by Mr. Bailey's observations at the Portsmouth observatory. On the 19th of December 1787 the last time of its being examined on shore, it was 1 minute 52.5 seconds too fast for mean time, and then losing at the rate of 1.1 seconds per day; and at this rate I estimate its going when we sailed.
>
> *At* Cape Town The error of the time-keeper was 3 minutes. 33 seconds too slow for the meantime at Greenwich, and its rate of going 3 seconds per day, losing.
>
> Arrived at Tahiti The ship was 3° 22' in longitude to the eastward of the dead reckoning, which the time-keeper almost invariably proved to be owing to a current giving us more easting than the log.

At the time of the mutiny, when Bligh and the members of the crew who elected to stay loyal to their captain were preparing to leave the Bounty:

> Mr. Samuel ... was forbidden, on pain of death, to touch either map, ephemeris, book of astronomical observations, sextant, time-keeper or any of my surveys or drawings. Mr. Samuel attempted to save the time-keeper, and a box with my surveys, drawings, and remarks for fifteen years past, which were numerous; when he was hurried away, with 'Damn your eyes you are well off to get what you have.'

Thus, without his precious chronometer, Bligh was forced to begin, in an open boat, his epic voyage to safety – one of the great feats of seamanship.

After the mutiny, Christian and the other mutineers searched for a place to settle. When they accidentally found Pitcairn Island, they noted

Bligh cast adrift by the mutineers; from the 1935 film, Mutiny on the Bounty.

Pitcairn Island.

that Captain Philip Carteret, its discoverer, had not charted its location correctly. On Admiralty charts, Pitcairn Island was placed 3 degrees of longitude, some 170 miles away from its true position, the contemporary equivalent of a two-day voyage under fair conditions. The mutineers had the K2 chronometer and were able to determine the island's true position. They knew that future expeditions sent to capture them would also have chronometers and would be unlikely to find the island, a good reason to settle there as they were likely to remain undiscovered.

The K2 chronometer remained with the mutineers on Pitcairn until Captain Mayhew Folger of the American whaling ship Topaz of Boston came upon the island in 1808 and discovered the women, children and the one surviving mutineer, John Adams. Folger purchased the chronometer from Adams, who, Folger records, received a 'small silk handkerchief he prizes' for the chronometer and the Bounty's azimuth compass.

On their way to Valparaíso, Folger and his ship arrived at Juan Fernández Island. The Spanish governor confiscated the chronometer and imprisoned Folger and his crew until a new governor arrived some months later and set the Americans free. According to Folger's log, written in Valparaíso on 10 October 1808: 'Smith [alias John Adams] gave to Capt. Folger a Chronometer, made by Kendall, which was taken from him by the Governor of Juan Fernandez. (signed) Wm. Fitzmaurice'.

The chronometer appears next at Concepción in Chile, where it was purchased for three doubloons by an old Spanish muleteer by the name of Castillo. It was kept by Castillo until his death in Santiago in 1840. His family, by arrangement with Alex Caldcleugh of Valparaíso, sold it to Captain Thomas Herbert R.N., of HMS Calliope for 50 guineas. Herbert had the watch examined by Mr Mouat, a 'chronometer maker' in Valparaíso.

The chronometer was then conveyed to the United Service Institution in London upon Herbert's behalf by Captain Newman of H.M. Sloop Sparrowhawk. Newman notes: 'I was at Pitcairn Island in the Sparrowhawk this time last year, and perhaps that has contributed to the interest I feel in this affair. I have some tappa or native cloth manufactured by the hands of Polly Adams Herself.' K2 can now be seen at the National Maritime Museum.

The Mudge 'Green' chronometer.

We have seen that by the mid-eighteenth century, great progress had been made in building clocks that fulfilled these requirements. The temperature-compensated pendulum made an excellent time controller when impulsed by the dead-beat escapement, which kept the pendulum going with very little interference. Regulator clocks, which kept time reliably to a second or so per month, were built not only for observatory use, but were soon to be found in large households and clock- and watchmaker's establishments.

Accurate portable timekeepers were a much more difficult problem. The pioneering work of Harrison and Mudge had shown that the balance wheel with some form of temperature compensation could be a suitable time controller. However, the escapements they used to drive the balance were really developments of the common verge escapement used in watches of the time. These escapements added friction, which spoilt the timekeeping qualities of the balance wheel. Only with the addition of highly complex devices did these makers succeeded in getting good results from their marine timekeepers. What was needed was a breakthrough in escapement design, which would give the balance a sharp impulse and then detach itself completely from the balance wheel, leaving it free to oscillate until the next impulse; a successful 'detached' escapement became the holy grail of marine timekeeping.

During the third quarter of the eighteenth century, Pierre Le Roy and Ferdinand Berthoud experimented with sea clocks with encouraging results. However, Le Roy abandoned this branch of horology and Berthoud's progress was slow. It was in England that the most important developments took place.

RIVALRY

The elusive goal of developing a simple and reliable chronometer design, which could be produced at a price that would make it an affordable piece of equipment for seagoing vessels, fell to two rival compatriots.

John Arnold

John Arnold was born in 1736 in Bodmin, Cornwall. As the son of the local watchmaker, he was naturally apprenticed to his father. However, it seems that the provincial life did not suit John, so he broke his indentures and ran away to Holland, where he found work in the trade. At age twenty, he travelled to London, where he made a precarious living until he made the acquaintance of a Mr McGuire, who advanced him the capital to set himself up as a watchmaker. Arnold proved himself to be a good businessman as well as a fine craftsman and his business prospered.

Arnold's knowledge of German, which he had picked up in Holland, proved useful when he obtained an audience with George III and in 1764 he gained considerable fame with the presentation to the King of a most remarkable watch. Fitted into a finger ring about 12mm diameter, it not only kept good time but was a 'quarter repeater', sounding the time to the nearest quarter hour on tiny gongs. This was an incredible achievement and understandably caused a sensation at the time. Arnold received the sum of 500 guineas as a reward and refused an offer of double this from Catherine the Great of Russia to make a similar watch, giving as his reason that he wanted King George's watch to remain unique.

This success in business would have given him the freedom to experiment and he soon turned his attention to marine timekeepers. In 1770, he submitted a machine to the Board of Longitude, as the minutes for 26 May record: '... Mr Arnold, a Watchmaker in Pall Mall, attended with a Timekeeper of a new construction, which he showed to the Board and strongly recommended. He was told that if he constructed one of the kind it should be tried.'

Arnold duly built a second timekeeper and presented it to the Board the next year, reporting that its cost was only about 60 guineas, a fraction of the cost of previous timekeepers by Harrison, Kendall and Mudge. The Board advanced him £300 on condition that this sum should be deducted from the cost of any timepieces supplied by him to the board.

John Arnold *by Mason Chamberlin,* c. *1767.*

The balance arrangement and temperature compensation of Arnold's early timekeepers was on the same lines as Harrison's; however, he used a form of pivoted detent escapement, which was a considerable improvement on the designs of Harrison and Mudge. This escapement appears to owe little to those of Le Roy, who was working on a similar design. Whilst lacking the elegant simplicity of the French designs, it does show that Arnold was independently making progress along the same lines. It is improbable that Arnold could have known anything about the French experiments, which would have been kept secret, and to suspect him of industrial espionage is fanciful in the extreme.

At this time, the Admiralty was fitting out two ships, the *Resolution* and *Adventure* for Cook's second voyage to the Southern Oceans. Kendall's K1 was already destined to accompany the expedition and Arnold was keen to have his timekeepers tested on the voyage. Accordingly, three of Arnold's timekeepers were tested. However, the results were not what Arnold hoped, as all three performed very badly, showing wild variations in timekeeping. The problem appears to have been with his temperature compensation, which seems to have ceased to operate; this would account for the large errors at different temperatures. Understandably, the Board refused to make Arnold any further disbursements 'until they have better proof of the merits of the watches they have of him, or are satisfied that he has made some very considerable improvement'.

Arnold, undismayed by this setback, continued working to improve his chronometers. Several important developments came in 1776. He adopted the helical form of balance spring and a new form of temperature compensation using bimetallic strips built into the balance wheel. He also developed a simplified and much improved form of pivoted detent escapement. At this time, Arnold decided to protect his improvements with patents. However, these early patents were so vaguely drawn that they would have offered Arnold very little protection. They would also have prevented him from getting any further support from the Board of Longitude, as a condition of applying to them was that inventions should not be patented.

It soon became apparent that these improvements were a great success and Arnold embarked upon producing a number of pocket chronometers, no doubt seeing an opportunity for a new market for his timepieces. Unlike a marine chronometer, which is suspended in gimbals to keep it constantly in a horizontal position, a pocket watch has to be adjusted to keep time accurately in several different positions. Despite this severe disadvantage, Arnold's pocket chronometers performed exceptionally well – one that was officially tested for over a year in normal use never varied more than 3 seconds per day.

It is not clear exactly when Arnold came up with his design for a spring detent escapement, but it later became an issue of bitter dispute with Thomas Earnshaw, who asserted that he had the prior claim to this important development. Eliminating the pivots and the associated spring of the earlier detent reduced friction and the need to oil the detent pivots, making the whole arrangement more robust and reliable.

John Arnold's spring detent.

At the same time as he introduced his spring detent escapement, Arnold developed his final form of compensated balance, patented in 1782. This form of balance wheel uses the bimetallic compensation strips to form the rim of the wheel, with movable weights attached that could be used to adjust the amount of temperature compensation. With later improvements by Earnshaw, this design of temperature-compensated balance became the model for all balance wheels in both chronometers and high-grade watches for the next century and a half.

Wrangling with the Board of Longitude continued without any progress on Arnold's claims to the award of prize money. In the meantime, Arnold was busy establishing a manufactory for chronometers and in 1785, he moved the business to Chigwell in Essex. This was a most important development, in that he was at last producing reliable chronometers of a comparatively simple design at a fraction of the cost of previous instruments. In 1790, he took his son John Roger, who had spent time in Paris training with Abraham-Louis Breguet, into partnership of the flourishing business.

The elder Arnold died in 1799 at the comparatively early age of 63. An obituary notice in *The Times* records that:

> On Sunday morning last died Mr John Arnold, of Well Hall near Eltham in Kent. As a mechanic his *abilities* and industry will be remembered by his *country*. He was the Inventor of the *Expansion Balance*, of the *present detached escapement*, and the first artist who applied the Gold Cylindrical Spring to the balance of a Timepiece. He retired

John Arnold's 'S Type' compensated balance.

> from business about three years since, but his active mind still labouring on the completion of his favourite object, and for what he called the ultimatum of timepiece making, has produced a *Chronometer,* far different and infinitely superior to anything yet made public. *His Son* who succeeded him, we understand is in possession of *all* his father's drawings and models, and from *him* we now hope for the completion of that grand object – the discovery of the Longitude by Time-keepers.

Needless to say, these extravagant claims were bitterly disputed, particularly by Thomas Earnshaw, who, as we shall see, had an equally good claim to many of the important developments in chronometer design. Sadly, John Roger Arnold was not the craftsman nor businessman his father had been and his mother appears to have taken a leading role in the business. In spite of a belated award of £1,678 given by the Board in recognition of his father's achievements in 1806, the business languished. In 1830, John Roger took into partnership the talented E.J. Dent, who revived the firm's reputation. John Roger

John and John Roger Arnold.

died in 1843 and the business was taken over by Charles Frodsham.

Thomas Earnshaw

Earnshaw was born in Ashton-under-Lyne in 1749 and served his apprenticeship as a watchmaker, probably in London. He soon became known as a first-rate craftsman and worked as a watch finisher for several eminent makers, including John Brockbank and Thomas Wright. He later came to specialise in watch jewelling, making ruby bearings and escapement parts.

In his book *Longitude, an Appeal to the Public* published in 1806, Earnshaw claimed that whilst working for Brockbank in 1780, making pivoted detent escapements on the same lines as those developed by Berthoud and Arnold, it occurred to him that he could improve the design. He realised that the pivots and return spring of the detent could be replaced by mounting the complete detent on an integral spring; this would flex to allow the detent to move sideways and return it to its original position after the impulse had been given. Earnshaw claimed that in 1782 he showed his new escapement to Brockbank under pledge of secrecy. Unfortunately, Earnshaw, who had a large family to support, could not afford the 100 guineas it cost to take out a patent. In 1783, he came to an arrangement with Thomas Wright, who would take out the patent and allow Earnshaw to produce watches with the new escapement on payment of a royalty to Wright of one guinea per watch. In the meantime, Earnshaw claimed that Brockbank had broken his promise of secrecy and revealed the invention to Arnold, who within days took out a patent on a very similar escapement, a year before the Wright patent.

Thomas Earnshaw *by Martin Archer Shee.*

Earnshaw's second important innovation was an improved method of constructing compensated balances. Arnold's method of making the bimetallic arms was to solder the strips of brass and steel together, bend them into shape and screw them on to the wheel. Earnshaw developed a method of fusing the brass and steel together, which made the arms much more stable.

Earnshaw's design for temperature compensation soon became the standard for watch and chronometer balances for the next two centuries. The arms bend inwards in rising temperatures, causing a gaining rate and compensating for the lowering elasticity of the balance spring. In falling temperatures, the spring becomes stronger, causing a gain, which is compensated by the outward expansion of the balance arms.

Priority for these inventions was hotly disputed and never resolved; however, Earnshaw's pattern proved more successful. Unlike Arnold's design, which needed oil on the escape wheel teeth, Earnshaw's design did not need lubrication, which was a considerable advantage. Earnshaw's design was also easier and, consequently, cheaper to produce. It was some years before he could set up business on his own account. Lacking the connections and business acumen of Arnold and other leading London makers, Earnshaw was compelled to earn his living making chronometer movements for other makers to sell under their names.

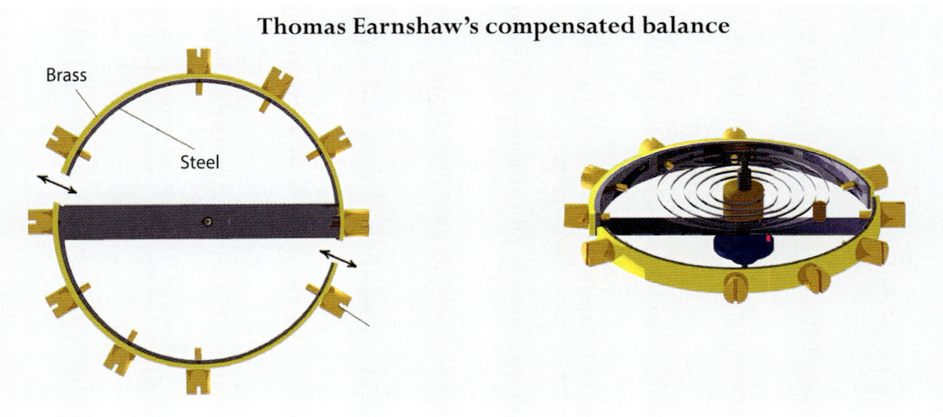

Earnshaw, always looking for ways to improve his financial position, turned his attention to the Board of Longitude's prize of £10,000, which was still available to any maker who could comply with the very strict rules of the trials. Nevil Maskelyne was persuaded to make a private trial of one of Earnshaw's pocket chronometers, though he was no doubt taken aback by the maker's name 'Wm Hughes' on the instrument. Earnshaw explained that he 'was under necessity of making them for other watch-makers who had customers for them … although they had no more to do with the making of the timekeeper than the person who bought it off them'. The irascible Maskelyne seems to have formed a good impression of Earnshaw and went out of his way to speak well of him to the Board. He was impressed with the performance of the chronometer, and there was some talk of a commission for two more machines to submit for formal trial, but nothing came of it.

Eventually Earnshaw was able to free himself from his obligations to other makers and set up in business on his own account. By 1791, trade was good enough for him to employ several workmen to assist him in the production of both pocket and larger box chronometers. That year, Captain William Bligh was sent on a second expedition to the South Seas to collect the breadfruit plants he had first attempted to collect on the ill-fated *Bounty*. The Admiralty instructed him to purchase a timekeeper and he accordingly invited makers to send samples of their chronometers for trial at Greenwich. Earnshaw entered five pocket chronometers, while Arnold and Brockbank entered box chronometers. Bligh eventually selected one of Earnshaw's instruments and issued the following certificate:

> This is to certify the principal Officers and Commissioners of His Majesty's Navy, That Mr Tho. Earnshaw has delivered into my possession a Metal Case Chronometer, No. 1503, at the price of forty guineas. And I do further certify that this Chronometer was compared at Flamsteed House [*the Royal Observatory*], with other watches of much higher prices, and that its rate was preferable, and on that reason taken by me on the Government account.
> July 1791 [*signed*] Wm Bligh

Earnshaw's relationship with the Board of Longitude continued to be difficult, to say the least. He objected that the conditions they imposed for the award of the longitude prize made it almost impossible to compete successfully. He was by now enjoying considerable success. After years of competing in trials he reasonably considered unfair, he gave up hope of winning the prize and simply petitioned the Board for whatever award they deemed appropriate.

Although the Board admitted that Earnshaw's machines consistently outperformed those of other makers, he had to respond to charges from his competitors that he had stolen some of his improvements from Arnold. The Board held an enquiry into these charges and the resulting vitriolic accusations of other members of the trade did them no credit. Eventually, the entire Board, with the exception of their chairman Joseph Banks, who was an enthusiastic patron of Arnold, came down on the side of Earnshaw. They concluded that the balance of evidence favoured Earnshaw and although he could not prove absolute priority for his developments, they were original.

The Board eventually decided to give equal awards of £3,000 to both Arnold and Earnshaw in recognition of their achievements. Reluctantly, Earnshaw accepted the award, but decided to petition Parliament for the justice he felt was due to him. Thus, the sorry episode continued with years of wrangling, with the supporters of both parties indulging in extravagant publications. Earnshaw himself published a 300-page book, setting out his case often in the most intemperate terms. The Parliamentary committee tasked to examine the various claims concluded that it was impossible to decide the priority of the various inventions on the evidence available and that they had no grounds to interfere with the Board of Longitude's conclusions.

Despite the time and effort wasted in these disputes, Earnshaw did more than any other of the early makers to put English chronometer manufacturing on a firm footing. His design proved the most successful and soon dominated the trade. After his death in 1829, his son continued the business until 1850.

Spring detent escapement

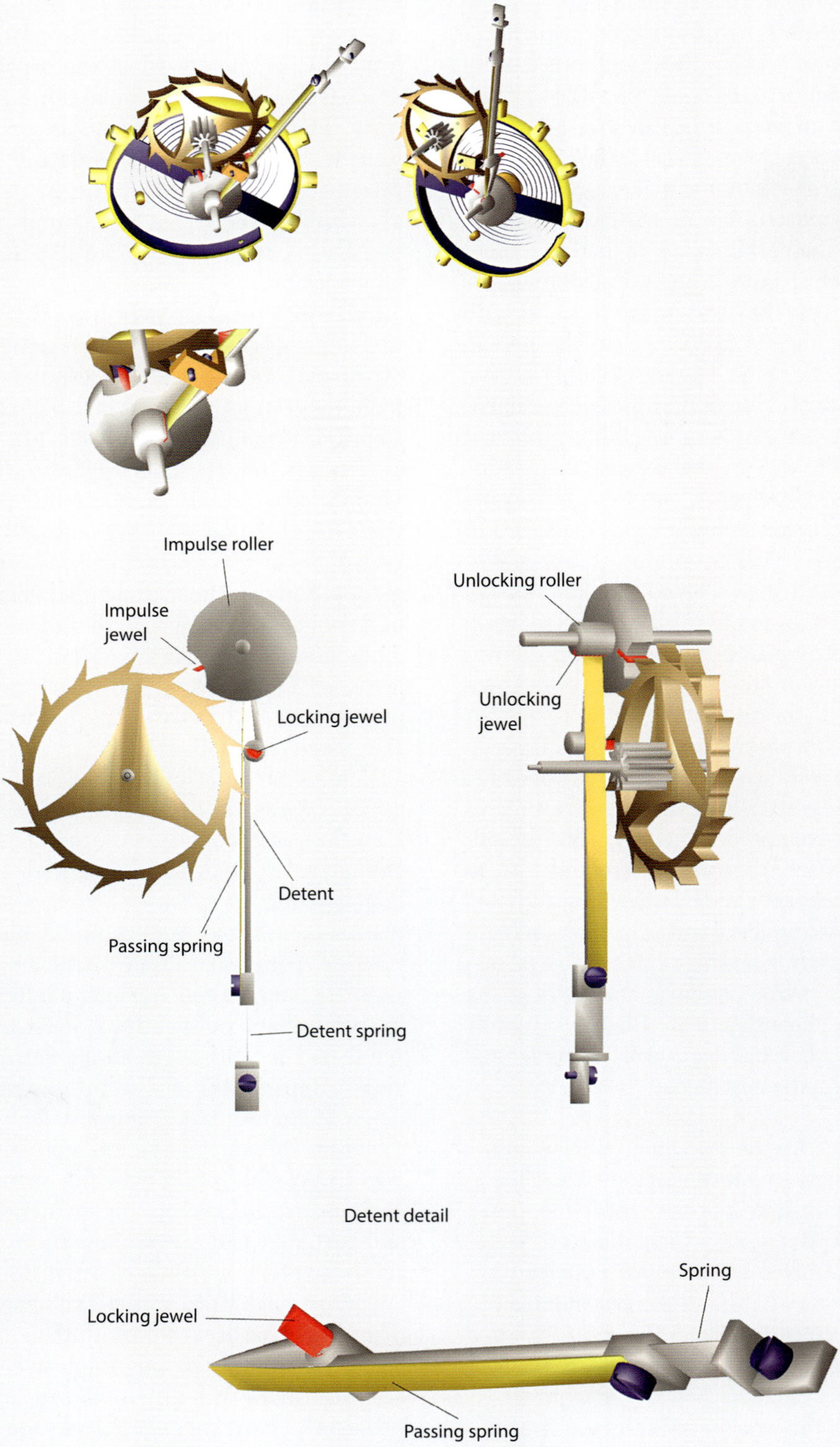

Impulse roller

Impulse jewel

Locking jewel

Detent

Passing spring

Detent spring

Unlocking roller

Unlocking jewel

Detent detail

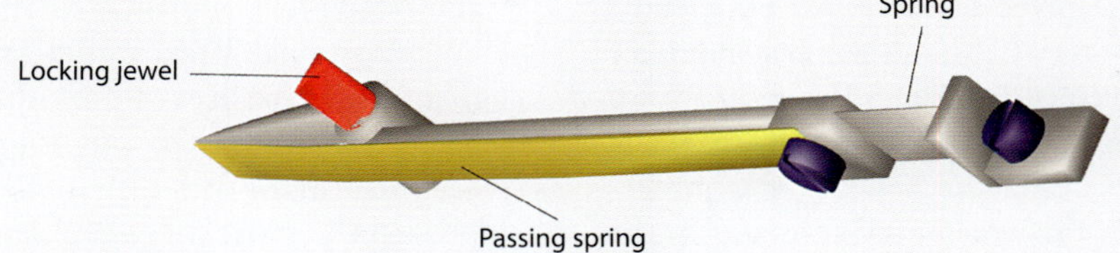

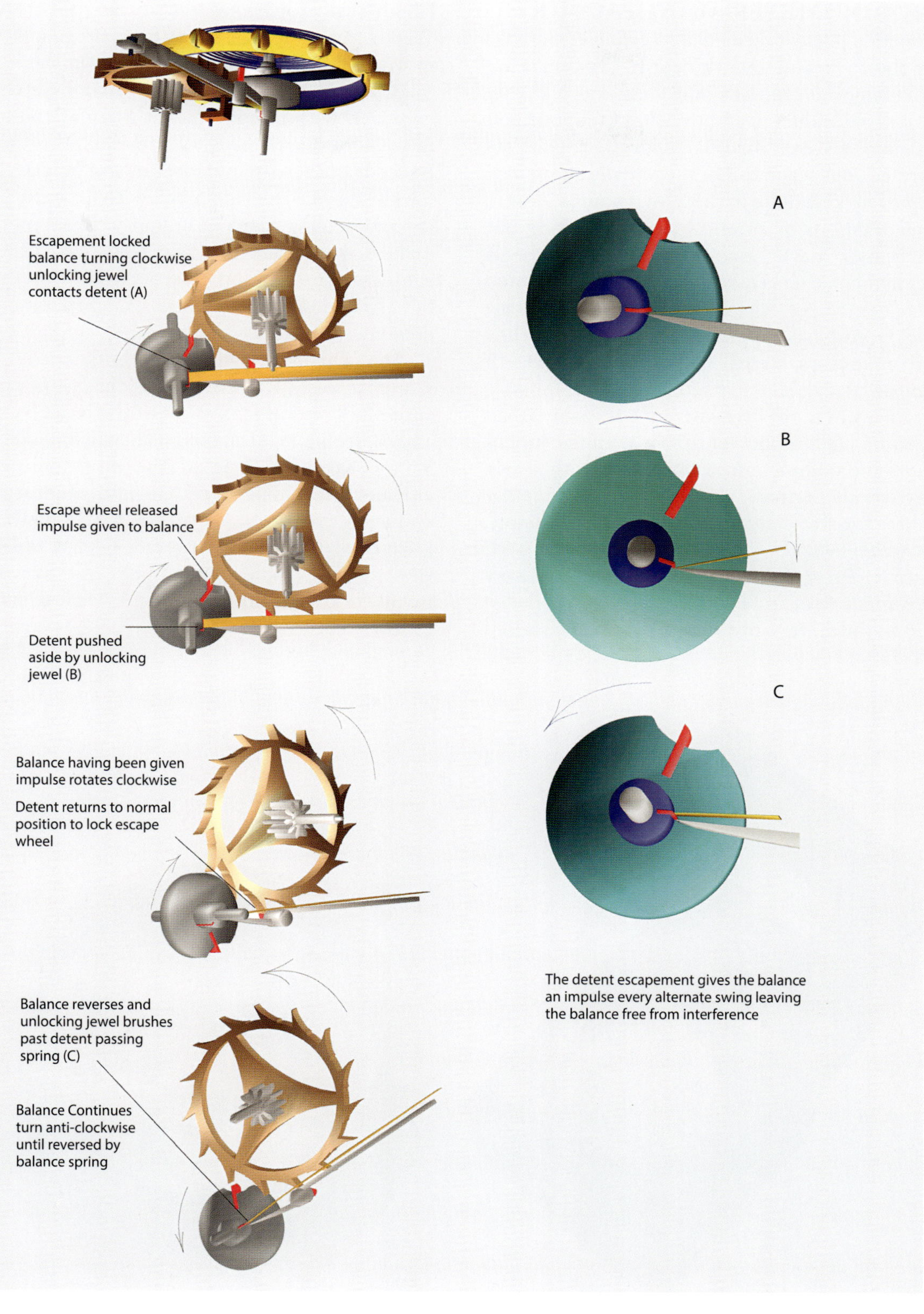

The detent escapement gives the balance an impulse every alternate swing leaving the balance free from interference

CHRONOMETER MANUFACTURE

By the early nineteenth century, the making of chronometers, like watches, was a highly organised industry and division of labour had reached an extraordinary level. Specialists carried out each aspect of manufacturing; some worked alone in their own homes, others in workshops or small factories, turning out particular parts like mainsprings, wheels or hands. Clerkenwell in London became the centre of the chronometer industry and from here supplied most of the world's chronometers until the mid-twentieth century.

The town of Prescott in Lancashire had become very important for the manufacture of parts and complete movements from the early eighteenth century. Liverpool was an early centre for watch manufacturing after London. However, land was in short supply and, nearby, Prescott had an established industry that made files and other tools. The town also had the advantage of a supply of suitably skilled labour ready for training in horological crafts. Watch manufacturers in Prescott supplied movements, finished or partly finished to 'makers' all over the country; many watches engraved with London maker's names contain movements partly or wholly made in Prescott. Records of these manufacturers are practically non-existent, particularly with regard to chronometers, and London chronometer makers were notoriously secretive as to their sources of supply. The Prescott trade directory for 1875, however, includes six 'chronometer movement makers'.

The chronometer movements made in Prescott were not complete; they generally supplied London makers with the basic frame and wheelwork. Luckily, the workbooks of Victor Kullberg, one of the most eminent chronometer makers of the late nineteenth and early twentieth centuries, have survived. Each instrument has a separate page detailing the cost of each component and process involved in its production. A typical page follows from 1864:

Earnshaw's chronometer.

1864 No. 1572

Movement	*Preston 2 Day*	*2 - 2 - 0*
Escapement	*Sibley*	*2 - 8 - 6*
Escape wheel		*2 - 6*
Jewelling escapement Gale		*16 - 0*
Balance		*12 - 0*
Brass box		*9 - 0*
Finishing	*Foster*	*3 - 0 - 0*
Mainspring	*Meredith*	*11 - 0*
Chain		*2 - 6*
Jewelling holes		*4 - 0*
Box	*Mahogany*	*1 - 0 - 0*
Gimbals		*14 - 0*
Engraving		*7 - 0*
Engraving name		*10 - 0*
Engraving badges		*3 - 6*
Engraving tablets		*2 - 0*
Stud		*2 - 0*

The supplier of the 'movement' was Joseph Preston & Sons, a company listed as one of the six chronometer movement makers in Prescott in 1875. The company was established in 1829 and continued to supply parts to the chronometer industry until World War II. From the list of parts, we can deduce that the 'movement' supplied by Preston for Kullberg no. 1572 consisted of the main plates, complete with wheelwork, fusee and mainspring barrel and so on, but without the escapement, balance, mainspring and fusee chain. It is also interesting that the finishing cost more than the movement, indicating that it was supplied in the rough. This makes sense, as the London workers would concentrate on the processes requiring high levels of skills and training, leaving the heavy machining to specialists in Lancashire where it could be done more cheaply. The photograph of the Preston factory probably dates from the 1930s and it was perhaps the last survivor of the Prescott watch industry, which had supplied a great deal of the watch and chronometer trade.

A typical chronometer movement after it arrived from Prescott made a complicated journey around the various specialists, mostly located around Clerkenwell in London. Jewel bearings were fitted in one workshop, the mainspring supplied by another. The balance, escapement, motion work and all of the other parts were made and fitted by highly skilled craftsmen who performed just one process in the overall jigsaw puzzle. Once all of the various parts had been fitted, the movement finally returned to the chronometer maker's workshop. The instrument was assembled 'in the grey'; that is, the parts were not polished and old screws were used. Then the 'springer' took over. He was the key craftsman in the operation and would adjust the balance spring, forming the terminal curves and then fitting it to the balance wheel, ensuring that it 'breathed' in and out perfectly in operation. The escapement was adjusted and the initial testing and rating began – this was the longest operation and took many months of daily checking and adjusting. The rate at different temperatures was noted and the compensation weights on the balance were adjusted to reduce the temperature error to the minimum.

Joseph Preston's factory in Prescott.

Once the chronometer was running properly and maintaining a satisfactory rate, it was completely dismantled for final finishing. This was a matter of great pride – a fully finished chronometer movement was an object of great beauty. The high level of finishing was not only for aesthetic reasons; it had been found that highly polished parts resisted rust and corrosion much better than unpolished components.

Richard (Dicky) Doke.

A typical chronometer took around a year to complete and whilst we ascribe instruments to particular makers, it is clear that most of the components were made by independent workers. A chronometer by one manufacturer might well have been made by the same collection of craftsmen as that of another maker. For instance, according to Frank Mercer, almost all chronometer wheels in the late nineteenth century were cut by Dicky Doke of Prescott. Richard Doke (1823–1906) had an unrivalled reputation for fine gear cutting and making beautiful escape wheels.

It was in the final finishing and adjustment that chronometer makers gained their reputation. If they could succeed in the Admiralty trials, this would surely stimulate business and many makers proudly engraved 'Maker to the Admiralty' on their dials. Unlike domestic clocks, which were made in a wide variety of styles and qualities, English chronometers from the mid-nineteenth century to World War II appear for the most part to be identical, although some makers adopted a particular form of detent or balance. Without the maker's signature and number, it would often be impossible to ascribe an instrument to a particular manufacturer. This is further confused by the common practice of makers supplying finished movements or complete chronometers to other makers, or to the many retailers of navigation equipment known as Nautical Opticians, who had the dials engraved with their own names and numbers. It is known that Thomas Mercer often supplied movements to Victor Kullberg and other makers and that Kullberg in his turn supplied to several retailers. If a maker had more orders than he could fulfil, he would simply buy in instruments from other makers. What is not in doubt is that English chronometers were almost without exception of the highest quality and if properly looked after would give a century or more of reliable service in the most extreme conditions.

SOME IMPORTANT MAKERS

The Frodsham Dynasty

One of the most prolific families in the chronometer trade descended from William Frodsham (1728–1807). He was a journeyman watchmaker and watch jeweller and was a friend of both Harrison and Earnshaw. The name of Frodsham appears on fine chronometers and clocks throughout the nineteenth and early twentieth centuries.

Parkinson & Frodsham

After the firms of Arnold and Earnshaw pioneered commercial chronometer making in the late eighteenth century, the next important manufacturer was Parkinson & Frodsham, established in 1801. It was William 'the younger' and William James, sons of William Frodsham senior, together with William Parkinson, who founded the firm. They specialised in making both marine and pocket chronometers at 4 Change Alley, Cornhill, London. They were both admitted to the Worshipful Company of Clockmakers in 1802 and W.J. Frodsham was elected Master in 1836 and 1837.

In 1818, two of the company's chronometers were taken on the Northern Expedition to find the North West Passage; this was the beginning of a long association of the firm with Arctic exploration. Four of their instruments went with John Ross on his 1819 expedition and all performed well despite exposure to temperatures of 40° below zero. In 1831, two of their instruments, a pocket chronometer No. 1081 and a marine chronometer No. 571, reached the North Magnetic Pole. The firm continued in business until 1947, although it had long ceased to manufacture its own instruments, using movements by Johannsen, Poole, Mercer and other makers.

Charles Frodsham

Charles Frodsham (1810–71), the third son of William James, joined the firm as an apprentice and showed his exceptional talent when, in 1830, he entered two marine chronometers for the Admiralty Premium Trials, for which he was awarded the second prize and £170, a significant sum at the time. In 1832, he left the business and started production on his own account, soon becoming recognised as one of the leading makers. The company continued from strength to strength and, in 1843, Charles purchased John Roger Arnold's firm and later acquired Benjamin Louis Vulliamy's business upon his death in 1854; this business came with the Royal Warrant.

The 1872 *Post Office Directory* listed Charles Frodsham as: '84 Strand, WC. Makers of marine and pocket chronometers, watches, clocks and horological instruments of every description by special appointment to Her Majesty the Queen and HRH the Prince of Wales'. In addition to his business, Charles was in demand as a lecturer and made several important contributions to horological literature. He also invented some ingenious devices, including one for testing the properties of oil. He served as Master of the Worshipful Company of Clockmakers in 1855 and 1862.

Other members of the family engaged in chronometer making included: Charles Mill Frodsham (1836–81), George Edward Frodsham (1831–1903), George William Frodsham (1831–1903), all of London; and Henry Frodsham (1802–58) of Liverpool.

Charles Frodsham.

E.J. Dent

Edward John Dent (1790–1853), a successful chronometer maker in the 1820s, went into partnership with John Roger Arnold in 1830 and the firm of Arnold & Dent was in business until 1840. During this time, the firm produced about 600 marine and pocket chronometers, supplying instruments to many polar and tropical expeditions, including No. 633, which went aboard the *Beagle* with Charles Darwin in 1831, and No.1800, owned by David Livingstone and used on his African expeditions. Later, H.M. Stanley wrote to Dent that 'The chronometers supplied by you, and which were taken across Africa in my last expedition, proved of a very great service and were in every way thoroughly satisfactory and reliable.' The Royal Warrant was granted in 1841 and the company also supplied the Emperor of Russia.

In 1840, Dent left the partnership and set up on his own at 82 Strand and various other addresses. The firm also made regulator clocks for the Royal Observatory, including the first clock to provide the 'pips' that the BBC started broadcasting in 1924. The firm branched into Turret clock manufacture and built the clock for the Crystal Palace in 1851 (now at King's Cross Station). However, their most famous project was undoubtedly the commission to build the great clock for Charles Barry's new Houses of Parliament in 1852. Unfortunately, Dent died in 1853 and the project was continued by his stepson Frederick; it was completed in 1854 at a cost of £2,500 and finally installed in the tower in 1859. (The official Parliament website has an excellent section on the clock, including a first-class animation.) The firm is still in existence and won the contract for the platform clock at the new St Pancras station in 2006.

E.J. Dent.

E.J. Dent's chronometer movement, 1845.

'Poole's Auxiliary' movement, 1860.

John Poole

Born in 1818 and established as a chronometer maker in 1840, John Poole became one of the great makers of the nineteenth century, not only under his own name but producing movements for many other firms. In 1854, his chronometer No. 1585 came top in the Greenwich trials with a maximum weekly error of just 4.5 seconds. In 1850, he introduced the auxiliary compensation device, which became the most successful of its kind and was soon taken up by other makers. It was known as 'Poole's Auxiliary'. Sadly, soon after winning the gold medal from the Paris Exhibition in 1867 he took his own life, leaving his brother James and his son Sidney to carry on the business.

Victor Kullberg

Born in 1824 in Visby Island, Gotland, Sweden, Kullberg moved to Copenhagen in 1843 to work for the eminent watch and chronometer maker, Louis Urban Jürgensen. In 1851, he came to London to visit the Great Exhibition and stayed on, working as an escapement maker for several London makers. He set up his own firm in Islington in 1856 and soon became recognised for the superb quality of his work, becoming one of the leading suppliers to the Admiralty. From the 1880s,

Victor Kullberg.

Thomas Mercer.

Kullberg's instruments came to dominate the Greenwich trials, coming top no fewer than 22 times between 1881 and 1914.

Victor Kullberg died in 1890, leaving the substantial sum of £13,555. The business was carried on by his nephew, Peter John Wennerström, and later by his partner, Sanfrid Lundquist, who continued working until 1947.

Thomas Mercer

Born in 1822 in St Helens, Lancashire, Thomas Mercer founded the most successful of all chronometer-making businesses. He was trained by his grandfather William Walker, whose business specialised in making watch wheels. Young Thomas' duties included feeding the chickens and cleaning out the family pigs and, once a week, he would walk to Liverpool with watch movements to sell for finishing. Later, Thomas moved to Liverpool to work for Thomas Russell, a large manufacturer of high-class watch movements and chronometers, acquiring the skills needed to finish complete movements.

Mercer moved to London in 1851 and took a job with the chronometer maker John Fletcher, where he learned the art of chronometer finishing and springing. By 1856, he was ready to set up on his own account with a small workshop in Clerkenwell and in 1858, he sold his first chronometer, No. 500, to Joseph Sewill in Liverpool. The business flourished, but in 1874, suffering from chest problems, Mercer decided to move away from the London smog to the healthier air of St Albans, Hertfordshire.

The new factory in St Albans included a steam plant to provide power for the machinery needed to manufacture larger parts such as chronometer bowls. However, many of the parts for the chronometers were still made by outworkers in Prescott and London, so Thomas made a weekly trip to the city, where he maintained a shop in City Road. Two of Thomas' sons, Tom (1876–1935) and Frank (1882–1970), came into the business. By the time of his death in 1900, Thomas Mercer had reached the pinnacle of the trade

The Mercer factory in St Albans.

and had produced some 5,000 chronometers. This left the two inexperienced brothers in charge of a flourishing and complex business; they clearly needed help, so Thomas Dodd, a skilled chronometer maker, was employed for the next three years to run the business, giving Tom and Frank Mercer the breathing space and support they needed to take over production. In 1903, the firm employed a staff of thirteen.

Frank was clearly the most enterprising of the two brothers and had travelled widely from the age of eighteen, when he was sent to Switzerland to study commerce. In 1905, he travelled to America and visited the famous watchmaking centre of Waltham, where he was greatly impressed by their progressive methods and extensive use of modern machine tools. This was a stark contrast to outmoded English manufacturing methods, where an obsession with tradition had resulted in an ailing watch industry steadily losing ground to more efficient and advanced American and Swiss manufacturing.

By 1907, Thomas Mercer Chronometers was producing over 300 chronometers per year

Frank Mercer.

and the brothers decided to build a modern factory to house new machinery, so that more of the parts could be made in-house. However, the firm still relied on many outworkers in Lancashire and Clerkenwell. In 1912, the new factory was built at Eywood Road, St Albans at a cost of £800; it was properly heated, although still lit by gas. The machine shop, powered by a 6½hp gas engine, was now separated from the finishing shop. Engineers and craftsmen were recruited, many from the north of England, and by 1913 the staff had increased to 30.

With war looming, the government was putting pressure on chronometer makers to increase production and Mercer, by far the largest manufacturer, was well placed to take the lead in reorganising the industry. At the outbreak of war, Frank, a keen territorial soldier and very much a man of action, volunteered for the Army. He served in the Herts Yeomanry and saw action in 1915 in Gallipoli, where he narrowly escaped with his life. In 1916, he was promoted from the ranks to Second Lieutenant and was stationed in Egypt. There, he received a telegram from the Admiralty requesting him to return to England to take charge of the chronometer industry.

By 1916, shipping losses had reached crisis levels and the nation's survival depended on replacing ships and their essential chronometers at record-breaking speed. It was agreed that production at the St Albans factory was to be increased to 500 per year and one of Frank's most important jobs was to persuade the other makers to cooperate and increase their production. This was no mean task, but, to Frank's credit, he persuaded and cajoled many rival makers, wedded to traditional manufacturing techniques, into accepting more modern production methods and cooperating with each other to pool resources. Mercer used its modern machinery to turn out parts for other makers and held large stocks of finished parts for distribution around the trade. The Admiralty was insistent that only chronometers of the highest standard would be accepted, capable of keeping time to within half a second per day in all conditions. It was a great credit to the industry's workers that they met the challenge and kept the nation's shipping supplied with the instruments vital to their safety and the war effort.

After the war, the demand for chronometers naturally took a steep downturn and many of the smaller makers went out of business. With the order book for new chronometers almost empty, Mercer needed to diversify or go under. Amongst its new products were surveying chronometers equipped with electrical contacts and dials reading sidereal and Solar Time, also several types of precision timing devices for scientific work. Electrical time systems were made for ships with a series of 'slave' clocks controlled by a master chronometer.

One interesting project was the restoration in collaboration with Rupert Gould of Harrison's H1 sea clock in the early 1920s; this involved making many replacement parts, as the clock was in a sad state of disrepair. Gould, who became a regular visitor to St Albans supervising the work on the Harrison instruments, later wrote: '. . . no one can say that I didn't take pains with the reconstruction of No. 1. But while I could plan this portion of the work, I gravely doubt whether I could have possibly executed it. Mercers did this for me magnificently and refused to take a penny.'

With World War II's outbreak, chronometer production was once more of strategic importance and Mercer expanded considerably, equipping the factory with the latest machine tools. Such was the importance of the work that a Mosquito aircraft made trips to Sweden to obtain supplies of special steel for mainsprings and pinions; other small parts came from Switzerland in diplomatic bags. Due to a shortage of jewels, some were secretly imported from France by way of Spain. The factory luckily escaped bomb damage, producing more than 2,000 finished chronometers and precision parts for other applications throughout the war.

After the war, the firm was left as the only surviving British chronometer maker and continued producing instruments to the high standards demanded by the Admiralty and merchant fleets, together with various scientific instruments and electric clock systems. The 1960s saw the firm at its zenith, employing over 500 workers and making 300 to 400 traditional chronometers per year and a range of scientific instruments. However, despite an attempt to enter the electronic age, producing quartz crystal chronometers under licence from Patek Phillipe, by the 1980s it was clear that economic chronometer manufacture was no longer possible at St Albans and, in 1982, production ceased. Two years later, the metrology division was taken over by the American machine tool company, Brown and Sharpe, who moved production of dial gauges to the USA and sold off the factory site for housing, ending 126 years of fine craftsmanship during which time the firm had produced some 30,000 chronometers.

The last marine chronometers, produced in the 1980s, were essentially the same as the instruments developed in the 1780s. It is a great tribute to the early makers that no significant improvements were made in over 200 years until the coming of modern electronics. Indeed, most large ships still carry several traditional chronometers, wound every day, to provide a back-up to externally vulnerable satellite navigation systems. It could be argued that the invention of the marine chronometer was the most important single technical achievement of the eighteenth century, transforming navigation and saving countless lives. Without accurate navigation, world trade, essential to modern civilisation, would not have developed in the way it did.

Mercer chronometer, 1955.

Chapter 8
Provincial Clocks

Provincial makers, mainly producing lantern clocks and simple 30-hour longcase clocks, had appeared in most counties by the early 1700s. Some were self-taught craftsmen from other trades, mostly blacksmiths; others were London makers moving their businesses to regional centres, producing what were essentially London clocks.

EARLY MAKERS

John Williamson was a respected London maker who moved to Leeds in 1683. The marquetry longcase clock shown here has all the hallmarks of a fine London clock of the 1690s. Another London maker who moved to York in 1679 was Thomas Cruttenden. These makers generally produced high-quality eight-day longcase clocks aimed at the wealthy residents of major provincial cities. Such makers would be few, as the market for such expensive clocks would necessarily be small.

Marquetry longcase clock by John Williamson, Leeds.

Locally schooled clockmakers were mainly from the solid regional metalworking traditions such as the blacksmiths or 'whitesmiths' (craftsmen who specialised in smaller iron items polished white). The epitaph of a self-taught Gloucestershire clockmaker who became mayor of Berkeley and died in 1665 reads:

> Here lyeth Thomas Pierce whom no man taught,
> Yet he iron, brass, and silver wrought;
> He jacks, and clocks and watches (with art) made
> and mended too, when others' work did fade
> …

Since the earliest period of clockmaking, the link with the blacksmith trade had been strong and the Worshipful Company of Blacksmiths regulated the early London clockmakers. Some ambitious provincial blacksmiths also tried their hand at clockmaking. A recently discovered lantern clock is signed: 'John Baxter fecit 1670 … of Conderton, blacksmith' and engraved with the rhyme 'John Baxter did me make And I will goe well for his sak'.

Eight-day longcase clock by Thomas Cruttenden, York, c. 1685.

These early indigenous craftsmen mainly produced 30-hour lantern and wall-mounted clocks; longcase clocks began appearing in the 1690s. Recent research is throwing light on makers such as Walter Archer of Stow-on-the-Wold, Gloucestershire. He came from a family of blacksmiths and gunmakers in nearby Moreton-in-Marsh and seems to have moved to the larger town in the 1690s to set up business as a clockmaker. Around 60 clocks by Archer have been identified. He appears to have started with lantern clocks, later branching out into longcase styles. Archer continued to use the earlier 'bird cage' construction method for his movements, which London makers were abandoning in favour of the more advanced two-plate design.

The photograph shows one of Archer's early longcase movements. Note that he uses a 'tic-tac' escapement, a form of anchor escapement used by Joseph Knibb, who had worked in Oxford, where Archer may have seen an example. Like many other rural clockmakers, Archer did his own engraving to keep costs down and it is possible to identify the individual style of his work.

Walter Archer's movement, c. 1695.

Walter Archer's dial, c. 1700.

Archer's longcase, early eighteenth century.

The Archer 30-hour dial features a boldly engraved chapter ring and corner spandrels of the same type as used by London makers around 1700; these would have been purchased from London brass founders.

Archer's eight-day longcase clock is more sophisticated, with a seconds dial and calendar work. The ringed winding holes are similar to London work of the period. As with most provincial work, the case is of plain oak.

QUAKER CLOCKMAKERS

Many famous London clockmakers, such as Thomas Tompion, Daniel Quare and George Graham, were Quakers. The Religious Society of Friends grew rapidly during the mid-seventeenth century and attracted many supporters from the merchant and artisan classes. The Society's founder was George Fox. He established a close and efficient organisation during his extensive travels preaching around the country and overseas. The Quakers not only survived the turmoil of the time, but thrived.

As Quakers were denied access to universities and thus the professions, many naturally turned to business and technology. The Quaker philosophy, which emphasised education, apprenticeship, travel and trade, played a significant role in the success of Quaker clockmakers. They were great travellers and the habit of attending regular meetings nationwide enabled them to build up a network of trustworthy business contacts. These clockmakers soon gained a reputation for producing consistently good products at a fair and fixed price. For a Quaker, bargaining was regarded as an admission that the price demanded was untrue and thus was dishonest.

Apprenticeship was an important aspect of Quaker education; in addition to learning their trade, youngsters attended meetings and were brought up in the Quaker way of life. These apprenticeships were sometimes paid from Quaker funds, or arranged between Friends groups. The accession of William and Mary in 1688 made life easier for the Quaker community, as it resulted in the 1689 Act of Toleration, which granted full liberty of conscience to all religious dissenters. Having experienced the dangers of religious intolerance in continental Europe, William wisely realised that this was necessary for stable government and a thriving economy.

Identifying provincial Quaker clocks can be difficult, as many were unsigned – Quaker makers often considered that signing their work was a mark of vanity, although some were modestly signed with initials only. An important family of Quaker clockmakers has been identified in North Oxfordshire. Thomas Gilkes set up a business in the village of Sibford Gower around 1700 and his three sons followed him into the trade, moving to other towns in the area. Shown here is a 30-hour longcase clock by John Gilkes, who moved to Shipston-on-Stour.

George Fox.

Longcase clock by John Gilkes, Shipston-on-Stour.

Abel Cottey, a Devon clockmaker, was born in Tiverton in 1655 and is known to have been working in Crediton in the 1680s. He is notable for being the New World's first clockmaker, sailing with William Penn in 1682 and settling in Philadelphia. Cottey was the first of the so-called 'Six Quaker Clockmakers' working in New England during the eighteenth century.

Another Quaker clockmaker who emigrated to Philadelphia was Peter Stretch (1670–1746). He came from a family of clockmakers in Leek, Staffordshire, and arrived in the New World with his family in 1703. The two tall-case clocks illustrated here show how his style evolved. The first is a simple single-handed 30-hour clock from *c.* 1703, while the second clock from *c.* 1715 is a much more sophisticated eight-day clock in the latest London style; indeed, the finials appear to have been cast in England.

English lantern clock by Abel Cottey, c. *1695.*

Eight-day tall case clock made by Abel Cottey in Philadelphia, c. *1705.*

CLOCK MANUFACTURING IN THE PROVINCES

We have seen in Chapter 4 evidence that clockmaking machinery was being manufactured in Lancashire in the seventeenth century, including tools for wheel cutting, fusee making and drawing pinion wire. Literacy standards amongst watch and toolmakers were high in Lancashire. In the mid-eighteenth century, parish clerks' records show that over 94 per cent were able to sign their names, compared to 59 per cent in the textile industry and just 13 per cent of miners. The high status of horological craftsmen was also reflected in consistently higher apprenticeship fees than other trades.

When we look at the Walter Archer movement illustrated earlier, it is clear that the wheel teeth were cut with the aid of a wheel-cutting engine such as the ones described in Chapter 4. Did he have his own wheel cutter, or did he purchase ready-made wheels and pinions? We know that firms in Prescott such as Thos. Hampson of New Street were supplying the London trade with pinions at prices ranging from seven to twelve shillings per dozen.

Liverpool had become a centre of watchmaking very soon after London and the nearby town of Prescott had long been renowned for the quality of the files made there. By the early eighteenth century records exist of craftsmen in that part of Lancashire supplying watch parts and complete movements to prominent London makers. In a recently discovered notebook written by Richard Wright of Cronton (a village near Prescott) covering work done from 1713 to 1736, he records that he supplied 31 complete watch movements to prominent London makers. He clearly was not the only craftsman in the area supplying parts and services such as finishing for other makers.

The division of labour was well advanced in the industry by the early eighteenth century and many sources describe the large number of sub-tasks involved in the production of parts. Alongside the flourishing watch and clock trade, the area became famous for producing the high-quality tools and machinery that the industry demanded.

Clockmaking enterprises in country districts varied greatly from small blacksmith/clockmakers, making many of the parts themselves but buying in items such as wheels and pinions, to much larger-scale operations with considerable resources of machinery and foundry equipment – no doubt they would supply the smaller country makers. Many of these were working on a part-time basis; occupations such as farming were seasonal and the slack winter months were an opportunity to supplement the family income. Spinning and

Two Philadelphia Quaker clocks by Peter Stretch.

weaving were popular, but some farmers with a mechanical bent might take up clockmaking, buying in parts and raw materials such as brass plates for basic 30-hour clocks using locally made cases. Lancashire workshops from the late seventeenth century would be capable of supplying any parts required by London or provincial makers. Improved communications enabled nationwide trading networks to grow rapidly. For example, the regular coach service from Warrington to London took about eight days in the eighteenth century.

By the end of the eighteenth century, the fast-growing English clock trade was broadly divided between London makers who provided higher quality timepieces and provincial craftsmen catering for their local customers with more modest resources. However, as we have seen, some fine clocks were made outside London.

A London Coaching Inn *by William Hogarth, 1747.*

Chapter 9
Changing Styles

By the mid-eighteenth century, all of the main technological developments in clockmaking were well-established and clock mechanisms changed little until the introduction of electricity to clock making from the late nineteenth century. For over 200 years, clockmaking became a question of style rather than improvements in the mechanism. The main development during this period was lowering the cost of clock production, making domestic clocks increasingly available to the fast-growing middle classes rather than status symbols for the wealthy.

LONGCASE CLOCKS

Longcase clocks, introduced in the 1670s, began with the classical designs of makers such as Fromanteel and East. These clocks were a little over 6ft tall, mostly made with fruitwood or ebonised cases. The trend for larger houses with high ceilings required proportionately larger clocks, so that 7ft or even 8ft cases became common. Elaborate inlay work and Chinese lacquer replaced the earlier, more conservative seventeenth-century styles. Mahogany, imported from the West Indies, became available from the mid-eighteenth century and rapidly gained in popularity. By the nineteenth century, the elegant proportions and restrained decoration of earlier cases had given way to the heavier, more elaborate designs characteristic of the furniture of the Victorian era.

Painted Dials

The type of dial developed during the seventeenth century was made of several elements. One element was a brass back plate, which was finished by 'matting', a form of decoration applied by a special punch. The chapter ring had the numerals engraved and filled with black wax. Cast corner spandrels completed the design. This is often known as a composite dial. The chapter ring needed silvering for clarity and the silver coating was lacquered to prevent tarnishing – this would need restoring every twenty years or so.

From the middle of the eighteenth century, simpler single-sheet dials began to appear. They were made from a single sheet of engraved brass, entirely silvered, which gave a steely white appearance. The fashion for single-plate dials was during the 1770–1800 period and we see many examples from London and the provinces. Whilst they were very elegant and clear, they still needed regular resilvering and good engraving was expensive.

At the same time, experiments were made with enamelled clock dials. This method involved melting white enamel on to a copper base; the numerals were then painted on and fired permanently on to the surface. However, these dials were very delicate and costly to produce, so very few have survived.

In his book, *Painted Dial Clocks*, Brian Loomes reproduces an advertisement by Osborne & Wilson in the *Birmingham Gazette* of September 1772, offering for sale 'White Clock Dials in imitation of Enamel, in a manner entirely new.'

Longcase clock designs.

1750 1770 1780

1790 1800 1810

Seventeenth-century brass composite dial.

Single-plate dial type.

WHITE CLOCK DIALS.

OSBORNE and WILSON, Manufacturers of White Clock Dials in Imitation of Enamel, in a Manner entirely new, have opened a Warehouse at No. 3, in Colmore-Row, Birmingham, where they have an Assortment of the above-mentioned Goods. Those who favour them with their Orders may depend upon their being executed with the utmost Punctuality and Expedition.

N. B. The Dial Feet will be rivetted in the Dials, and such Methods used as will enable the Clock-Makers to fix them to the Movements.

Advertisement for painted dials.

Enamel dial, c. 1770.

Japanning

This technique for decorating all types of objects, including furniture, was copied from the ancient craft of lacquering developed in Japan and China. The European technique uses varnishes with a resin base, similar to shellac, applied in heat-dried layers, which are then polished to give a smooth, glossy finish. A large industry emerged in the Midlands during the eighteenth century to manufacture Japanned ware, such as boxes and trays. Trade directories for 1818 list twenty firms of 'japanners' in Wolverhampton and fifteen in Bilston. According to Samuel Timmins' book, *Birmingham and the Midland Hardware District*, published in 1866, there were 2,000 people employed in the japanning and tin-plate industries in Wolverhampton and Bilston at the time. As far as we know, the firm of Osborne & Wilson in nearby Birmingham was the first to apply the technique to the production of clock dials.

The last part of the Osborne & Wilson advertisement indicates that the dials were provided with an easy method to fix them to a clock movement. In fact, this development was almost as important as the new method of painting the dials. It ensured such success for these new colourful dials that they soon became the most popular form, particularly for provincial longcase clocks.

Early painted dial by Osborne & Wilson, Birmingham.

The diagram shows how the dials were supplied ready to attach to the clock movement. The dial had three or four pillars riveted to the plate before painting; a separate cast-iron fixing plate was supplied to fit the dial pillars. The dial plate generally had three substantial brass pillars that fitted into the movement's front plate, giving clearance for the striking work. It appears that the usual procedure was for a clockmaker to keep several complete dials in stock and his finished movements would be drilled ready to fit the dials. The customer would choose a dial and the clockmaker would then assemble and case-up the components – sale made! A flourishing trade in this new form of dial soon became established, mostly in Birmingham. Brian Loomes has identified over 130 dial makers in Birmingham alone, working from the 1770s to the 1890s. There were also over twenty makers in Edinburgh and Glasgow.

From the 1790s, the majority of provincial longcase clocks had painted dials – the bright new designs appealed to customers in contrast to the comparatively dull engraved brass dials. Provincial clockmakers, who were essentially engineers trained to construct the working parts of clocks, had found dials a problem. They had the choice of paying for expensive professional engraving or learning to engrave for themselves, with varying results. Clockmakers would have been delighted to have the option of a ready supply of standardised dials and wholesalers soon appeared, giving customers a wide choice of designs. Samuel Deacon, a clockmaker working in Leicestershire, has left notebooks that provide a rare insight into this business. He records a visit to Birmingham in 1785, presumably to find suppliers for his business. A later entry details an order for dials:

> Ordered the following dials:
> 12 – 12inch square, varied, neat corners, open mouth, written figgers, 30hours Deacon Barton
> 4 – 13inch arched 30hour, open mouth
> 3 – 13inch arched 30hour, two with figgers in arch, one with an urn
> 1 – 13inch with moon
> Let some of the 12inch have a bird above the centre.

The photograph shows one of Samuel Deacon's 30-hour longcase clocks with an arched dial; the 'open mouth' in the list refers to the calendar aperture. We can see that this is a 30-hour clock by the absence of a seconds dial and winding holes – 30-hour clocks are wound by pulling the chain or rope holding the single weight, which powered both the strike and going trains.

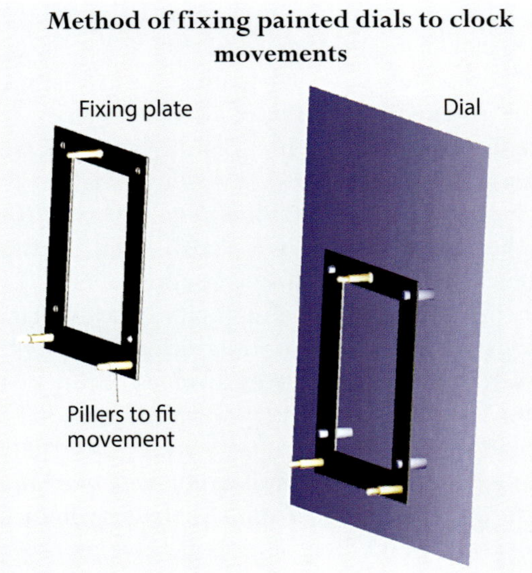

Samuel Deacon's dial and movement.

This type of clock was economical and reliable and was produced in large quantities by provincial makers. Eight-day clocks had two weights wound through the dial and normally had a seconds hand. Interestingly, the early painted dials were more expensive than the traditional brass dials, reinforcing the impact these dials had on customers, who were willing to pay extra for the new fashion. Later, painted dials came down in price, though this is reflected in the quality.

The freedom to add painted decoration to longcase dials led to a profusion of images. Earlier square dials with floral designs or exotic birds gave way to break-arch dials with added space for rolling moons or automata, such as rocking ships using a simple link to the pendulum. Idealised rural scenes and country cottages were very popular and as they were hand-painted, no two are exactly alike. Whilst the artistic quality is not high, they often have great charm. The fashion for painted dials lasted well past the mid-nineteenth century before taste reverted to eighteenth-century style composite dials and reproductions of classical case types.

A distinctive, more restrained style of Scottish clock evolved from the late eighteenth century, often featuring round dials with very little decoration, unlike the colourful painted dials popular across the border.

A selection of early nineteenth-century painted dials.

In England, the classic proportions of the seventeenth and eighteenth centuries gave way to a taste for wider cases and heavy carving; sometimes, some older cases were elaborately re-carved to fit the new taste. This resulted in some very charmless, badly proportioned clocks, which soon went out of fashion in favour of a return to seventeenth- and eighteenth-century styles.

The newly wealthy, building large houses, created a demand for extravagant clocks designed to impress. Huge three-train clocks upwards of 8ft high and chiming on tubular bells were made by London firms such as F.W. Elliott, often with cases made by well-known furniture makers such as Maple & Co.

By the twentieth century, domestic English longcase clock production was largely taken over by modestly priced mass-produced clocks. Ceilings were generally too low to accommodate earlier clocks, although it is not uncommon to find eighteenth- and nineteenth-century country clocks that have been cut down to fit in modern houses. So-called 'grandmother' clocks, which stood little over 5ft, became very popular, often with three-train spring-driven Westminster chiming movements, using the same movements as the ubiquitous mantle clocks popular as wedding presents. At the upper price range of the market, F.W. Elliott became the dominant maker and survived until the 1970s. Various makers, including Smiths Clocks, emerged in the 1920s and 1930s, continuing production into the 1960s when furniture makers imported cheaper German-made movements to fulfil the remaining demand for 'grandfather' clocks.

Scottish longcase styles.

A selection of nineteenth-century longcase clocks.

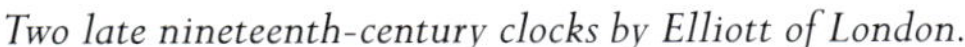

Two late nineteenth-century clocks by Elliott of London.

Some twentieth-century longcase styles.

TABLE OR BRACKET CLOCKS

At around the same time as the first longcase clocks were introduced in the mid-seventeenth century, spring-driven clocks were developed for standing on a table or a wall bracket. These clocks retained the traditional verge escapement with a short pendulum and generally struck the hour on a bell. They had a clear advantage over longcase clocks, as they could be easily moved between rooms without specialised setting up. The earliest examples by makers such as Edward East and Joseph Knibb were, like their longcase clocks, generally ebonised in plain architectural form cases. Later in the century, more elaborate cases with gilt brass decoration appeared, often with a repeating work to strike the previous hour by pulling a cord – suggesting that they were often placed near the bedside when lighting a candle was a laborious process.

In the early eighteenth century, square dials gave way to break-arch dials with an extended top, which might include a dummy pendulum or strike/silent feature; a calendar as well as a repeating work was also generally included. Lacquered cases became popular around 1710–1730, giving way to mahogany by the mid-century.

The late eighteenth century and Regency period is characterised by round, painted dials and a change in case shape, abandoning the handle at the top. The left-hand clock shown in the illustration is from the late eighteenth century and known as a balloon clock, a style that became increasingly popular in the nineteenth century. Also, we see the influence of the Gothic revival with the lancet-shaped cases from the 1820s. By now, the makers of these clocks had abandoned the old verge escapement and bob pendulum in favour of the anchor escapements and longer pendulums on suspension springs, improving accuracy. These clocks, particularly from London makers, are always of high quality with double fusees. Increasingly, gut fusee lines were replaced with chains.

Later in the nineteenth century, the cases of table clocks reflected the fashion for heavy carving and gothic-influenced styles, as we have seen in longcase clocks. However, in the

Seventeenth-century table clocks.

Early eighteenth-century styles.

Regency-style table clocks.

mid-century, some London makers produced elegant drum-shaped clocks that were always of the highest quality.

The twentieth century marked the end of the traditional English fusee table clock. The high cost of producing movements of the quality of typical nineteenth-century clocks could not be maintained against the cheaper French clocks and budget-priced, mass-produced American and European clocks that took the lion's share of the market. A few English makers, such as Elliott and Garrard, found a niche in the upper end of the market of mass-produced clocks. Smiths, in the post-war years, fulfilled the demand for budget-priced chiming and striking clocks, which took pride of place on many working-class mantlepieces. The examples shown here start with an Edwardian balloon clock strongly influenced by the fashionable art nouveau style and sold by stores such as Liberty's in London. Later mantle clocks from the 1920s to the 1950s, typical of Garrard and Elliott, are illustrated with the ubiquitous Westminster chimes.

TAVERN CLOCKS

From the mid-eighteenth century, a distinctive clock style was developed as part of furnishing taverns and inns around the country. At a time when few people had watches and the only source of time for most was the local church clock, the convenience of a good clock in the local hostelry would clearly be an encouragement for trade. Always looking for ways to increase revenue, William Pitt's government in 1797 decided to tax watches and clocks, which resulted in a charge of five shillings per year on all such clocks. This has resulted in the misnaming of tavern clocks as 'Act of Parliament Clocks'. In fact, the Act proved most unpopular and threatened the watch and clock trade to such an extent that it was repealed within a year and replaced by Pitt's new income tax to raise funds to pay for the wars with France.

Tavern clocks were essentially wall-mounted longcase clocks, with a seconds pendulum, and were consequently around 6ft in length. Earlier styles illustrated on the left were typically decorated in the popular chinoiserie style; later clocks, like the 1840s example on the right, had plainer mahogany cases.

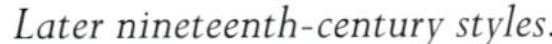
Later nineteenth-century styles.

Twentieth-century styles.

Tavern clocks.

SKELETON CLOCKS

The English skeleton clock style originated in France in the late eighteenth century, when great makers such as Breguet produced magnificent clocks for the aristocracy. These clocks were designed to impress, not only with the quality and richness of the case, but also to display movement. The illustration (left) shows one of the famous Breguet *Sympathique* clocks. The fortunate owner placed his watch in the cradle at the top and the clock automatically wound and set the watch to time. Only Breguet produced such extravagant timepieces, built to demonstrate its owner's status and fabulous wealth. On a more modest scale, he commissioned a series of 'Three Wheel' clocks (right) from other French makers, influencing English makers in the early nineteenth century. These clocks were generally displayed either under a glass dome or in a case with glass sides and top.

The first English skeleton clocks were simply timepieces with a single fusee and anchor escapement, generally with a pendulum of approximately 9.87in beating half seconds. This style of simple skeleton timepiece remained popular throughout the nineteenth century and shown here is a nice example by Dyson of Leeds from around 1870. Note the high standard of finish, with the nicely blued screws and chain-operated fusee typical of these clocks, which were designed for display.

An example of a skeleton striking clock by Savory of Cornhill, *c.* 1850, is shown here. It is still of comparatively simple design, with a double fusee movement striking the hours on a bell and a simple silvered dial with Roman numerals. However, by the mid-nineteenth century, more elaborate styles of skeleton clocks became popular and some examples are represented here. They generally struck the hours on a bell and showed a distinct gothic influence. Some were built in the style of famous buildings, such as St James's Palace and Westminster Abbey.

Perhaps the ultimate development of the skeleton clock is the magnificent three-train chiming clock by John Moore of London. Given the date of the clock, it was probably built to be displayed at the Great Exhibition of 1851, which celebrated British industry and manufacturing. The fashion for skeleton clocks lasted until the end of the nineteenth century. Later examples often featured unusual escapements such as duplex and lever types, which dispensed with the pendulum; even a few were made with chronometer escapements, making such clocks true table regulators capable of high accuracy.

Early nineteenth-century 'Great Wheel' skeleton timepiece by Whitehurst & Son, Derby.

French skeleton clocks.

Skeleton timepiece by Dyson of Leeds, c. 1870.

Skeleton striking clock by Savory of Cornhill, London, c. 1850.

Architectural styles of skeleton clocks.

Chiming skeleton clock by John Moore of London, 1851.

Breguet carriage clocks.

ENGLISH CARRIAGE CLOCKS

The term 'carriage clock' refers to small portable clocks with a fitted case that enables the clock to be easily packed and transported; their origin was in the early spring-driven clocks that were developed in the fifteenth century. In the late eighteenth century, Breguet took up the idea, ever searching for new luxury timepieces to amaze his aristocratic clients.

Other French makers, such as Berthoud, took up the idea and began producing clocks of a similar design – although none matched the superlative quality of Breguet's masterpieces. Over the next century, the French carriage clock became the most popular form of small clock, selling particularly well in Britain and is still produced today. The success of this type of clock is not surprising as it can be produced in a variety of qualities, from modestly priced simple timepieces to high-grade luxury models. They made a perfect souvenir and vast quantities were sold to British tourists in Paris. Every clock shop in Britain sold a selection of French carriage clocks, often with the name of the retailer on the dial. The clocks look good in any surroundings and it is not surprising that they are still sold in large numbers.

Amongst the vast numbers of carriage clocks produced in the nineteenth century,

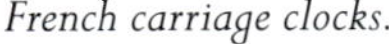

French carriage clocks.

a handful of English makers, mostly chronometer specialists, marketed a small number of these clocks designed for the luxury end of the market, where only the highest quality and standard of accuracy would do. These clocks were larger and more expensive than even the best French clocks and were generally made to special order, exhibiting the finest craftsmanship and latest technological innovations. The size of these clocks was not a consideration at a time when the travelling arrangements of the wealthy involved a vast amount of heavy luggage and a retinue of servants.

The clocks fall into two main types, the earliest from the 1820s with lever escapements and those with chronometer escapements, which came a little later. The lever escapement is more robust than the detent escapement used in marine chronometers and some pocket watches; this would have made it more suitable actually for travelling. There is a view that these chronometer clocks were mostly intended for domestic use, although they were always provided with travelling cases. One can imagine a wealthy gentleman ordering a fine chronometer clock to grace his desk or library table.

The 'hump-backed' carriage clock by J.F. Cole shows one of the earliest and finest of all these clocks. Clearly inspired by Breguet's *pendules de voyage*, it is at least equal to them in quality. Indeed, Cole has been called the 'English Breguet'. This clock, one of a series, has many additional features, including a perpetual calendar that shows the times of sunrise and sunset. Another less extravagant clock by Cole, retailed by Garrard, is also shown.

Silver 'hump-backed 'carriage clock by J.F. Cole, 1823.

Carriage clock by J.F. Cole, c. *1840.*

Carriage clock by James McCabe, mid-nineteenth century.

James McCabe was another notable carriage-clock maker; the example shown was made in the 1850s. This strikes the hours and quarters and has a fine lever escapement with temperature-compensated balance. Like all the best English work, it has chain-driven fusees. The brass-bound box has a sliding panel on the front, which could be removed to display the time while keeping the clock protected; this became a common feature in such cases.

E.J. Dent was one of the leading makers of marine chronometers, adapting their chronometer technology to produce highly accurate carriage clocks. These were mostly simple timepieces, as the striking work would have added friction to the gear train, affecting accuracy. The example shown is from around 1850 and has a spring detent, Earnshaw type escapement with Dent's patent 'staple' compensated balance.

Chronometer carriage clocks continued to be produced in small numbers well into the twentieth century. Thomas Mercer, the last remaining English chronometer maker, produced some fine examples into the 1970s. The company had hoped to find a market for their products once electronic instruments, and eventually satellite navigation, replaced traditional marine chronometers. Sadly, the cost of these chronometer clocks was prohibitive and the firm closed down in 1982.

Chronometer carriage clock by E.J. Dent, c.1850.

Strut clock by Thomas Cole, 1850s.

Chronometer carriage clock by Thomas Mercer, St Albans, 1970s.

Oval strut clock by Thomas Cole, 1850s.

Strut Clocks

A more compact form of travelling clock, known as the strut clock, was developed in the mid-nineteenth century. It was a flat clock that could be easily removed from its leather case and stood up on a folding bracket, with the winding key built into the back. The strut clock shown here is from the 1850s and is by Thomas Cole, the brother of J.F. Cole, who appears to have invented this design. Cole designed and produced these clocks in many different styles; the example oval strut clock was probably intended to appeal to feminine taste. The inset shows the fine lever escapement; a door in the back of these clocks could be opened for regulating.

The convenience of this type of clock led to them being made in a great variety of styles well into the twentieth century. The example shown is from the early twentieth century featuring a shagreen case, a leather made from shark or stingray. Simple travelling clocks of this kind had large Swiss pocket-watch movements, often eight-day, generally in leather travelling cases and were often known as 'Goliaths'.

Early twentieth-century strut clock.

Chapter 10
The Great Westminster Clock

Without a doubt the most famous clock in the world, commonly known as 'Big Ben', has become an iconic symbol, not only for London but for Parliament and Britain. The clock tower was conceived as part of the new Palace of Westminster, which replaced the old Houses of Parliament destroyed by fire in 1834.

THE COMMISSION

In November 1835, a select committee of the Commons was formed to consider rebuilding the Palace after the fire and an open competition to design a new building was announced. In order to harmonise with the ancient Westminster Hall, which had survived the fire, and nearby Westminster Abbey, the building should be in either Gothic or Elizabethan style. The committee examined over 90 entries before awarding the contract to Charles Barry, regarded by many as the leading architect of the day. The original plan did not include the provision of a clock; however, a revised plan, in collaboration with Barry's assistant Augustus Welby Pugin, was drawn up to include the addition of a clock in the northern tower. The committee approved the scheme in April 1836 to provide a Great Clock with four faces, each 30ft in diameter, an hour bell weighing 14 tons and eight quarter bells.

The designs for the tower by Barry and Pugin evolved over the next few years before the final version was exhibited at the Royal Academy in 1844. Despite some opposition as to the cost and desirability of having a clock at all 'when almost every mechanic carries a watch in his pocket', the Ministry of Works stuck to its original specification to produce 'a noble clock, indeed a king of clocks, the biggest the world has ever seen, within sight and sound of the throbbing heart of London'. Unfortunately, the plans from the 1844 exhibition have not survived – shown here are two sketches from the late 1830s and a later drawing that indicates the design's development.

The clock tower of the Palace of Westminster.

Barry initially approached Benjamin Louis Vulliamy, Master of the Worshipful Company of Clockmakers, to prepare a design for the Great Clock. However, under pressure from George Airy, the Astronomer Royal, the Ministry of Works put the tender out for

Charles Barry (left) and Augustus Pugin.

competition, appointing Airy as referee for the design. Airy took up the task with great enthusiasm and eventually made a list of fifteen provisions, including an electromagnetic connection to the Royal Observatory to check the clock's timekeeping twice a day and to provide electrical impulses to regulate other clocks in the Palace.

This was not a problem; however, the stipulation that 'the striking machinery is to be so arranged that the first blow for each hour shall be accurate to a second of time' caused great consternation in the horological world. This kind of accuracy was possible only in delicate observatory clocks and marine chronometers. To match this standard in a huge turret clock with four dials and hands open to the weather was considered by most clockmakers to be impossible. In the event, just two clockmakers accepted the specification: E.J. Dent, a successful chronometer maker who had recently built a fine clock for the Royal Exchange; and a respected Derby clockmaker, John Whitchurch.

DENISON AND DENT

At this stage, a third character enters the scene, Edmund Beckett Denison QC (later succeeding his father as Baron Grimthorpe), an eminent and influential lawyer with a passion for horology who had published several works on the subject. He was later elected President of the British Horological Institute – which he accepted on condition that he would not be required to attend its dinners. Unlike the amiable Airy, Denison was by all accounts an aggressive and unpleasant character, but his talents ensured that he was appointed co-referee, an honorary position without payment. Denison favoured Dent's design, but proposed several improvements, which amounted to redesigning the original plans.

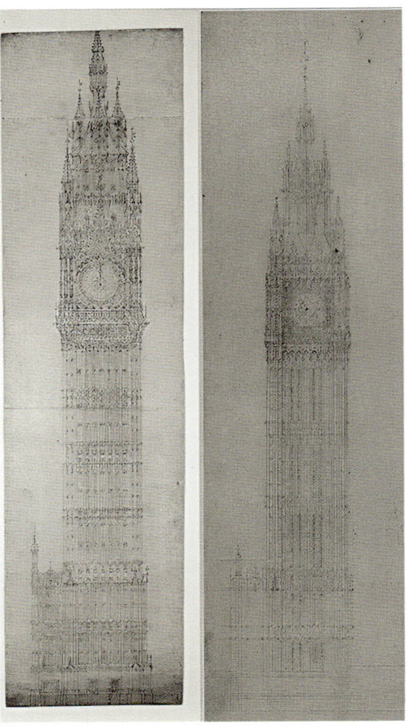

The evolution of the clock tower design.

'Edmund Beckett Denison', Vanity Fair, *1889.*

Double three-legged gravity escapement

Denison's most important improvement to Dent's design was for a revolutionary new escapement, without which the level of accuracy demanded would never have been achieved. This escapement uses two arms pivoted at the point of suspension of the pendulum. At each vibration the pendulum lifts and releases a gravity arm, which allows the arm to push the pendulum, giving it an impulse – as one arm drops, the escapement raises the opposite arm. Whilst other escapements rely on the power of the train for the strength of the impulse, this has the great advantage of using the force of gravity for the impulse.

Following are the details of the action as shown in the diagram on the following page:

A. Shows the pendulum moving to the right, having just had its impulse from gravity arm A.
B. Shows the front escape wheel held against locking block B. The gravity arm B has been raised by one of the three lifting studs and is locked in position.
C. Here, the front escape-wheel tooth has been released from locking block B and has rotated 60 degrees clockwise, raising gravity arm A, which locks on the rear escape wheel. The pendulum is being pushed to the left and will make contact with gravity arm A, releasing it for the next impulse.
D. Shows the side view.

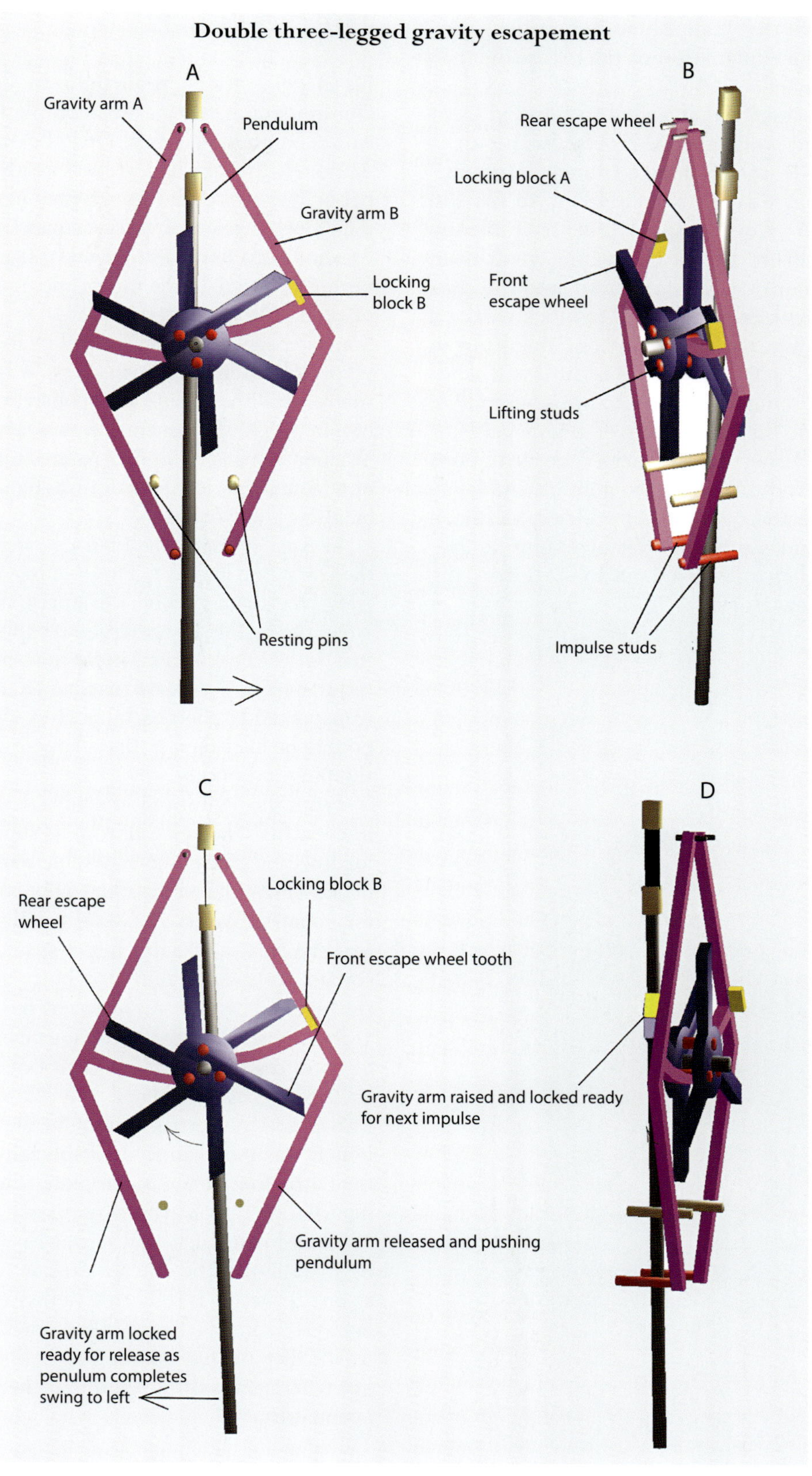
Double three-legged gravity escapement
A
Gravity arm A
Pendulum
Gravity arm B
Locking
block B
Resting pins
B
Rear escape wheel
Locking block A
Front
escape wheel
Lifting studs
Impulse studs
C
Rear escape
wheel
Locking block B
Front escape wheel tooth
Gravity arm raised and locked ready
for next impulse
Gravity arm released and pushing
pendulum
Gravity arm locked
ready for release as
penulum completes
swing to left
D

Simulations that can be found online provide further explanation of the escapement in action.

The contract was awarded to Edward Dent in 1852 and work on the movement began at the firm's Royal Exchange branch. Unfortunately, Dent died in March 1853, so his son Frederick took over responsibility for finishing the mechanism. In the meantime, Dent's old rival, Vulliamy, whose failure to land the contract still rankled, attempted to block work on the clock. He took legal action, resulting in Dent's contract being declared null and void. This left Frederick with an almost complete mechanism, but no means of being paid for the work. However, he carried on with construction and finished the job in 1854, by which time the contractual position had been resolved and many months of extensive factory trials began, carried out by staff from the Royal Observatory.

E.J. Dent.

THE GREAT BELL

In 1855, Airy reported to the Chief Commissioner that he was completely satisfied and recommended that Dent be paid his fee. Although the mechanism was ready, the clock tower was still under construction. After more than twelve years of work, it was less than half finished and Dent was obliged to store the clock without charge. In the meantime, the Great Bell needed to be manufactured; at 14 tons, no bell of this size had ever been cast in England. Denison, who had studied campanology, was appointed referee for the design and construction of the bell in 1854. The contract was awarded to John Warner & Sons, who had recently opened two new foundries in Stockton-on-Tees capable of handling the work.

In August 1856, the furnaces were fired and the Great Bell was cast. The opening of the mould was always going to be a dramatic moment and when the bell finally emerged complete, one can imagine the celebrations in the foundry. The bell, it transpired, weighed a massive 16 tons and was transported to the nearby port of West Hartlepool to be loaded on to the schooner *The Wave* for shipping to London.

From the beginning, the voyage was far from uneventful. The bell fell from its support during loading and caused considerable damage to the deck, which forced the ship to put into dry dock for repairs. When *The Wave* finally set out to sea, she was caught in a heavy storm. Rumours spread around London that both the ship and the bell had been lost. However, on 21 October 1856, the ship, with its precious cargo, arrived to great rejoicing at the Port of London.

Large crowds turned out to witness the transportation across London of the Great Bell, which was to be hung on a specially built gantry at the foot of the incomplete tower for testing. The bell was struck regularly throughout 1857 and it seemed that it was finally ready to be installed in the tower. This was not to be, as on 17 October 1857, the bell cracked whilst being struck. The cause of the crack was a matter of dispute until after the bell was broken up, when it was discovered that the casting had been faulty.

THE GREAT WESTMINSTER CLOCK.

Fig. I.

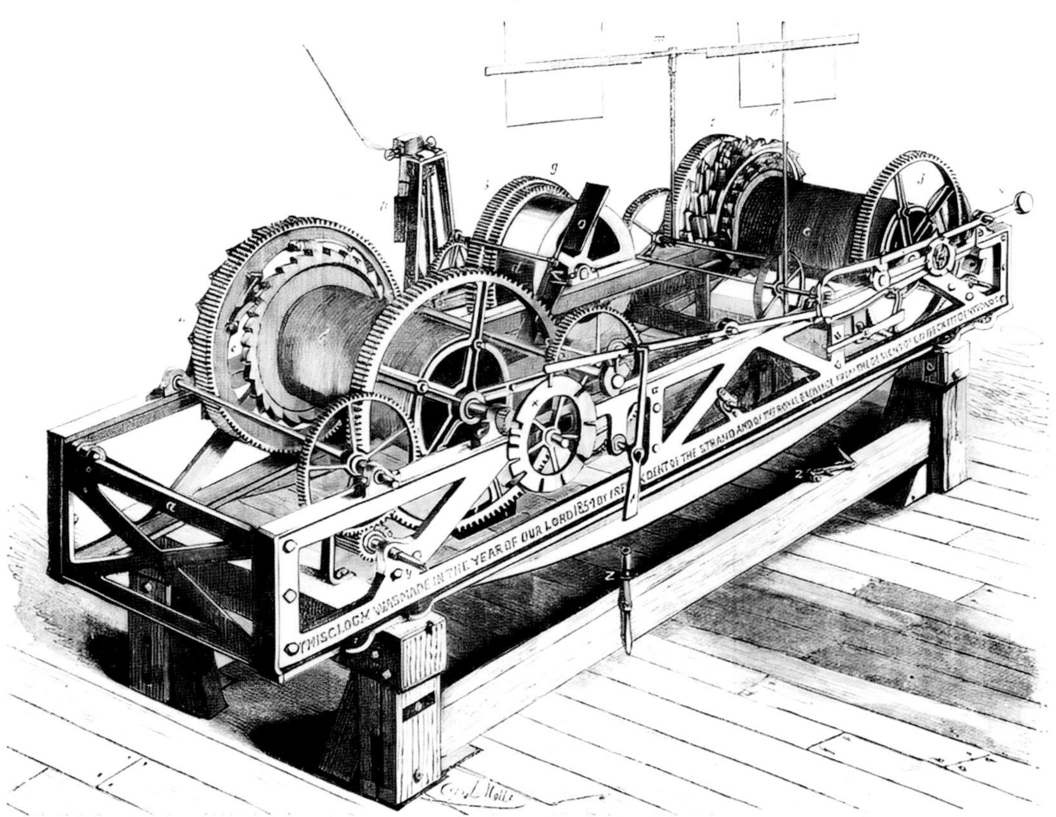

Early drawing of the mechanism.

Transporting the Great Bell.

The Great Bell crossing Westminster Bridge.

The Office of Works duly put out a new tender for the Great Bell. This time, the Whitechapel Bell Foundry, run by Charles and John Mears, having missed out on the original tender, won the contract over Warner & Sons. This had the advantage of casting the bell in London, avoiding transport problems. A little rhyme circulated in London, which summed up the feelings of the public at the time:

> Poor Mr Warner is put in a corner
> For making a bad Big Ben
> Good Mr Mears, or so it appears
> Will make us a new one, but when?

The broken pieces of the old bell were transported to Whitechapel and on 10 April 1858, the furnaces were fired up and the casting began. To the relief of all, the bell emerged complete and was found to weigh 13½ tons, very close to the original specification. The bell sounded the note E, the same as the first bell; this was very convenient, as the four quarter bells had already been cast to harmonise with that note. The new bell was transported to Westminster, but as the bell tower was still not yet finished, it was hung on the gantry at the base of the tower for testing.

This bell was considered to have a superior tone to the old one and was lavishly decorated with the Royal Coat of Arms, with the following inscription around the skirt in iron lettering:

> The bell weighing 13 tons 10 cwt 3 qrs 15 lbs was cast by George Mears of Whitechapel for the clock of the Houses of Parliament under the direction of Edmund Beckett Denison Q C in the twenty-first reign of Queen Victoria and in the year of Our Lord MDCCCLVIII.

By 12 October 1858, the clock tower was ready to receive the Great Bell to join the four quarter bells already in place. It was a laborious task taking several days. The shaft's width was only just sufficient for the bell and it had to be raised on its side in its cradle to get it safely into the belfry.

'Testing the Great Bell', Daily Mail.

The belfry with all five bells in position.

Sir Benjamin Hall.

The bell, originally known simply as the Great Bell, appeared to have gained its present name sometime before October 1859, as the name 'Big Ben' appeared in the *Daily Telegraph* at that time. It had long been the custom to name important bells and the most likely explanation for this bell's name is that during a special sitting of Parliament to choose a name in the summer of 1857, the Honourable Members present were getting weary of the tedious nature of the debate. Sir Benjamin Hall MP, Commissioner of Works, a very popular member who was known as 'Big Ben' due to his height of 6ft 4in and substantial girth, launched into his speech. At some point, a backbencher shouted out, 'Why not call it Big Ben?', much to the acclaim of the House, and the name stuck. Unfortunately, the story cannot be substantiated, as there is no record of it in *Hansard*.

INSTALLATION

During the early months of 1859, the clock mechanism was raised to its place in the tower and assembled. Provision was made for a massive two-second pendulum, which required a drop of 13.05ft; the pendulum bob weighs 202kg. The temperature compensation needed was of the zinc and steel type.

This length of the pendulum governs the timekeeping and as the temperature changes, the length of the pendulum changes. Various methods have been described earlier to solve the problem. This type of compensation depends on the differing rates of expansion of two metals – zinc and steel. The steel (or, in the case of the Westminster Clock, iron) rod expands downwards, lowering the bob, which causes a losing rate. At the same time, a zinc tube resting on the adjusting nut expands, dragging the bob upwards and making the clock gain. Thus, the bob remains in the same position regardless of changing temperatures.

Now that the problems of timekeeping had been largely solved, the clock needed to have a means of adjusting the small errors that inevitably arose. The adjusting nut below lengthens and shortens the pendulum to bring it to time. The problem, however, is that the clock must be stopped for adjustment. If a tray is placed at the pendulum's centre of gravity, a small weight dropped on to the tray will raise the centre of gravity, causing a gain. The Westminster Clock uses old pennies; dropping one coin on to the tray makes the clock gain two-fifths of a second per day, or slows the clock if removed. Thus, minor adjustments can be made without stopping the clock. The photograph shows the escapement and upper part of the pendulum; the tray with the adjusting weights can be seen below the engineer's knee.

Now that the clock and bells were in place, a tune for the quarter chimes had to be chosen. The choice fell again to Denison, who had admired the chimes of Great St Mary's during his time in Cambridge and selected this tune for the Westminster chimes, not realising that this would become one of the world's best-known tunes, adopted by millions of chiming

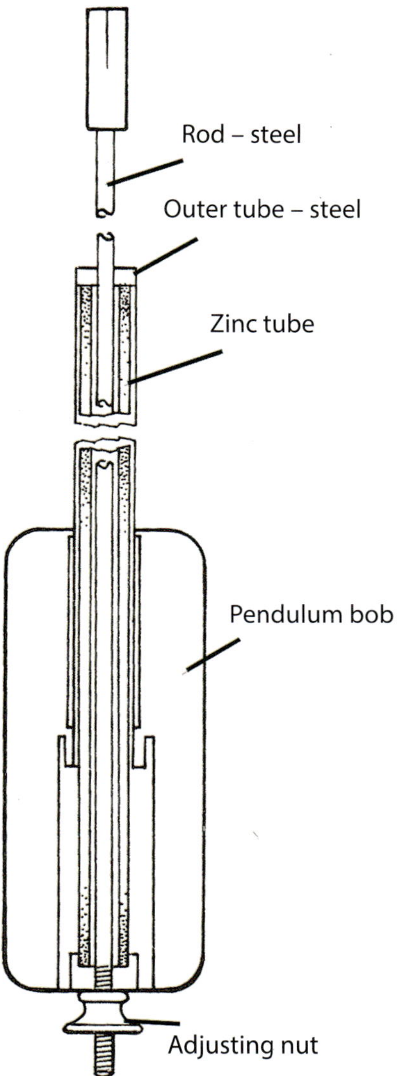

Zinc and steel pendulum.

The escapement and pendulum.

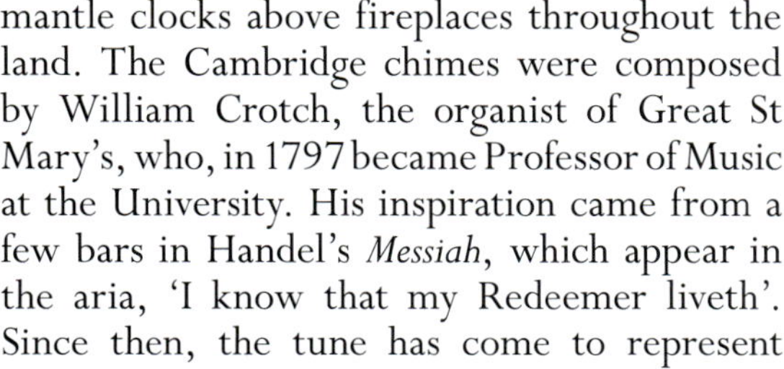

mantle clocks above fireplaces throughout the land. The Cambridge chimes were composed by William Crotch, the organist of Great St Mary's, who, in 1797 became Professor of Music at the University. His inspiration came from a few bars in Handel's *Messiah*, which appear in the aria, 'I know that my Redeemer liveth'. Since then, the tune has come to represent London and England throughout the world and many composers have quoted it to instantly evoke the city, including most memorably Vaughan Williams in his *London Symphony*. The BBC began daily broadcasts of the Westminster Chimes worldwide in 1924 and during World War II they became even more significant as a symbol of resistance and national survival.

Chapter 11

Twentieth-Century Developments

The twentieth century saw sweeping developments in clockmaking. These included the development of electrically driven clocks, followed by quartz crystal technology. After World War II, constant-force springs were introduced and mass production of clocks gathered pace.

Electric clock by Alexander Bain.

ELECTRICITY IN CLOCKMAKING

The first application of electromagnetism to clocks was made by Alexander Bain, a clockmaker and inventor from humble origins in Caithness, Scotland, who settled in London in 1837 and attended lectures at the new Polytechnic Institute. He patented his first electric clock design in 1841, when he described a clock that utilised electromagnetic impulses rather than a traditional mechanism to impulse the pendulum. The power came from an earth battery consisting of zinc and copper plates buried in the ground.

The pendulum of the Bain clock contains a permanent magnet. The magnet passes into one of the two coils as the pendulum swings. A simple switching system attached to the pendulum rod sends a pulse of current to each coil in turn, giving an impulse to maintain the pendulum. A simple ratchet system turned the hands of the clock.

Various other clocks were produced using the same principle and several makers made both wall-mounted and table clocks. However, the performance was disappointing for two reasons:

1. As the power output of the primitive batteries varied, it affected the impulses given to the pendulum and, thus, the timekeeping.

2. Any interference with the free motion of a pendulum will spoil its timekeeping properties.

Before the performance of electric pendulum clocks could be improved, a design that separated the magnetic apparatus from the impulsing of the pendulum was required.

Synchronome Clocks

The first precision electrically maintained clock was produced mainly for industrial and commercial use as a master clock to drive a number of 'slave clocks' – basic dial clocks whose hands were advanced by a simple ratchet system every 30 seconds. Frank Hope-Jones (1867–1950) took out a patent in 1895 for his 'Synchronome switch', which enabled a pendulum to be maintained electrically with hardly any of the disturbance from which earlier electric clocks suffered.

Bain's design took advantage of the latest advances in conventional clock technology, particularly the development of Invar by the

Frank Hope-Jones.

Synchronome master clock.

Swiss scientist Charles Édouard Guillaume. This alloy of iron and nickel had an almost zero coefficient of expansion. It was ideal for making precision pendulum rods that were superior to existing compensation systems, such as the zinc and steel pendulum used in the Westminster Clock described earlier. An improved design was patented in 1905 and Hope-Jones' Synchronome Clock Co. continued to develop the master clock and slave system until 1918, when they went fully into production. It remained the most successful system of its kind until 1980.

The Synchronome system used a gravity arm to impulse the pendulum every 30 seconds; the gravity arm falls away and is reset by an electrical contact, leaving the pendulum free from interference. The diagram explains the

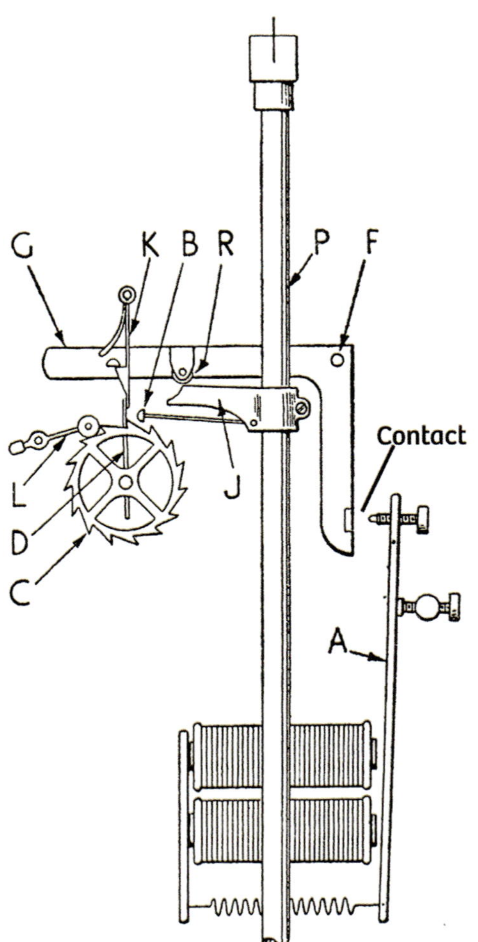

The Synchronome impulsing system.

W.H. Shortt.

system further (from Hope-Jones' *Electrical Timekeeping*, 1940). The pendulum P has an impulse pallet J attached, which transfers the impulse every 30 seconds. The gathering hook B moves the count wheel C clockwise, one tooth every 2 seconds; the lever L prevents the wheel from reversing. A vane, D, attached to the wheel, comes into contact with the release catch every 30 seconds. This catch releases the gravity arm C to fall on to the impulse pallet and the roller R rolls down the curve of the pallet, impulsing the pendulum. When the roller drops away from the pallet, the gravity arm falls and makes an electrical contact with arm A; this activates the coils and resets the gravity arm. This 30-second pulse of electricity is used to power the slave clocks.

Whilst the Synchronome clock was extremely accurate, keeping time to within a second per week, Hope-Jones was not satisfied and continued experimenting with designs to build a 'free pendulum' system

The Shortt-Synchronome free-pendulum system.

that would eliminate even the very small interference to the pendulum caused by the impulsing system of the Synchronome clock. He fortunately met up with a kindred spirit, a railway engineer, W.H. Shortt soon after World War I.

For many years, Shortt had been experimenting with ideas for producing a free pendulum, impulsed by electrical means. He joined Hope-Jones in his Synchronome works. Hope-Jones describes in his book, *Electrical Timekeeping*, the many problems they had to overcome before they produced in 1921 a working clock that was set up in the Edinburgh Observatory. It caused a sensation in the horological world, having a variation of less than one-hundredth of a second in a year. The Shortt-Synchronome system became the ultimate time standard between the Wars, used in observatories worldwide. It was soon adapted to control broadcast time signals and other innovations, such as the 'Speaking Clock'.

Free pendulum.

The photograph shows the two elements of the system. On the left is the master pendulum sealed in a vacuum chamber, connected to an adapted Synchronome clock. By enclosing the master pendulum in a partial vacuum, barometric error – the changing of air pressure, which affects the rate – is eliminated. On the right is the clock with the slave pendulum that operates the slave dials.

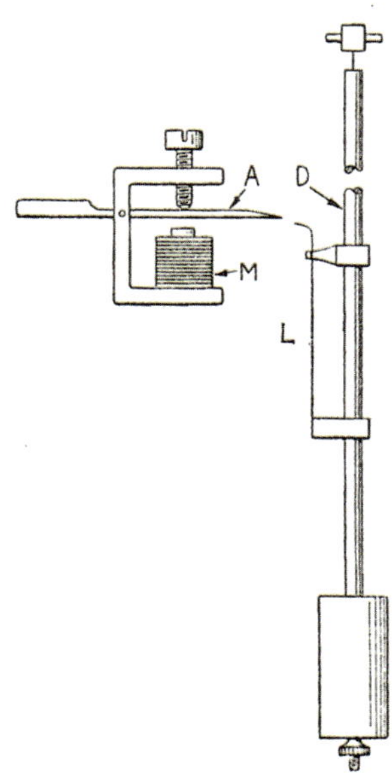

Shortt's 'hit-and-miss' synchroniser.

Synchronome complete system plan

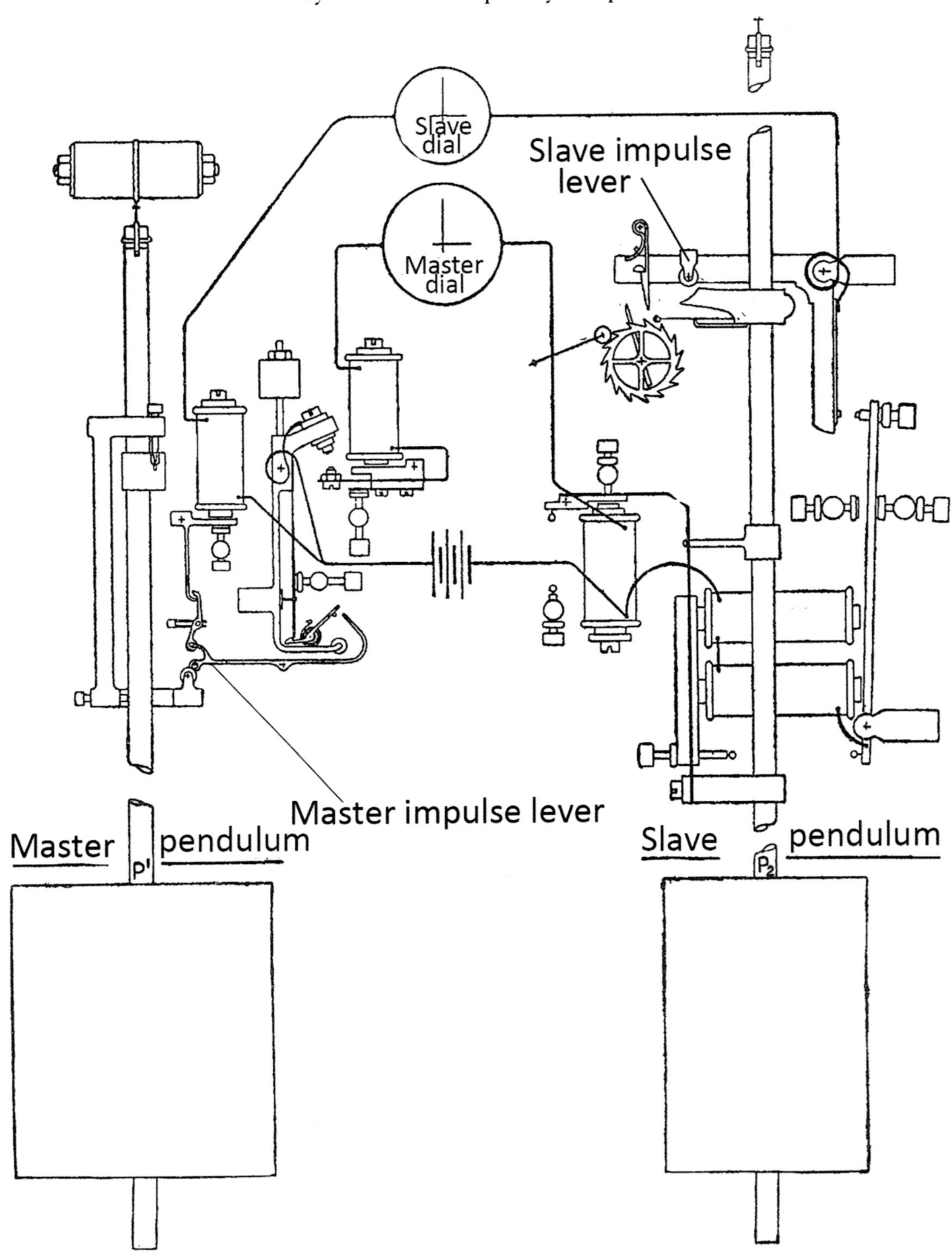

The second photograph shows the chamber with the dome removed. The upper part of the pendulum is visible with the gravity lever, which impulses it every 30 seconds. This lever is released by an impulse from the Synchronome slave clock; when the lever falls off, it sends a precise pulse back to the slave clock.

The main problem was that in order to release the impulse lever of the master pendulum at the exact time, the pendulum of the slave clock must be kept in synchronisation with the master pendulum. To solve this problem, Shortt invented his 'hit-and-miss' synchroniser. The hit-and-miss synchroniser is attached to the pendulum of an otherwise standard Synchronome master clock. The system is explained in the diagram earlier in this chapter. Every 30 seconds, the master clock sends a pulse to the coil M, which momentarily pulls down the lever A before releasing it. If lever A is in the down position when the pendulum D swings to the left, the spring L will contact the lever's tip – a 'hit'. This flexes the spring and slightly reduces the pendulum arc, causing a temporary gaining rate. The pendulum is regulated to lose slightly; in this state, the spring will make contact with A every 30 seconds.

However, if the pendulum is made to move slightly faster, the spring will pass underneath A before the next impulse comes – a 'miss'. The slave pendulum is adjusted so that when a hit happens, the pendulum speeds up and at the next 30-second impulse from the master pendulum, the spring misses the lever. The pendulum slows back down by the time the next pulse arrives and a 'hit' takes place.

Thus, the hit-and-miss cycle, controlled by the impulses from the master pendulum, keeps the slave pendulum in step with the master, ensuring that the gravity arm falls at the correct moment so that when it drops, it makes the contact to send the next impulse to the slave pendulum. The plan shows the complete system.

Synchronous Electric Clocks

The long-distance transmission of electricity was made possible by the development of synchronous generators, which replaced earlier dynamos that produced direct current (DC) electricity, that is, current with a constant flow. The first industrial application was pioneered by the firm of Elkington & Co. in 1844 for commercial electroplating. DC dynamos were widely used in industry; however, DC current was not suitable for long-distance transmission. Alternating current (AC), which periodically reverses polarity in the form of a sine wave, is much easier to produce and can be transported efficiently over a long distance.

From the late 1880s, power stations were set up using the new synchronous generators to produce a reliable AC electricity supply. The frequency of the current was soon standardised in Britain to 50Hz, that is, completing a cycle of polarity 50 times per second.

At the same time as synchronous generators were developed, a type of electric motor came into use, using the alternating polarities of the generators to drive the rotating element of the motor. This meant that the motor's speed was always synchronised with the generators in the power station. The applications of this new synchronous motor soon became obvious – any machine part that needed to rotate at a fixed speed could use a synchronous motor.

The National Grid began supplying power in 1926 and domestic synchronous clocks and commercial wall clocks were manufactured in large numbers. Two firms, Smiths and Ferranti, dominated the British market.

Ferranti International was a large electrical engineering company founded in 1885. Dr Ferranti designed the equipment for the first truly modern power station at Deptford, which began the large-scale distribution of AC electricity in 1890. In the 1930s, the firm branched out into 'brown goods',

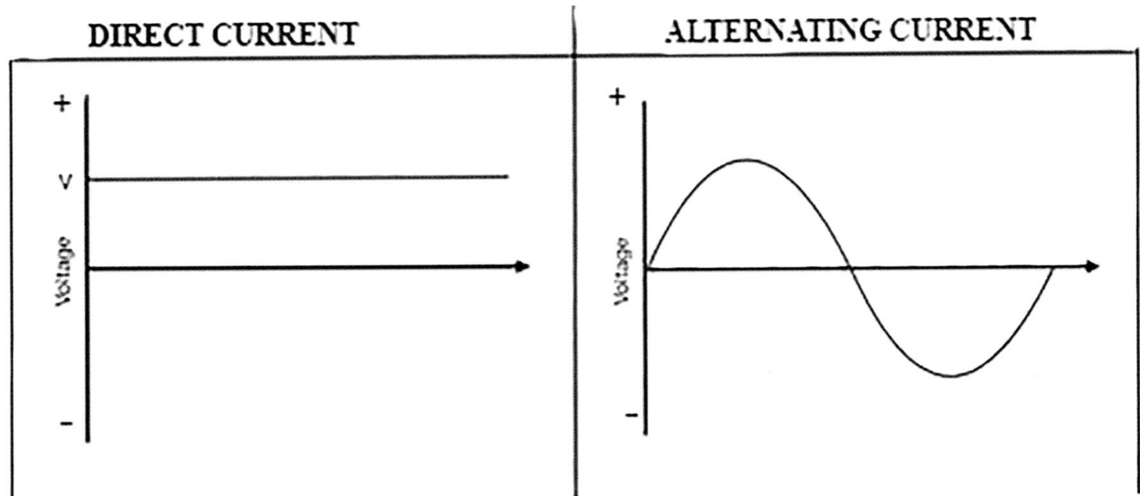

Direct and alternating current.

Westinghouse Electric Co. advertisement, 1888.

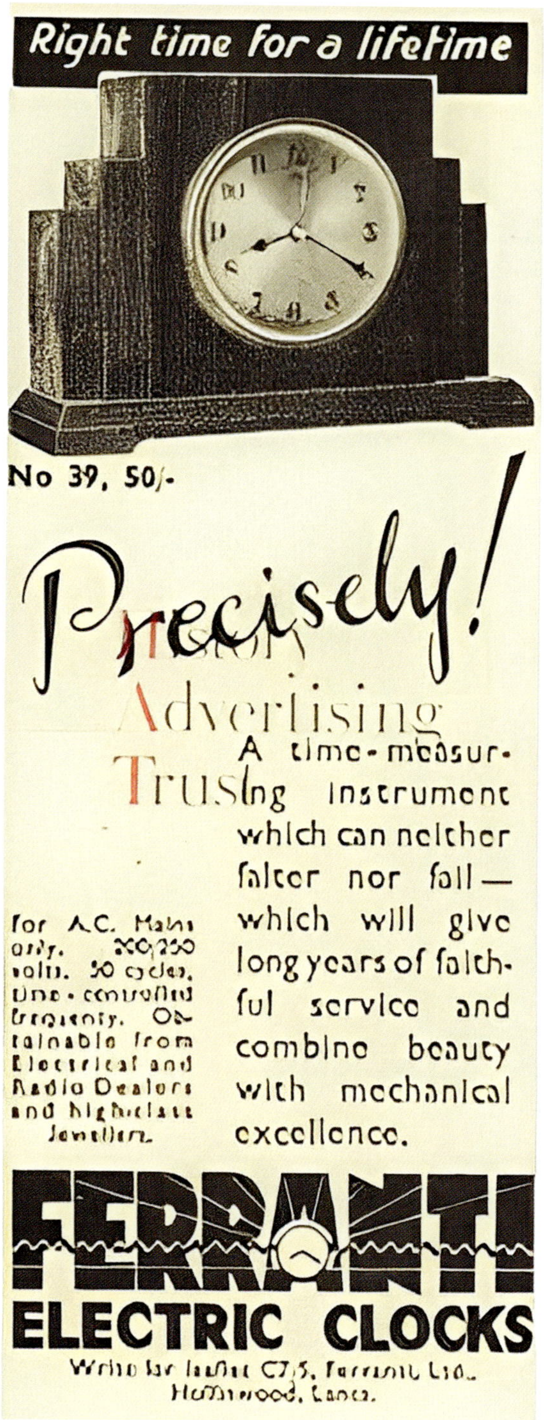

Ferranti advertisement.

such as radios, clocks and later televisions. Its first clock, the Model 1, was introduced in 1932 and the company remained in clock production until 1957.

One problem with the early synchronous clocks was that they were not self-starting. The back of the Model 1 clock had a knob that had to be turned to start the motor. Later in the 1930s, self-starting motors were developed. From the early beginnings, more stylish clocks were introduced in the popular Deco style. The convenience and accuracy of these timepieces ensured their popularity until battery clocks took over the market in the 1970s.

Smiths entered the synchronous clock business at the same time as Ferranti. S. Smith & Son Ltd specialised in motor accessories and, in 1931, it opened a clock division and started producing an extensive range of synchronous clocks. To add to the early Bakelite models, Smiths – who adopted the brand 'Sectric' in 1937 – produced a vast range of clocks, dominating the British market until the 1960s. Alarm models appeared in the late 1930s and even an electric chiming clock was introduced. The old English dial clocks seen in most schools, offices and stations in the country became obsolete and the more convenient and accurate electric wall clocks began to replace them.

QUARTZ CRYSTAL TECHNOLOGY

Walter Guyton Cady (1874–1974), a noted American physicist and electrical engineer, became interested in the piezoelectric properties of crystals when working with the General Electric Company during World War I. He discovered that a quartz crystal could be made to vibrate constantly at a specific frequency. This work resulted in a series of patents in the early 1920s of quartz resonators and their use as radio frequency standards. It was soon realised that a piece of quartz cut to

Ferranti synchronous clocks.

Smiths synchronous clocks.

The first quartz oscillators used by the US Bureaux of Standards, 1929.

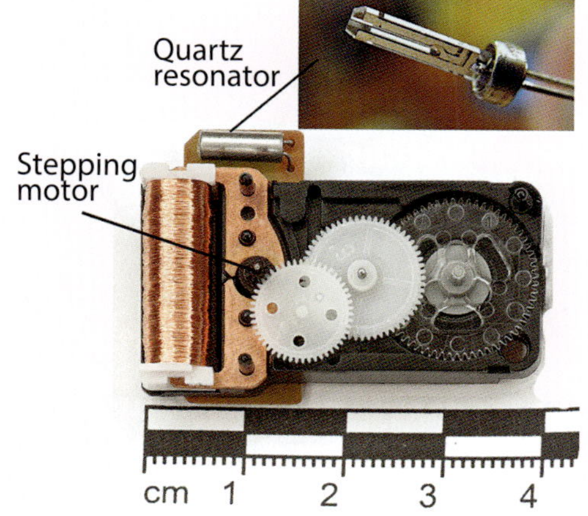

Quartz clock movement, 1970s.

a particular shape and electrically stimulated could produce pulses of electricity at a steady frequency

Work at the Bell Telephone Laboratories by J.W. Horton and W.A. Marrison resulted in the first quartz clock in 1927. This had a crystal that resonated at 50,000 cycles per second, which was reduced by a device called a submultiple controlled frequency generator to a frequency low enough to drive a synchronous motor. Bell Telephones, in 1929, built a set of four precision quartz oscillators for the US Bureaux of Standards, which became the first electronic frequency standard. It achieved an accuracy of about 1 second error in four months.

The early quartz clocks were too bulky and expensive for domestic use. However, over the next 30 years, quartz and microchip technology improved to the extent that by the 1970s, small, cheap quartz mechanisms became available for both domestic clocks and watches. The convenience of these clocks, which did not need mains wiring, soon ended the market for synchronous clocks. The 1970s quartz battery clock movement has a quartz resonator mounted on a dividing circuit used to control a stepping motor that drives the clock hands.

Constant-force springs.

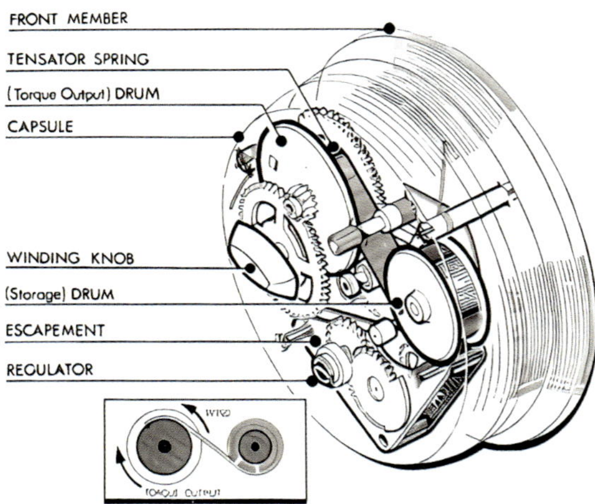

Tensator constant-force spring in a Smiths clock, 1970.

The author's tensator-powered chronometer carriage-clock movement.

CONSTANT FORCE SPRINGS

In the post-World War II period, advances in stainless-steel technology made its application possible in watch and clock springs. One notable product had its origin in a 1930s US patent, which at the time was not viable as the types of spring steel available were not suitable. The idea was taken up in the 1960s by the Tensator company in the UK for a revolutionary constant-force spring, which has since found many applications, from wind-up radios to retractable winding electrical cables in many household appliances such as vacuum cleaners.

A constant force spring behaves in the reverse of a traditional clock spring. From the diagram, we can see that it comes in a tight coil and that is the shape it tries to return to if uncoiled. A traditional leaf spring starts as a strip of spring steel coiled up inside the spring barrel; when it is wound, the spring coils are pulled into the centre of the barrel and the uncoiling action rotates the barrel and drives the mechanism. This uncoiling action creates a great deal of friction, which needs lubrication; also, the power output – the torque – varies as the spring runs down. This was well understood in the sixteenth century when inventions such as the stackfreed and fusee were introduced to make the torque more constant.

Chronometer carriage clock by John Cronin, 1995, commissioned by J.W. Benson.

In the diagram earlier in this chapter, the spring is shown wound on to the storage drum. The torque output drum is wound anticlockwise to wind the spring, which is trying to resume its original shape wound around the storage drum. The pulling force of this action provides the torque to turn the output drum, which powers the clock. As the coils of the spring ribbon do not slip against adjacent coils, the spring winds and unwinds with virtually no friction, at a constant torque and needs no lubrication. The problem was that this, an ideal power source for mechanical clocks (it is too bulky to use in watches), came too late, as cheap battery-operated electronic movements took over from budget-price clocks at the same time as this technology was developed. Smiths abandoned the idea in 1971 and soon stopped mechanical clock production altogether.

In the 1990s, some interest emerged in the possibility of using a constant force spring in high-quality mechanical clocks, such as chronometer carriage timepieces. The author produced a small number of tensor-powered chronometer carriage clocks, which proved to be considerably more accurate than the earlier chronometer clocks – maintaining a rate of a second or so per week, using both spring detent and pivoted detent escapements. A Tensator powered chronometer carriage clock was commissioned by J.W. Benson from the author in 1995.

Mantle clock by Seth Thomas, 1880.

Shelf clock by Eli Terry, 1825.

Junghans factory, 1925.

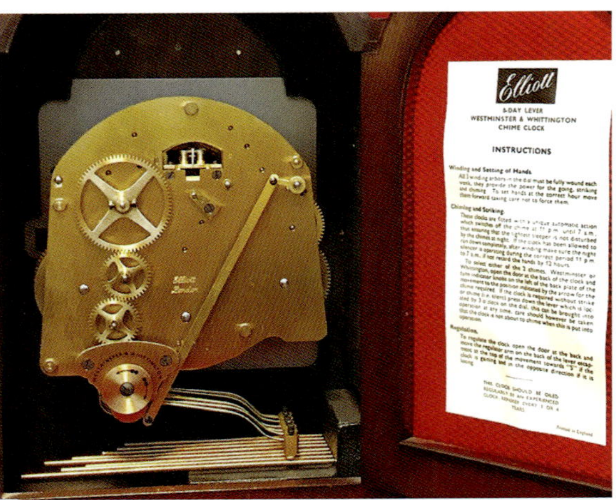

Chiming clock by F.W. Elliott, 1960s.

MASS PRODUCTION

Like most consumer goods, the mass production of clocks began in the nineteenth century and transformed them from a mark of status into a commonplace item in the home. Most English clockmakers opposed the importation of cheap foreign timepieces, stubbornly persisting in producing high-quality clocks for those who could afford the price. It was not until well into the twentieth century that serious attempts were made to compete with cheaper imports from America and Europe.

Eli Terry (1772–1852), an American clockmaker from Connecticut, is considered the pioneer of clock mass production. In the 1790s, he began developing water-powered machinery to produce more or less interchangeable parts, made largely from local materials, which could be assembled without skilled labour. In 1806, he signed a contract to build 4,000 clock movements. It has been claimed that these clocks were the first mass-produced mechanisms with interchangeable parts. Other firms soon followed, such as Seth Thomas, producing large quantities of budget-priced clocks that were exported worldwide, undercutting European makers and opening up new markets.

Inspired by American manufacturers, German makers such as Junghans became involved in mass production towards the end of the nineteenth century. Arthur Junghans spent a good deal of time in the USA studying the latest production methods, which enabled the firm to become Europe's leading producer of watches and clocks by 1903, employing over 3,000 workers.

British companies such as J.J. Elliott and Gillet & Johnson had some success in producing high-quality clocks in the late nineteenth century; these two firms amalgamated in 1923 and became F.W. Elliott. The firm established a market with customers who were prepared to pay a premium for a higher quality English product than German and American makers provided. F.W. Elliott continued producing fine clocks in Croydon, London, until the 1970s.

Another firm making similar clocks to Elliott was Garrard, originally Garrard Engineering & Manufacturing Company, founded in 1915 to manufacture war materials such as bomb sights. After the war, the company began making clockwork gramophone motors and clocks from 1931 to 1960.

In 1929, the Enfield Clock Co. was formed to manufacture clocks in England, directly competing with the German clocks that dominated the British market. Machinery and core workers were brought in from Germany and the first movements were ready for sale in 1932. Competition from lower priced German-made clocks made trading difficult.

Sriking clock by Garrard, 1930s.

Enfield striking clock, 1930s.

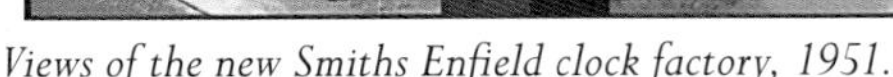

Views of the new Smiths Enfield clock factory, 1951.

S. Smith & Sons, who had recently started manufacturing synchronous electric clocks, bought out the shareholders and absorbed the company. The Enfield name continued and clocks were sold both as Enfield and Smiths Enfield.

After World War II, Smiths, by then a large industrial group, moved the majority of its clock and watch production to South Wales and built a factory in Ystradgynlais, Swansea. The Smiths Enfield factory was built in 1948 on the same site as the new Anglo-Celtic Watch Company (later Smiths Watches) and in 1949 production of a new range of striking clocks began.

Smiths became the largest British clock producer and its striking, chiming and alarm clocks competed successfully with imported timepieces. Over the next twenty years, a vast range of clocks was produced. The company's demise was due to changes in fashion and the low-priced battery clocks imported from old rivals Junghans, which supplied movements to what was left of the British clock industry. The largest of these enterprises was the Metamec clock company in Dereham, Norfolk, which, from 1947 for about 50 years, produced a range of clocks with imported movements. In the last decades of the twentieth century, English-made carriage clocks were produced in substantial numbers by Gluck Engineering of Croydon, with Swiss platform escapements; these were sold under various names, including large retailers. What has remained at the high end of the market is a handful of small enterprises and individuals making high-quality clocks, mostly to order.

Smiths clocks from the 1950s.

Further Reading

Alix, C. and Bonnert, P., *Carriage Clocks* (Suffolk Antique Collectors' Club, 1974 & 1981)

Betts, J., *Harrison* (National Maritime Museum, 2007)

Betts, J., *Time Restored* (Oxford University Press, 2006)

Britten, F.J., *Britten's Watch and Clockmaker's Guide* (Bloomsbury, 1978)

Cronin, John, *The Marine Chronometer* (The Crowood Press, 2010)

Daniels, George, *The Art of Breguet* (Sotheby's Publications, 1975)

Gazeley, W.J., *Clock and Watch Escapements* (The Crowood Press, 1992)

Jones, Barry M., *S. Smith & Sons Ltd, The Golden Years: Part One: Clocks and Watches* (pamphlet)

Lands, David S., *Revolution in Time* (Harvard University Press, 1983)

Loomes, Brian, *Brass Dial Clocks* (ACC Art Books, 1999)

Loomes, Brian, *Painted Dial Clocks* (ACC Art Books, 1994)

Macdonald, Peter, *Big Ben* (The History Press, 2004)

May, W.E., *A History of Marine Navigation* (G.T. Foulis, 1973)

Mercer, Tony, *Mercer Chronometers* (Mayfield Books, 2003)

Radage, D., Meinen, W. & Radage, L., *Through the Golden Age* (Three O'Clock Publishing, 2016)

Rawlings, A.L., *The Science of Clocks and Watches* (British Horological Institute, 1993)

Roberts, Derek, *British Skeleton Clocks* (ACC Art Books, 1987)

Robinson, Tom, *The Longcase Clock* (ACC Art Books, 1999)

Symonds, R.W., *Thomas Tompion his Life and Work* (Spring Publications, 1969)

Glossary of Horological Terms

Action A term used to denote the extent of the arc of vibration of the balance, that is, how far the balance rotates on each swing – for example, a 'good action' when the angle is large, say above 200 degrees.

Adjusting The act of regulating a watch or clock to keep time. Watch adjusting can be in different positions, for example dial up, dial down, pendant up and so on. High-quality watches are adjusted in five or more positions and for variations in temperature. Pendulums are adjusted by shortening or lengthening, turning the adjusting nut below the pendulum bob.

Arbor The shaft or axle that carries a clock or watch wheel, which often contains the pinion or gear that drives the wheel; the balance arbor is normally called a staff.

Automatic winding A device that uses the movement of the wearer to wind the mainspring of a watch.

Balance The controller or governor of a watch or clock escapement. Usually in the form of a wheel, which is made to oscillate, or 'vibrate' by an attached 'balance spring' and is maintained by impulses from the escapement.

Balance cock The bracket that contains the upper bearing for the balance, which holds the balance in place and to which the balance spring and regulator assembly is generally attached.

Balance spring Generally, a fine spiral spring attached to the balance, often known as the hairspring.

Balance staff The shaft or spindle that holds the balance, balance spring and roller.

Banking pins In the lever escapement, the pins on which the lever banks or rests. In a cylinder escapement, a banking pin is attached to the rim of the balance to prevent overbanking, that is, the balance turning too far and locking the escapement.

Barrel The cylinder containing the mainspring. It may be a plain barrel around which the fusee chain is wound, or it may have gear teeth cut into the periphery to drive the gear train directly – this is known as a going barrel.

Barrel arbor The steel shaft on which the barrel revolves. It contains a hook to which the inner end of the mainspring is attached and is used to wind the mainspring.

Beat The 'tick' of a watch or clock caused by the action of the escapement giving the impulse.

Bezel The rim that holds the glass of a watch or clock.

Bimetallic Two dissimilar metals, usually steel and brass, fixed together to form a strip that will bend with changing temperatures; used for the arms of a compensated balance, or a compensation curb.

Black polish The ultimate finish imparted by heating to hardened or tempered steel, as opposed to a bright surface gloss. Often used for watch and clock hands.

Bluing The process of heating polished steel until the surface turns to a blue colour.

Bow The pivoted loop of a pocket watch case used for hanging or attaching a chain.

Cannon pinion The pinion to which the minute hand of a watch or clock is attached. It fits friction-tight over the centre arbor and allows the hands to be turned.

Capped bearing A type of bearing with a cap, usually a flat jewel or endstone, which limits the endshake, or up and down movement, of the wheel.

Carriage The rotating frame that carries the escapement of a tourbillon. A carriage clock is a small portable clock, usually in a case designed for travelling.

Chapter ring The circular division of a clock or watch dial on which the hours and minutes are marked.

Chaton The ring, or bouchon, into which a watch jewel is set.

Chronograph A watch with a means of recording a time interval, normally by providing a mechanism to stop a seconds hand and return it to zero.

Chronometer A term given to high-precision timepieces. Originally used to describe a timepiece with a detent or chronometer escapement developed for navigation. Later, it was the term given by the Swiss to any watch that had passed prescribed tests and been given an official timing certificate.

Collet A small metal ring, usually cut to allow it to fit friction-tight over a shaft. Used to attach the centre coil of a balance spring to the staff, allowing adjustment.

Compensation balance A type of balance designed to compensate for the changing elasticity of the balance spring, which causes a gaining or losing rate. The rim of the balance is formed from a bimetallic strip that is cut to allow the rim sections to bend in and out; this changes the rate to provide temperature compensation.

Compensation curb A bimetallic strip, usually a steel and brass strip fixed together, so that they bend with the change of temperature. Used to provide automatic regulation to compensate for changing elasticity of the balance spring.

Contrate wheel A wheel with teeth cut at right angles to the plane of rotation. Used to transfer drive through 90 degrees.

Crossings The spokes of a wheel made by crossing out a wheel blank, cutting away sections to lighten the wheel.

Crown wheel escapement The name given to the verge escapement when applied to a clock.

Curb pins The two pins attached to a watch regulator arm, which embrace the outer coils of the balance spring and can be moved to alter the effective length of the spring.

Cylinder escapement A frictional rest escapement developed by George Graham from earlier experiments, principally by Thomas Tompion in the 1690s.

Damascene Originally described as decorative steel work from Damascus. In watch work, refers to complicated ornamental work on plates and bars.

Detached escapement A type of escapement in which the balance is detached from the escapement during its supplementary arc, that is, when the balance is not being given its impulse.

Detent A locking piece, usually a form of lever that locks a wheel by catching its teeth.

Detent escapement A detached escapement used in chronometers and other precision timekeepers. A detent releases the escape wheel to impulse the balance on alternate swings, leaving the balance free to oscillate without interference from the escapement.

Dial The face of a clock or watch containing the hour markers; subsidiary dials can be included for showing seconds, date and so on.

Draw In a lever escapement, after locking the pallets are advanced by a small angle (the angle of draw) to rest firmly against the banking pins, protecting against accidental release due to shock.

Drop The free rotation of an escape wheel after impulse has been given until locking takes place.

End shake The amount of up and down movement of a wheel between upper and lower bearings.

End stone A jewel fitted to form a cap to a bearing; the end of the pivot rests on it to reduce end shake.

Engine turning Sometimes called guilloché, a form of machine engraving used to decorate dials and cases.

English lever escapement The name given to the ratchet-toothed form of the lever escapement favoured by English makers until the club-toothed form superseded it.

Entry pallet The pallet stone in a lever escapement on the advancing side of the escape wheel; the opposite stone on the departing side is called the exit pallet.

Equation of time The difference between Solar Time (as shown on a sundial) and Mean Solar Time (clock time). Due to the Earth's elliptical orbit around the sun, the length of a day changes during the year. The average length of a solar day is called Mean Solar Time (used by clocks). The difference in the two times can be calculated using an equation table, which indicates the minutes to be added or subtracted to Solar Time to work out mean time. These are often seen on good sundials and some watches have an equation dial that shows the difference.

Escapement The mechanism that controls the speed of rotation of the gear train and thus the hands of a clock or watch and at the same time provides the time controller (for example, a watch balance or pendulum) with regular impulses to keep it in motion.

Fob A decorative attachment to a pocket watch used in place of a chain. A fob watch refers to a small watch hanging from a brooch or clip.

Front plate The plate of a watch nearest the dial, opposed to the top or back plate.

Full plate A form of watch with two main plates of similar size containing the wheels and escapement, with the balance positioned above the top plate supported by the balance cock.

Fusee A spiralling grooved pulley of reducing diameter used to equalise the varying power of the mainspring as it runs down.

Gilding The process of covering base metal with a coating of gold. Before electroplating, items were covered with an amalgam of gold and mercury and heated to drive off the mercury. leaving a coating of gold.

Gimbals (Gymbals) A form of universal joint used to maintain a chronometer in a horizontal position.

Guard pin In a lever escapement, the pin attached to the fork of the pallets, which in conjunction with the roller prevents the lever getting out of position.

Hardening The process of making steel hard by rapid cooling from a high temperature by immersing it in water or oil. Generally accompanied by tempering, which is reheating to reduce the hardness to the desired level.

Hog's bristle Used before the invention of the balance spring as a buffer against the arms of the balance, which gave some measure of regulation as it was moved towards and away from the centre of the balance.

Hooke's Law '*Ut tensio, sic vis*' – as is the tension, so is the force. Robert Hooke's fundamental law of springs.

Hunter A watch with a sprung cover to protect the glass; a half- or demi-hunter had an opening in the centre of the lid to enable viewing of the hands without springing open the lid.

Impulse pin The pin, usually a jewel, fixed to the roller of a lever escapement, which engages the fork of the lever and impulses the balance.

Impulse roller The part of an escapement attached to the balance, which transmits the impulse.

Isochronism An oscillating system, for example a balance, which can complete varying arcs of vibration in equal times.

Jewelled A term which indicates that a watch or clock contains bearings or surfaces that are made from jewel stones, usually corundum – sapphire or ruby.

Karrusel A form of revolving escapement, similar to the tourbillon, but more robust and slower moving.

Keyless work A mechanism to allow a watch to be wound without a key.

Lepine calibre A form of watch movement in which each wheel is supported by a separate cock, with a cylinder escapement. The design allowed very slim pocket watches to be made.

Lever escapement A detached escapement invented by Thomas Mudge in 1754. During the nineteenth century it became, in various forms, the almost universal watch escapement.

Lift Refers to the angle of the impulse pallets of a lever escapement. The tooth of the escape wheel traverses the incline of the pallets to impulse the balance.

Locking The action of arresting the rotation of the escape wheel after the impulse is given.

Mainspring The principal spring in a watch or clock. It takes the form of a strip of steel coiled into a barrel that powers the mechanism.

Maintaining power The mechanism that keeps a fusee watch going whilst winding when the power is lost; a separate spring is engaged automatically during the winding operation.

Mean Time The average length of all the solar days of the year. The usual time shown by watches and clocks.

Minute repeater A repeating watch that strikes the hours, quarters and minutes on the depression of a button or lever.

Motion work The gears that turn the hour and minute hands of a watch or clock.

Movement The complete mechanism of a watch or clock.

Oscillation A complete cycle or period, or repeatable alternation of a reciprocating body, for example a watch balance or clock pendulum.

Overcoil The upraised coil of a Breguet balance spring.

Pair case A pocket watch with two cases; the movement is fitted into one and this fits into the outer case.

Pallet The part of the escapement upon which the escape wheel operates and transmits the impulse to the balance or pendulum; or a rotating part of a striking mechanism.

Parachute A shock-resisting device invented by Breguet to protect the balance pivots.

Passing spring A thin spring attached to a chronometer detent, which flexes to allow the balance to pass in one direction and operates the detent on the return swing.

Pawl A detent, or click, used to lock a wheel with ratchet teeth and prevent it reversing; it is held against the ratchet by a click spring.

Pendant The part of a pocket watch case to which the bow is fitted. In a wrist watch it refers to the position of the winding crown for timing purposes, for example pendant up or down.

Perpetual calendar A mechanism that shows the date and adjusts for the length of the months and leap year.

Perpetuelle The name Breguet gave to his self-winding watches.

Pinion A small gear, usually the driven member of a pair of gears on a wheel; the teeth of this wheel are referred to as leaves.

Pinion wire Extruded wire in the shape of pinion leaves, made by drawing several times through specially shaped dies. Sections are cut off to form the arbor and pinion of a wheel.

Pin lever escapement A type of lever escapement where the impulse jewels are replaced by steel pins; also called the pin pallet escapement.

Pivot The end of an arbor, which is reduced in diameter to turn in a bearing.

Pivoted detent escapement A form of chronometer escapement where the detent is pivoted from an arbor instead of a spring detent.

Poise In equal balance. In horology, it describes a balance that has an equal distribution of weight around the rim; it is then said to be 'in poise'.

Positional error The change in rate of a watch when it is in different positions. Precision watches are regulated generally in five positions: dial up; dial down; pendant up; pendant left; and pendant right.

Potance A bracket, such as that which supports the lower balance pivot in a full plate movement.

Push piece The part of a watch case that is pushed to release a catch and open the case; also the pin that is depressed to engage a keyless work, or the piece to acuate a chronograph mechanism.

Rack A segment of a circle having teeth cut in the periphery, usually used to count out hours, minutes or quarters in a repeating or striking mechanism.

Rack lever escapement A type of lever escapement, where the lever has a toothed rack that gears with a pinion on the balance staff.

Rate The daily average timekeeping of a watch or clock.

Remontoir A device with a small spring that is wound by the gear train at regular intervals, providing constant force to the escapement.

Repeater A watch or clock that sounds the hours, quarters or minutes on demand by pressing a button or pushing a slide on the watch case.

Roller The disc attached to the balance staff of a lever escapement that contains the impulse pin.

Shake A term denoting the working clearance of a wheel, that is, end shake and side shake.

Shellac A resinous substance that is used to secure small parts such as pallet stones; it softens with heating and sets hard as it cools.

Shock-resisting watch A watch with spring-loaded bearings that protect the balance pivots from damage due to shock.

Slide The thumb-piece on the side of a repeating watch, which is pushed to operate the mechanism.

Spotting A form of decoration for watch or chronometer plates consisting of a series of circular rings.

Spring detent A detent in a chronometer escapement that is supported by a spring rather than the pivoted type.

Stackfreed An early device to equalise the varying force of the mainspring, superseded by the fusee.

Staff The arbor of a balance.

Stopwatch A watch with a provision for stopping the balance to note intervals of time.

Stop work A device to control the number of turns of the winding of a mainspring.

Stud The block into which the outer end of a balance spring is fixed.

Supplementary arc The continued vibration of a balance after unlocking and impulse have occurred.

Terminal curve The curve applied to either end of the balance spring, intended to improve isochronism.

Temperature compensation A device designed to compensate for the effects of changing temperatures on the timekeeping of a watch or clock.

Tourbillon A revolving carriage invented by Breguet to carry the escapement and balance of a watch, which slowly revolves to counteract poising errors of the balance.

Train In horology, a series of wheels and pinons in a watch movement.

Vibrations In horology, the term used to describe the swing of a pendulum or balance in one direction. The count of a balance is generally described in vibrations per hour.

Index

First published in 2025 by
The Crowood Press Ltd
Ramsbury, Marlborough
Wiltshire SN8 2HR

enquiries@crowood.com
www.crowood.com

British Library Cataloguing-in-Publication Data
A catalogue record for this book is available from the British Library.

For product safety-related questions contact productsafety@crowood.com.

ISBN 978 0 7198 4504 8

Typeset by Simon and Sons
Cover design by Blue Sunflower Creative
Printed and bound in India by Thomson Press

Photograph credits
Cambridge University Press, p.8; National Trust, p.28 (bottom); V&A Dundee, p.38 (right); Metropolitan Museum of Art, New York, p.67 (top); Leeds City Museum, p.82 (right); Royal Museums Greenwich, p.86.

Frontispiece captions
p.2 (frontispiece 1): Table clock by Thomas Tompion, c. 1690.

p.4 (frontispiece 2): The Great Clock of Westminster.